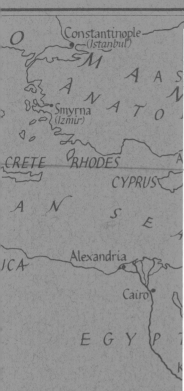

Boswell, James
18, 22, 24, 68-69n
287-90, 293, 296

Samuel Johnson
17-19, 35, 49, 95-96
137, 185, 188-90, 293-4
305.

D1336420

JOURNEYS

TRAVELLER
EXTRAORDINARY

James Bruce aged 32, from a painting by Pompeo Batoni in the
Scottish National Portrait Gallery.

TRAVELLER EXTRAORDINARY

The Life of James Bruce of Kinnaird

——⟫•❦•⟪——

J. M. Reid

THE HISTORY BOOK CLUB

Printed in Great Britain by
W & J Mackay & Co Ltd, Chatham

Contents

Illustrations

---⊃•◉•⊂---

PLATES

The engravings used as chapter endpieces are all by James Bruce from drawings he made during his Ethiopian journey. (Reproduced by kind permission of Lord Bruce.)

MAPS

by W. Bromage

ACKNOWLEDGEMENTS

The author and publishers are grateful to the following for kindly allowing us to reproduce copyright photographs. The Trustees of the Scottish National Portrait Gallery for frontispiece and Plate 16, the Trustees of the National Library of Scotland for Plates 1 and 4, Lord Bruce for Plates 2, 3, 6a, 6b, 7a, 7b, 12, 13, and 14, the Imperial Ethiopian Government, Ministry of Information, for Plates 5, 10, and 11, and the Trustees of the British Museum for Plates 8 and 9.

Foreword

This book is the story of a man and his adventures. It might not have been written if James Bruce had told his own story more clearly a century and three-quarters ago, for in that case his book *Travels to Discover the Source of the Nile in the years 1768, 1769, 1770, 1772 & 1773* would surely have been one of the accepted classics of travel, to be reprinted for each successive generation of readers.

He was a vivid, exciting and amusing writer as well as an explorer of remarkable determination and courage; but he did not know how to arrange the vast flood of material – autobiography, history, geography, biology, to say nothing of essays on a whole series of loosely related topics – which he finally gave to the world in five fat volumes. As a result of this literary weakness, the thread of his experiences is difficult to follow. Names of people and places disappear for a hundred pages or so, and are not easily recognized when the reader meets them again. An important fact about his own career may be found only in his note on an Ethiopian plant. His book fascinated readers in many countries when it first appeared, even though most of them could scarcely believe what it had to tell. It has had a few devoted readers ever since. But it has not been reprinted in full since 1813. If another complete edition ever does appear, it is likely to be among the specialized publications of some university or learned society.

Many abbreviations or selections from the *Travels* have, indeed, been published, the earliest in his own day, the latest in 1964.[1] No volume of quotations which covers only part of his journey, however, can give an adequate account of his adventurous progress or of its extraordinary setting in the lands through which he passed. Above all, no such book can give a sufficient portrait of the man, James Bruce, the first of the scientific explorers of Africa; a big man in every sense, greatly ambitious, but with certain weaknesses which made him a tragic comedian at his life's end.

The story is too good to be half-forgotten. James Bruce's own words must, indeed, be quoted where, as often, he described incidents and people better than any other writer could do. The basis of his biography must still be the editions of his *Travels* edited by Alexander Murray. These contain not only his book with revisions made before his death in 1794 but also a number of letters, extracts from his journals and other documents, with appendices and notes and a long essay on his life and writings by the editor.

The MSS used by Murray have scarcely been consulted for more than a century: it has been supposed, indeed, that they had disappeared when Kinnaird House was sold by James Bruce's descendants in 1895: it was subsequently demolished and rebuilt. I had begun to write this book when I learned through my friend, Dr Douglas Young, that many of these documents and a mass of other material, besides some of the drawings, arms and instruments which the explorer brought back from Africa, were at Broomhall, Dunfermline, the home of Lord Bruce whose grandfather, the 9th Earl of Elgin, acquired them from his half-sister, Lady Thurlow, James Bruce's great-great-granddaughter. Lord Bruce has generously and most helpfully allowed me to examine them, to quote from unpublished letters and to use drawings as illustrations.

The Delvine MSS in the National Library of Scotland, Edinburgh, include numerous letters to John Mackenzie, W. S., James Bruce's legal adviser, which throw light on financial and family affairs and dealings with the Carron Company.

[1] *Travels to Discover the Source of the Nile*, selected and edited by C. F. Beckingham, Edinburgh University Press.

Modern books of particular value for the Ethiopian and Sudanese background to Bruce's travels are

> *An Introduction to the Economic History of Ethiopia* by Richard Pankhurst (1961)
>
> *The Ethiopians* by Edward Ullendorff (1960)
>
> *L'Empire du Prêtre-Jean* by Jean Doresse (1957)
>
> *The Fung Kingdom of Sennar* by O. G. S. Crawford (1951)
>
> *Lake Tana and the Blue Nile* by R. E. Cheeseman (1936)
>
> *A History of Ethiopia* by Sir E. A. Wallis-Budge (1928)

Most quotations from Murray's editions of the *Travels* are not specially indicated in this book. For the reader's convenience I have not hesitated to make some changes in Bruce's text. His Abyssinia is Ethiopia here, his King and Iteghe, Emperor and Empress, his Ozoro (today Woyzaro) I have made Princess. More modern transliterations of Ethiopian and Arabic names have been substituted for his, where this seemed suitable, though I have preferred the English equivalent of familiar personal names. The wording of conversations has often been modernized or condensed: talk in Amharic, Tigrinya or Arabic remembered after nearly twenty years and rendered into eighteenth-century English can scarcely be so absolutely authentic as to be unalterable.

Bruce's latest editor, Professor Beckingham, hints that his reputation among the learned suffered because he wrote 'for the general, not the academic, public'. No doubt this is so. One of the real weaknesses of his book is that it attempts to satisfy several types of specialist and the general reader at the same time. I hope that this account of his life will suffer from no such confusion. It has been written not for learned Africanists, historians or geographers but for men and women who can enjoy a character and a tale of exploits and experiences not much less surprising today than they were in 1790.

Eaglesham, 1967   J. M. REID

TRAVELLER
EXTRAORDINARY

I

———⊃∘◉∘⊂———

Lion-in-Waiting

It was on June 21st, 1774, that James Bruce of Kinnaird arrived in London. He was handsome, rather romantically travel-worn, six feet four inches tall and ready to be a lion. The town had not seen him for twelve years, but recently it had heard of him.

He had come, he said, from the source of the Nile. This was something that the educated men of his day were likely to find peculiarly exciting. It was a time when scientific exploration of the world was just beginning. The great voyages of discovery, culminating in Magellan's circumnavigation of the globe, had indeed taken place two and a half centuries earlier, or more than that. The shape of the earth and its chief land masses was known, at least roughly. But these earlier travellers had sailed in pursuit not so much of mere knowledge as of wealth and of heathen peoples who might be conquered and brought into Christendom. There were vast areas which remained unknown to Europeans behind the coasts round which the first great travellers had sailed and their successors traded and fought.

Most of Africa was a land of mystery filled on the maps with pictures of strange beasts and the names of half-legendary kingdoms. And to men brought up on the Greek and Latin classics the Nile was the most tantalizing mystery of all. They could read of the great river of Egypt whose annual floods gave life to the oldest civilization known to European men, but the classic writers had been able to guess at its source only vaguely. Since the days of the Pharaohs efforts had been made to follow the whole length of the river. Cambyses the Persian, Alexander the Great and his successors in Egypt, Nero of Rome had sent emissaries, sometimes armies, on this quest, but they had been defeated or had turned back or had gone astray.

Now this Scotsman announced that he had succeeded where all the ancients had failed. He had visited lands that were almost unknown and had brought back manuscripts in scarcely known scripts, chronicles, copies of the apochryphal Book of Enoch, seeds of unknown plants, drawings of unknown classical buildings, of animals, birds and fishes, strings of scientific observations and accounts of extraordinary adventures. He had been welcomed in France by the great M. de Buffon, the most admired of living biologists, and by other men of learning. He had given manuscripts and seeds to King Louis. And now he was bringing still finer things to King George III, with whose encouragement he had begun his travels.

King George's had so far been a peaceful reign – the great crises of the American and French Revolutionary Wars were still to come – and Englishmen could be proud to feel that it was opening new regions of the world to Western man, not by armed conquest but by peaceful exploration. Captain Cook and the group of scientists who sailed with him had just returned from the Pacific with accounts of unknown islands peopled by handsome, happy, friendly men and women – evidently the 'noble savages' described by philosophers of this optimistic age who wished to turn their backs on the Fall of Man. Cook and his companions had made their voyages in the King's ships with the Government's active support, but James Bruce's travels had been completed by himself alone, at his own expense, and solely for the sake of knowledge and glory. He could (and did) feel that his was one of the foremost achievements of the age, that he could expect to be welcomed and honoured as a great man and probably to spend the rest of his life – he was still only forty-four – in digesting and explaining his discoveries.

He was a Scotsman, indeed, and eighteenth-century London was apt to think that it saw too many Scotsmen. But he was a still unusual sort of Scot, one who could speak like an Englishman. He had gone to school at Harrow. He knew many of the right people. For a Scots laird he was prosperous. Like a good many of his countrymen, he considered himself to be, in a remote way, a sort of cousin of the King himself. A baronetcy and a pension would surely be a reasonable reward, with a secure place in the world of literary learning.

At first London was, indeed, interested to look at this giant and listen to him. The King received him and the splendid collection of architectural drawings from North African which he – or the young Italian he employed – had made for the royal collection. He was elected a Fellow of the Royal Society. But the atmosphere quickly grew cooler.

James Bruce talked, indeed. He spoke with assured authority, for no other living man from western Europe had been in the chief countries he had visited: Ethiopia and the Sudanese deserts. He persisted in talking of the most extraordinary things.

There was the story of the soldiers who cut a steak from a living cow and then patched the unfortunate animal up again. There was the chief who swathed himself in the entrails of animals. There were imperial hunting parties not only for lions, elephants and impossible long-necked 'giraffas' but also for human beings, black Shankalla from the eastern borderlands, whose sons, when captured and trained, proved to be better and more intelligent soldiers than their brown masters. There were whole tribes driven from district to district by clouds of flies. There were feasts where bellowing cattle were vivisected at the door while within princes and princesses crammed one another with raw beef and then made love in the dining-room.

It was true that no one had seen Ethiopia, but all educated Londoners knew something about it. They knew that the ancients had called its people wise and good. And then there was Dr Samuel Johnson's famous little book, *Rasselas, Prince of Abyssinia*, which almost everyone had read.

His was an Ethiopia as different as possible from James Bruce's. It was a country where princes and princesses lived in a Happy

Valley and could pass their time discussing problems of ethics with learned philosophers. No doubt this was a fable, but Dr Johnson did at least know something of the land he was writing about. His first publication had been a translation, from a French translation, of a Portuguese account of the country. Except among the most abstrusely learned, no one had a clearer idea of Ethiopian life than he had: and Samuel Johnson was the greatest literary figure of his age. It might be that, as James Bruce was to have no difficulty in pointing out, his views on Ethiopian geography were thoroughly confused: but he did at least realize that if Bruce had, in fact, reached the source of the Nile another European had been there before him.

The doctor did not think much of the explorer. 'He is not a distinct relater,' he told James Boswell, 'and I shall say he is neither abounding nor deficient in sense. I did not perceive a superiority of understanding.' This first reaction was comparatively mild; but as public scepticism of Bruce's supremely un-Rasselasian account of the Ethiopians grew stronger, Johnson took up a much more damning position. He doubted whether the traveller had ever entered Ethiopia at all.

For Bruce's hopes of honours and glory this was disaster. London had already begun to doubt, and to smile with the clever Miss Burney at 'the tallest man you ever saw in your life – at least *gratis* . . . not more elevated above the common man in his size than in his ideas of his own consequence.' Now it laughed. He was a figure for lampoons, even for darker hints that he might have murdered the young artist, Balugani, who was the only European witness of his travels.

In disgust he left London for his Scottish estate, to marry, to litigate, and finally, in his widowerhood, to pour out the long, confused, brilliant book of his travels which was read throughout Europe and revived the stream of criticism and satire again which was to flow till long after he was dead.

2

The Name of Bruce

Almost all that James Bruce told about himself and his astonishing journey was true as well as new. But not quite all. Behind the carefully noted facts about places and people, plants and animals, the laboriously calculated heights and distances, there was one basic illusion on which Samuel Johnson had fastened. Bruce had convinced himself, in the face of evidence which was known to him, that he was the first European traveller to reach the springs of the Nile. More excusably, since local tradition was on his side here, he had also closed his mind to a fact which seems to have been fairly obvious to his eyes – the fact that the Blue Nile, whose source he had visited, was not the main stream of the great river he followed into Egypt. The new knowledge he brought home, his courage and scientific observations, were extraordinary, but the supreme achievement that he claimed was the discovery of the Nile's source: and this claim was a double delusion. It was not the only illusion in his life.

The old house of Kinnaird, from which he first looked out as a solitary, motherless child, was a place where illusions could grow very naturally in the early 1730s. It was a laird's house, though an unpretentious one. From its low hill-top above the marshy levels of the Forth he could look to places and listen to stories full of the name of Bruce. A mile or so to the north was the castle of Airth, which had been his mother's home, and before that the home of his grandmother's Bruce ancestors, one of whom had brought there as his bride the granddaughter of a Stewart princess. Just beyond it was the field of Bannockburn, where the most famous of all Bruces, King Robert (also an ancestor) had won his decisive victory over a great English army. Against the background of the Highland hills which closed his view, a shaft of sun might show him Stirling Rock, with its palace-castle where other kings of the Bruce blood had reigned. Beyond the Forth were the lands of Bruce lairds whose possessors had fought for their kings.

The lairds of Kinnaird had an honourable history. Successively they had dared to take the dangerous side in public affairs: in spite of this, the family survived, even if it had not grown rich. The first of the line, Robert Bruce, son of a knight of Airth, had been one of the makers of Scottish Presbyterianism, an outstanding personality of the Kirk in the generation after its first reformers. For a time he was King James VI's chief clerical adviser and minister of the High Kirk of Edinburgh. But when the King tried to make himself master of the Church and to introduce bishops of the Anglican kind as his agents, Robert Bruce opposed him. He was an impressive figure, tall, majestic and immensely popular – indeed, much more kingly than James himself, who is said to have feared that he would claim the crown as namesake and heir of King Robert Bruce. He was forbidden to preach and was exiled from Edinburgh, but when he died in 1631 he had passed on his beliefs to the next generation of Covenanters, who defied Charles I.

His grandson, another Robert, died of his wounds after the battle of Worcester, where he fought as a captain of the guards of Charles II, when the Scots who had defeated the father made the son their king. His brother and heir, Alexander, survived the battle, but was almost ruined by Cromwell's exactions.

Sixty-four years later young David Bruce, son of the heiress of Kinnaird and her husband, David Hay, was still a king's man. There were no longer Kings of Scots at Stirling. Formally the kingdom of Scotland itself had disappeared, absorbed in the new kingdom of Great Britain. But there was a Stewart in exile who claimed to be King of Scotland, England and Ireland. In the Jacobite rising of 1715 David Bruce, with some of his neighbours, stood for this

King James. He was taken prisoner[1] and was to be tried for his life in England, for Scots juries could not be trusted to apply the savage English treason law introduced after the Union of 1707.

Whether they were Jacobites or not, Scots lawyers were angered by these trials of their countrymen beyond the Border, and organized the defence of the prisoners. They maintained, justifiably, that, under the terms of the Union, Scots should be tried only in Scottish courts.

'The most obstreperous', wrote the Bishop of Carlisle, a zealous courtier of King George, who sat beside the judges, 'is reported to be one Mr Graham, a person of great learning and eminence. He is the King's Judge of Admiralty in Scotland and (in the warmth of his zeal) has procured leave to be of counsel to the prisoners in order to dispute the points, which he declares he'll maintain to the hazard of his very life as well as his fortunes.'[2]

Though the Scots plea was not admitted, the court evidently found it wiser to be merciful. David Bruce was released. He believed that he owed his life to James Graham. Soon his defender acquired the estate of Airth and became his neighbour. Graham was at the head of his profession as Dean of Faculty. A few years later David Bruce became his son-in-law. James Bruce was the only son of the marriage, which ended sadly when the young wife died (apparently of tuberculosis) in 1733.

It was a formidable family tradition but now an embarrassing one for David Bruce, a kindly, perhaps rather puzzled man, as tall, impressive and ruddy as his ancestor, the minister of Edinburgh, had been and as his son was to be, but scarcely so firm in mind as either of them. After his escape from the gallows he had had enough of adventure. He was anxious to live quietly in troubled times.

He married again, and a second family, which was to number six sons and two daughters, began to appear at Kinnaird. With

[1] M. E. Cumming-Bruce, *Family Records of the Bruces and Cumyns*; and Peter Rae, *History of the Rebellion.*

[2] Bishop William Nicolson to the Archbishop of York, December 17th, 1716. *Miscellany of the Scottish History Society*, 1893, p. 536.

his father-in-law, Judge Graham, he was evidently concerned for young James. The boy's health was poor, and there was not much love between him and his stepmother. Scotland remained a troubled country. The union with England was still resented. Among the gentry there were still many who dreamed of King James and discussed schemes for another Jacobite rising. If this did happen, armies would surely move again along the roads below Stirling where men had marched and fought through the centuries – armies perhaps of government red-coats, perhaps of Gaelic-speaking clansmen from beyond the mountains within sight of Kinnaird. It might be difficult to sit quiet through a storm of this sort. An imaginative boy of the name of Bruce might be tempted to do as his father had done in 1715. James had better be removed from such dangers altogether. The best place for him would be at the other end of the island.

Scots lairds had not yet formed the habit of sending their sons to English schools. But at the English Bar, Scotsmen were already beginning to make that success in what was, to them, a foreign legal system which was to give London Scottish Lord Chancellors and Lord Chief Justices. David Bruce had a brother-in-law, Counsellor William Hamilton, 'of the Wishaw family', who was one of these legal pioneers. He had a son of James's age who was to make an unusual niche for himself in Parliamentary history as 'Single-Speech Hamilton'. It was decided to send James Bruce to London, where the boys could be brought up together.

For a child eight years old, the week-long journey to the south and the nine years that followed made a breach with all that he had known. Perhaps he was never to be completely at home again in his own part of the world, never to speak and think quite like his Scottish neighbours or to be properly understood by most of them.

Yet he felt like a Scot. Though like many Scotsmen of his time, he was apt to call himself English when he travelled. Scotland was always 'my own country'. He was intensely proud of his name. Many Scots gentry could claim, as he did, to be descendants of King Robert Bruce – this was the basis of James Boswell's tendency to feel that he should be treated *en prince* (or at least *en comte*) when he travelled abroad. Almost these remotely royal Scots, the Kinnaird lairds included, had Robert's grandson, the first Stewart king as their ancestor. But the heir of Kinnaird seems to have persuaded himself that his name made him, in a particular way, a successor of King Robert – though by strict descent that name should have been not Bruce but Hay. The imposing manner that was to earn him the nickname of 'His Abyssinian Majesty' was surely a reflection of this half-conscious delusion: so, perhaps, was his feeling that he was born to do something great in the world.

His years in London or near it seem on the whole to have been happy ones. He lived there among Scottish relatives and friends. Alexander Hamilton, a brother of his uncle by marriage, took a special interest in his education. When he went to Harrow school it was with his cousin, William Gerard Hamilton, and an uncle of his own age, William Graham, his grandfather's heir who, at Airth, was to be his closest friend and neighbour throughout their two lives. James was a rather delicate, studious schoolboy with a talent for languages which no doubt explains his headmaster's choice of him, in 1745, as Orator – the leading pupil who made an annual Latin speech to the school governors.

As he grew older his first ambition was to become a parson in the Church of England – an odd choice for the descendant of the Rev. Robert Bruce.

Meanwhile Scotland saw the Jacobite rising which David Bruce had feared. Within a mile or two of Kinnaird, Prince Charles and his Highlanders had passed south in 1745. At the beginning of the next year they had reappeared again to besiege Stirling Castle. Musket smoke had drifted among the rain on Falkirk Muir, a little to the south, when the Prince won his second victory. Then they had retreated beyond the Forth, and Kinnaird had seen the Duke of Cumberland's troops march north towards the battle that ended all at Culloden.

'We have both suffered extremely by the Highlanders,' wrote Judge Graham to Alexander Hamilton (February 13th, 1746), explaining why he had not been able to discuss James's clerical ambitions with David Bruce.

'For my part I should think it a great happiness that he had taken so lucky a turn; for altho' it will necessarily require a university education which is attended with great expense, yet it is a sure card at length, and all of us will endeavour our utmost, when he is fit for it, to procure him a comfortable settlement.'

Peace and comfort, however, were not to be the chief qualities of James's career. He had finished with Harrow, and there were doubts among his friends about Oxford and Cambridge, where 'such a general dissoluteness of manners prevails'. For the moment, 'as the rebellion is not yet quite extinguished in Scotland' he was sent to a private academy to learn French and other modern languages, besides fencing and polite accomplishments. Then, in May 1747, he was at last brought back to Scotland. He travelled to York or Newcastle by coach. The rest of the journey he must ride, but, wrote Alexander Hamilton, 'take care not to send a sholty [Shetland pony] for him lest with his long legs he should travel both on foot and horseback at the same time'.[1]

The boy was first to strengthen his health by riding and shooting and then to study at Edinburgh for the Scots Bar. Law was the most respectable profession for the sons of Scots lairds, and though Judge Graham had died, the grandson of a Dean of Faculty could expect to be well received in it. But James Bruce seems to have had no more enthusiasm for the work than James Boswell was to show a few years later. His textbooks were scribbled with Italian verses.

His family were less insistent on this career than the judge who was Boswell's father was to be. His health weakened again: he remained too tall for his strength and was thought to be threatened with the tuberculosis that had killed his mother. He went back to Kinnaird and the field sports that broadened him.

But this was not a very happy return or a hopeful one. He felt neglected and poor. His father's house was full of young step-

[1] To David Bruce, February 1747, Broomhall MSS.

brothers and stepsisters. David Bruce was trying to make provision for this family and could not find more than an occasional guinea for his eldest son.[1] James must make a living for himself. He studied military engineering. Then another prospect seemed to offer itself.

Scots were beginning to bring home fortunes from India. This seemed an interesting and adventurous way of life, but at twenty-two he was already too old to join the East India Company's service in the ordinary way. The company could, however, grant licences to 'free traders' who would work with them. To get this privilege he must go to London again – a journey which, as he thought later, might have ended in the Black Hole of Calcutta. A free trader needed some capital to invest in the goods which he would sell in India. James wrote rather pathetically to his father to ask for £500 on which he had a claim.

'Do me the justice you have often done me in conversation,' he begged, 'by owning I have not been an expensive Son to you . . . that it may not fare the worse with me for having all my life avoided all those Expenses that Gentlemen do ordinarily see their Sons run into without thinking them Unreasonable, or Extravagant . . . P.S. I am in great need of Cloathes . . . in your answer you may tell me whether to take off a suit and from whom.'[2]

He did not take his new suit to India: instead he fell in love in London. The girl was Adriana Allan, daughter of a Scottish wine merchant whose widow and son were carrying on the business after his death.

'She has had', he wrote to his anxious father, 'a most complete education, is in every respect perfectly amiable, and has a handsome fortune; which last, as is very necessary, I mention for your satisfaction, though it is, of all the advantages of which she is possessed, that which I value the least. Besides this, I am to be admitted a partner into the house, which being of the greatest

[1] Letter of James Bruce to John Mackenzie, W. S., August 17th, 1758. Scottish National Library; Delvine MSS, 1241.
[2] From Airth, March 27th, 1753, Broomhall MSS.

reputation in London, is of itself a fortune.'

What followed was a brief rapture. There is no doubt that James Bruce, who was always a romantic, had chosen his bride for her beauty and kindness rather than for the wealth she could bring him. There was love, there was comfort, there were sympathetic friends. But within a few weeks of the marriage it was plain that Adriana, too, was in danger from tuberculosis.

Her mother took her to the Hot Well, at Bristol, for treatment and her young husband wrote to her in passionate anxiety.

'Do not, my Dearest Life hurt your Breast by writing, I pay very dear for the pleasure of hearing from you if by so doing you increase the Pain. You may depend upon my frequent writing that I am Constantly thinking of you and that I shall never Cease Every hour to Love you more and more . . . I most Earnestly Entreat you to make yourself Easy and Content that your Cure may be more perfect as well as the time Shortened and do not Doubt were that done But I should make my Angel tho' not So Great yet fully as happy as any man Else, tho' with a much greater Fortune.'[1]

The Bristol waters were not effective, however.

She was advised to go to a warmer country for the winter, and at the end of September 1754, James Bruce set out with her for the South of France. They got no farther than Paris, where she died on the 10th of October.

'My mind', he wrote to his father, 'is so shocked, and my impressions of that dreadful scene at Paris so strongly fixed that I have it every minute before my eyes as distinctly as it was then happening. Myself a stranger in the country; my servants unacquainted with the language and country, my presence so necessary among them, and indispensably so with my dear wife; my poor girl dying before my eyes, three months gone with child, full of that affection and tenderness which marriage produces when people feel the happiness but not the cares of it; many Roman Catholic clergy hovering about the doors; myself unable to find any expedient to keep them

[1] From Mark Lane, London, June 25th, 1754, Broomhall MSS.
[2] From Mark Lane, London, November 12th.

from disturbing her last moments – Don't you feel for your son, dear sir, in these circumstances?'[2]

The British Ambassador, Lord Albemarle, had been helpful.

'The morning before my wife died, he sent his chaplain down to offer his services in our distress. After hearing the service for the sick and receiving the sacrament together, he told me, in case I received any trouble from the priests My Lord desired I would tell them I belonged to the ambassador. When my wife died, the chaplain came again to me, desired me to go home with him, and assured me that My Lord had given him orders to see my wife buried in the Ambassador's burying ground, which was accordingly done; and had it not been for this piece of humanity she must have been buried in the common ground, where the wood is piled for the town's firing.

'I could not, however, leave her as soon as dead, as is the custom in England, but having ordered the mournful solemnity with as much decency as is allowed in that country to heretics, at midnight, between the 10th and 11th ult., accompanied only by the chaplain, a brother of my Lord Foley's and our own servants, we carried her body to the burying ground at the Porte St. Martin, where I saw all my comfort and happiness laid with her in the grave.

'From thence, almost frantic, against the advice of every body, I got on horseback, having ordered the servant to have post horses ready and set out in the most tempestuous night I ever saw to ride for Boulogne, where I arrived the next day without stopping. There the riding, without a great coat, in the night time, want of food which, for a long time I had not tasted, want of rest, fatigue and excessive concern, threw me into a fever, but I recovered well enough to set out for London on the Wednesday. Thus ended my unfortunate journey, and with it my present prospect of happiness in this life.'

3

---∘◦∘---

Apprenticeship in Europe

It was an end, but it was also a beginning. In that midnight ride James Bruce dramatized his despair, as his nature often forced him to dramatize his experiences, but it was a dramatization of the truth as he felt it. For a while he threw himself into business. He had to find a new reason for existence. Trading in wine, he soon decided, was not enough to absorb him. He had money, and though he was never sorry to have more, money-making alone did not satisfy him. He felt he must do something great. But what was to be done?

The first thing, perhaps, was to see the world. His business gave him a reason for travel in the vine-growing countries and he prepared for this in ways that were not too closely connected with trade. He studied languages, particularly Spanish and Portuguese to begin with. He studied drawing: one of his best friends in London was Robert Strange, a Jacobite engraver who had designed bank-notes for Prince Charlie in 1745 and was now making a European reputation for his versions of the work of famous painters. He gathered ideas about art, and particularly about ancient architecture in which the mid-eighteenth century was deeply interested. Another friend was Robert Wood, an Irishman who had visited the legendary cities of Palmyra and Baalbek, publishing two successful books about them, and was turning from cultural exploration to politics.

And then there was the chance of military glory. The eighteenth century was the first age of world wars – of long, dynastic struggles in Europe which reached out into Asia, America and Africa, because Britain and France, always on opposite sides whoever their allies might be, were rivals for colonial wealth and power. In 1755 the great European powers had been at peace for seven years. But there was fighting between British and French in America and at sea, and new alliances were building up in Europe. It was the prospect of war which sent James Bruce to Guernsey to make plans for safeguarding stocks of wine which his firm had bought on the Continent. As his ship sailed down the Channel he could see signs of armament in the French ports and he passed British naval ships gathered at Spithead.

It was Bruce's plan, says his first biographer, to 'travel over the south of Europe in the character of a merchant, with the taste and science of a scholar'.[1] Before this commercial grand tour could begin, in July 1757, the Seven Years War was in being, but there was still peace in Portugal and Spain. On this first journey, and in spite of all his studious preparations, the future explorer was surprised by the sheer foreignness of foreign lands. At the naval port of Ferrol he was shocked to find that the Spaniards seemed to know too much about the latest British warships. And Portugal (scarcely beginning to recover from the terrifying Lisbon earthquake of 1755) was shocking altogether.

'There are many particular customs in Portugal', he noted in his diary, 'All of which may be known by this rule, that whatever is done in the rest of the world in one way is in Portugal done by the contrary, even in the rocking of the cradle, which I believe in all the rest of the world is from side to side, but in Portugal is from head to foot. I fancy it is owing to this early contrariety that their brains work in so different a manner all their lives after. . . . The smallest affront is never forgiven. This is the occasion of the many murders which are continually committed here. It is, indeed, the only country where it can be said that murder is tolerated. Every family has a son, a brother, or a nephew a priest or friar. These are

[1] Alexander Murray, *The Life and Writings of James Bruce*. Printed in his edition of the *Travels*.

the instruments. As soon as the friar has committed the crime, he flies to his convent: and in six months the thing is no more talked of.'

Bruce's inherited suspicion of Roman Catholicism had been strengthened by the attempt of French priests to reach his dying wife's bedside. In Ethiopia it was to be a welcome prejudice: it did not stand in the way of his friendly feelings for Frenchmen, even when France and Britain were enemies, but in 1757, when he knew so little of 'all the rest of the world', it sharpened his criticism of France's southern neighbours.

Having 'seen everything remarkable in Portugal', including its vineyards, he passed into Castile and Andalusia, Cordoba and Seville. Like many a northern traveller since, he was impressed by the relics of the Moslem past in the Spanish South. Here, he thought, was the subject for a great book – a history of the Moors in Spain and the decay of Andalusia after its conquest by the Catholic Kings.

There was a great collection of Arabic manuscripts in the Escorial which no foreigner had been allowed to examine. This might be the material for the work he wanted to do. To be sure, he had only begun to learn Arabic, but he had enthusiasm and self-confidence enough to believe that he could soon go farther. King Ferdinand's favourite minister was an Irishman, Richard Wall, who was anxious for peace and friendship with Britain. Don Ricardo seems to have been impressed by the eager Scottish giant and to have wished to keep him in Spain, if possible as a soldier; but Bruce did not think much of the Spanish Army, and even Wall could not offer him access to the Escorial manuscripts. Yet this gave a turn to Bruce's interest that was to be decisive.

Meanwhile his grand tour of the vineyards was still to be completed. In spite of the war he was allowed to pass into France, to spend some months in Bordeaux, where he enjoyed French society. He passed on into the Rhineland and then to Brussels, where he fought a duel that looked like having awkward consequences. He escaped into Holland, where he collected books on Arabic and other Eastern languages, among them the grammars and history of Job

Ludolf, an enormously learned German scholar who never seems to have been nearer Ethiopia than Rome; but with the help of an Ethiopian monk had worked out the only regular keys to the letters and language of an African country cut off by Moslem conquests from the rest of the Christian world.

This was Bruce's first step towards the Nile. It was taken, it seems, merely by chance, the result of the new interest in Semitic studies which Spain had aroused but had not satisfied. Yet almost at once Bruce was distracted from his books. In Holland he was close to a fighting front of the European war. Hanover, King George II's native principality, was just across the border. Having got rid of their royal general, the Duke of Cumberland, who had led them to defeat, and borrowed from Frederick the Great a more skilful commander, Ferdinand of Brunswick, the Hanoverians, with some reluctant British support, were striking back at the French. With some Scots officers in the Dutch service who wanted to see what was going on, James Bruce made an excursion into Germany. He arrived at Crefeld, in the Rhineland, on June 23rd, 1758, just when Ferdinand's army was meeting the Duc de Clermont's, which lay among the ditches, willow thickets and peat-bogs west of the Rhine. He watched the skilful manoeuvre by which the Hanoverian 30,000 held Clermont's 57,000 in front, while the French flank was turned and the whole force broken and dispersed. It was his first sight of war, a victory quickly won and complete, and it convinced him that a Bruce of Kinnaird must indeed find some more impressive way of life than the wine trade.

James was now Laird of Kinnaird. On the Continent he had learned of his father's death. He came back to London with plans for withdrawing from business and setting out decidedly on a new career.

There were difficulties at first. It seemed doubtful whether Kinnaird could give him the sort of income he would need if he was to be able to take a more independent way in the world. But the world was changing. The Kinnaird estate, like several of those round it, included a small colliery where a few families of miners, tied inescapably to their work under the seventeenth-century Scots law which made the men of this trade and their families something very like serfs, produced fuel to be shipped from the little Forth harbours. Already, in August 1758, Bruce, in London, was asking his agent in Scotland for information about the coal worked at Kinnaird.[1] Possibly he was even then in touch with the ingenious Dr Joseph Roebuck, a medical graduate of Edinburgh who practised as a physician and also as an industrial scientist in Birmingham.

Roebuck had unorthodox and ambitious ideas about iron production. Iron was normally smelted with charcoal: the great centre of the industry was in Sussex, though there was one furnace in Scotland where charcoal made from the wood of Highland forests was used to treat imported English ore. It had been proved, however, that coke made from the right kind of coal could be used in iron-smelting. Dr Roebuck saw great possibilities in the process. He and a Birmingham partner, Samuel Garbett, had already set up a sulphuric-acid plant at Prestonpans, near Edinburgh, and these two, with a Scots merchant, William Cadell, looked for a site in Scotland with a suitable harbour for exports and supplies of coal and ore within easy reach. They found this near the mouth of the Carron Water only two miles south of Kinnaird. The establishment they planned was to be the largest of its kind in Europe, and almost as soon as the Carron Company was established a contract for coal supplies was made with James Bruce on November 4th, 1760.

Scarcely fourteen years after the Jacobite army had passed that way this was the beginning of heavy industry in Scotland. Henceforth the night skies over East Stirlingshire would be lit with the glare of furnaces; and the Laird of Kinnaird would be free to look for the source of the Nile.

This was not his first project, however. William Pitt had just had his wonderful year of victories over the French, from Canada to India. It now seemed that the war would extend to Spain. From his visit to Ferrol, James Bruce had brought back a plan of this Spanish naval base and a belief that it could be captured by a British force

[1] National Library of Scotland, Delvine MSS 1241.

without much difficulty. Here was a chance to make a name for himself. His friend Robert Wood was now Pitt's Undersecretary of State – in the eighteenth-century style something between a politician and a leading civil servant. Bruce worked out his project in detail and persuaded Wood to submit it to the great minister.

It says something for the plan itself and more for the young Bruce's capacity for impressing powerful people that Pitt considered this proposal from a man who had no military experience. At first he rejected it, but soon Bruce was summoned from Scotland to discuss it again. Pitt's greatest days were almost over, however. George III was on the throne, determined to get rid of the Whig politicians who had managed his grandfather – and also to make peace as soon as possible. Pitt resigned, and the plan seemed to vanish with him.

The new ministers, however, found that war with Spain, which they had opposed, could not be avoided after all. Robert Wood, still Undersecretary of State, put Bruce's proposal before the King. There was another journey to London and meetings with the ruling triumvirate, George Grenville and Lords Egremont and Halifax. Bruce was more eager than ever. When it was suggested that there might be difficulty in landing at Ferrol, 'I, from no motive but of forwarding His Majesty's service, offered to fix an ensign upon the landing-place in the first boat that went ashore'.

After all, it was not to be. The force available for the expedition was intended, after taking Ferrol, to pass on to Portugal, an ally threatened by the Spaniards. When the Portuguese Ambassador heard of the plan he insisted that the defence of his country must come first. Kinnaird and a quietly studious country life, cushioned by the profits of his coal-mines might, it seemed, be the only end for James Bruce.

But, again, he had made an impression. George III's Government was anxious to prove that there could be a new age of glory – peaceful glory, if possible – under a king who was a king. Able and enterprising men who wanted to do something great were to be encouraged if they were prepared to be king's men. Too many of them were on the other side in politics. James Bruce had a sincere fellow-feeling for kings which was to show itself in Africa as well as in Europe. His friends, like himself, believed that he could make a stir in the world if he had the chance. His cousin, William Gerard ('Single Speech') Hamilton, who had been Chief Secretary for Ireland when the Earl of Halifax was Lord Lieutenant there, was sent to ask him to see Halifax, now a Secretary of State, before he left London.

The earl was flattering. It would be ridiculous, he said, if a man of Bruce's ability, still young and active, should decide to live lik a peasant in Scotland. The King favoured discovery and the arts: these were the keys to honour under George III. There was Africa, for instance, next door to Europe, but still unexplored. It was known that there were splendid remains of Roman architecture in the Regencies of Algiers and Tunis. These needed to be studied and recorded in properly measured drawings which could be added to the King's collection. At the moment, luckily enough, the British Consulate-General at Algiers was vacant. If Mr Bruce would accept this appointment and could travel through the country examining ruins and making drawings for the King, he could expect the same sort of reward that had been promised him when the Ferrol expedition was being discussed – there seem to have been strong hints of a baronetcy and a pension.

One may suspect that the mind behind this proposal was that of Robert Wood, the explorer and recorder of Palmyra, rather than George III's. The King, indeed, seems to have been inclined to think that 'a person acquainted with the Barbary States' would be more useful in Algiers than the most eager of antiquarians. But Wood's boldness and tenacity made him indispensable to the great men he served: he was to be their champion (and to some extent their scapegoat) in their long struggle against their formidable critic, John Wilkes. In this case the King finally accepted Wood's advice.

James Bruce had repeated discussions with both Halifax and Wood.

'The discovery of the source of the Nile was also a subject of these conversations,' he wrote in the introduction to his *Travels*, 'but it was always mentioned to me with a kind of diffidence, as if to be expected only from a more experienced traveller. Whether this was but another way of exciting me to the attempt I shall not say; but my heart in that instant did me the justice to suggest, that this, too, was either to be achieved by me, or to remain, as it had done for these last thousand years, a defiance to all travellers, and an opprobrium to geography.'

In fact, Lord Halifax's proposal was irresistible. It seemed to be made for Bruce's particular interests and talents – as, by Robert Wood, it probably was. He could carry on his Arabic studies with dignity in an Arabic-speaking land. He could travel adventurously, though 'under the protection of a public character', in little-known countries. He could make drawings and display his taste in architecture with a purpose. Above all, he could take a leading part in the rediscovery of the ancient classical world which his generation found absorbing.

Greece, and Rome, the languages and history of the Mediterranean before the modern nations existed, were still the bases of knowledge for all educated men. But the practical progress of their world had passed half of the Mediterranean by. While Western Europe grew strong and reached out to the Far East and America, most of the lands from which it took its origins fell half out of sight.

In a sense the Turkish Sultanate was the last successor to the empires of Alexander the Great and Rome, but it had been the conquering enemy of the West, and now, for half a century, it was in decay. Yet it contained the relics of greatness and art which classically minded Europeans could value most. Western Europe, which had built a new civilization for itself and had discovered beyond the ocean 'regions Caesar never knew', needed to search out the remaining traces of its own beginnings. Perhaps on the farthest borders of the classical world, in the Ethiopian Empire whose history reached back to Macedonian and Roman times, there might even be a living shadow of the seminal past. For the late Middle Ages, Ethiopia had been the kingdom of Prester John, a mysterious Christendom beyond Christendom. For Dr Samuel Johnson it was the platonic country where kings – or at least princes – were philosophers.

And here, for James Bruce of Kinnaird, was the chance of leading in the work of rediscovery with the support of the British Government, just emerging victorious from a world war. He was to be allowed to begin by travelling through Italy and seeing for himself modern arts and Roman antiquities. Then North Africa. Then, perhaps, the observation (from Algiers, or possibly from Armenia) of an astronomical phenomenon about which scientists were excited – the transit of Venus across the disk of the sun – for among so many other things he was an amateur student of astronomy. Or perhaps – he scarcely dared to breathe the thought publicly – the discovery of the source of the Nile.

It must have seemed almost too good to be true. He hurried home to settle his affairs at Kinnaird. And here, to crown all, he fell in love again – with the sister of a neighbouring laird, William Murray of Polmaise. Margaret Murray promised to wait for him while he travelled: she was only sixteen. The future seemed to fall into a happy pattern – first achievement abroad, then a settled life, fame and happiness.

But this new romance was no calm and calculated attachment. He left Scotland in March 1762, and was soon writing love letters. He worried about his Peggy's health, and also about the strength of her affection.

'My Dearest Love, I received the pleasure of your kind letter. My Dearest Life, do always produce kind letters. Your last was but middling. *Dear Mr Bruce* should have been *My Dear Husband* or *My Dearest Love.*'

Or again, 'You are packing up for Pencaitland [the home of a relative] and can write No More. I am packing up for two voyages and a land journey half the length of Europe. . . . What shall I say to My Dearest Love on this as it were Second Separation? My heart recoils at it far from being happy as usual at the thought of travelling – there is a Dead Weight upon my Heart and Nothing before me that presages good.'[1]

[1] From Warwick Court, London, May 4th and June 24th, 1762, Broomhall MSS.

In London he saw the King as well as friendly ministers. He equipped himself with 'a large apparatus of instruments' for scientific observation. Thus supplied, he sent out for Italy, travelling through France, in spite of the war, by special permission of Louis XV's minister, Choiseul. To justify the Italian journey it was decided that this totally inexperienced diplomat should visit Malta and warn its ruler, the Grand Master of the Knights of St John, that a British fleet would be coming to the island to demand an explanation of the Order's unneutral behaviour during the war. In fact, before the threatening message could be delivered the Grand Master had decided to apologize through an agent of his own.

The real object of Bruce's six months' Italian travel, as he and Wood had planned it, was his apprenticeship in the direct examination of ancient buildings and the development of his taste and knowledge of architecture and painting. He threw himself into this work with all his usual vigour. He visited most of the chief cities. He examined inscriptions, ancient coins, palaces, picture galleries. He began to write an essay on ancient and modern Rome – no small subject. He prepared a separate work on the ruins of Paestum. He talked with antiquaries and artists, notably Andrew Lumisden, a Scottish Jacobite exile who had been Prince Charlie's secretary during the Rising in 1746 and was now his father's. Lumisden had made himself a leading expert on Roman antiquities. His mother had been a Bruce and he became one of James's most useful advisers. The traveller met Roman nobles, British residents, ambassadors, consuls, men freed from slavery in Algeria, and learned what he could from them all.

But, with all this, he was still writing anxiously to Margaret Murray. 'I think I can always tell when you are ill by myself . . . I scarcely ever dream of you but uneasy troublesome dreams such as I have done constantly since your last and at the time I wish your letters most I am most afraid of them.'

He had convinced himself – against all evidence, since she said she could not live without him – that she had favoured his African expedition.

'My Dearest Love, you know that with much less persuasion because it was your will, I forsook all my happiness and undertook this accursed journey.' She was to have a portrait painted which could be sent on to him. He was sitting to the best painter in Italy – Pompeo Batoni, whose portrait is the frontispiece to this book. A miniature copy would be made and sent to her.[1]

At last, in March 1763, a British man of war carried him from Leghorn to Algiers.

[1] From Rome, 26th August, 1762; and Florence, February 25th, 1763, Broomhall MSS.

4

Apprenticeship in Barbary

In spite of his concern for the girl he had left behind him, his months in Italy had been a splendid beginning, exciting, informative, socially pleasant, and coloured by the prestige of a government mission. And now Bruce expected to be able to settle down in a city not too much out of touch with the world – and with a country house for relaxation – where he could study languages, collect manuscripts, plan journeys and, when he went off in search of Roman remains, leave a Vice-Consul to do the dull work of filling in official papers, clearing ships and listening to the demands and grievances of merchants.

But this picture was, in fact, a little too good to be true. The ministers who sent him out, and Bruce himself, had been inclined to think of the Algiers consulship as something like a sinecure in the familiar eighteenth-century style, a post whose holder could draw a comfortable salary and save his own time for more interesting things. James Bruce was not a man to shirk work he was expected to do, but for him the real purpose of his appointment was the recovery of Roman architecture. In fact, however, George III had been wiser than his ministers. Algiers was not a place made for studious retirement or a peaceful base for an explorer of the hinterland. It was a city full of difficulties, even of danger, for the spokesman of any European country. In fact, its Consulate-General needed 'a person acquainted with the Barbary States' – acquainted, too, with the ways of British governments whose habit in North Africa had been to speak firmly about principles and honour from a distance, but, in practice, to avoid trouble and expense on the spot.

The Algiers of 1763 was typical enough of the Ottoman Empire in decay. Formally, it was the capital of the Turkish Sultan's westernmost province, but the Sublime Porte in Constantinople had long ceased to have much detailed control over its affairs. Turkish soldiers did, indeed, rule the city, while the country behind it was inhabited by Arab and Berber tribesmen theoretically under their control, but for ordinary purposes the Regency was almost an independent kingdom. The Dey – who was often called King by Europeans – was chosen by the military leaders, though confirmed in office by the Sultan.

The State existed for and by war, a war that could never be ended, though treaties and truces could modify or interrupt it. There had been no real peace in the Mediterranean in the thousand years since Moslem conquerors overran the Middle East and North Africa. Christian and Moslem ships waylaid one another. The idea of further Moslem conquests by land or of Christian reconquest was always in the air. Turkish Algiers had risen to fame as the head-quarters of a fleet of corsairs which ravaged Christian coasts, cruised against European traders and navies, and captured and sold Christian slaves. Europeans on their side raided and enslaved almost as persistently. Between Spaniards and Moslems in particular the sea war was practically continuous. But as Turkish naval power weakened and the Holy War dwindled into something more like organized piracy, other Europeans (who could sometimes be the Sultan's allies) tried to limit it and safeguard their trade.

Algiers was an important market not only for slaves but also for corn. North Africa, which fed ancient Rome, could offer useful cargoes after the harvest. Treaties were made with Deys and with the rulers of Tunis and Tripoli, also the heads of semi-independent Turkish provinces. England, in particular, had a treaty of 1682 which was supposed to guarantee that British ships carrying 'proper passes' could visit Algiers safely and must not be attacked at sea. It was also claimed – though, perhaps, never fully admitted by the Algereins – that British subjects must not be enslaved.

Undoubtedly James Bruce had a high idea of his consular duty. He represented the King of Great Britain and believed that he must uphold the honour and prestige of a government which had just won a great war.

> Britannia rules the waves:
> Britons never shall be slaves . . .

He would have been ready enough to cheer these favourite boasts of a contemporary Scot. Perhaps his views of his duty and office were actually too high for his own good. British traders in Algiers were apt to expect that the Consul would support them in money-making schemes which would not bear much discussion, that he would even take a share in illegitimate money-making. Bruce had no sympathy for manoeuvres of this kind, and very little time for such traders themselves. 'In consideration of your family I warn you not to begin shuffling with me', he wrote to a merchant, Simon Peter Cruise, who had acted as temporary Vice-Consul before his own arrival in Algiers, and whom he suspected of cheating a widow in the matter of a shipload of corn. 'I said, and now repeat that if you do not furnish me an account, or if you furnish a false one, the consequences will fall on yourself.'

He suggested that his correspondent, an Irishman, might not understand English very well. Therefore he (Bruce) must put the position very plainly.

'I am a trustee for widows and orphans. Shall I send you a copy of some certificates of your character out of my chancery book to show how proper a man you are in point of morals for such a charge? You are hereby enjoined to make out your account. If you do not I will adjudge you to pay the sum of 8567 shillings, the sum with which you charge Mrs H – without a voucher.'

This was decisive enough, if not tactfully expressed: Bruce was never afraid to make decisions and to state them plainly either to British traders in Algiers or to the Dey himself. But this sort of decisiveness did not make for popularity, at any rate with the merchant community.

Meanwhile he threw himself into what he considered to be the real work he was sent to do, the preparation for travels to come. He spent long hours in the study of Arabic, learning to speak the language fluently in its North African form, so that he could pass, when this was necessary, as a native of the Maghreb. He gathered new apparatus, notably a portable camera obscura, sitting in which he could trace the outline of buildings and other objects as they were thrown on a screen. A doctor was attached to the Consulate's staff, and from him Bruce learned some of the principles and practice of medicine which could be most useful to a traveller. The Consulate should also have had a chaplain, but he was on a protracted leave.

'The Protestant ship-master who came into the port, and had need of spiritual assistance, found here a blank that was not easily filled up; I should therefore have been obliged to take upon myself the disagreeable office of burying the dead, and the more cheerful, though more troublesome one of marrying and baptizing the living: matters entirely out of my way, but in which the Roman Catholic clergy would contribute no assistance'. Luckily there was in the city an aged Greek priest from Cyprus, 'of a very social and chearful disposition', who became Bruce's private chaplain. Father Christopher could not only marry, bury and baptize: he also taught his host to speak Greek with the current pronunciation 'of which the generality of English scholars are perfectly ignorant'. This was a preparation for travel in the Greek islands, but it was to prove useful far beyond Greece, and Father Christopher's influence was to be more useful still.

It was in Algiers, too, that Bruce was joined by a yet more valuable assistant. He needed an artist who could join him in making architectural and other drawings for the King's collection, and had asked Andrew Lumisden in Italy to help him in finding such a man. After a prolonged search Lumisden engaged a young Italian, Luigi Balugani, who was to be Bruce's companion for seven years of travel that was usually dangerous and often exhausting. He was a faithful and industrious helper, the one western European to be with his employer on a main part of his journey. He was also a man of real talent – at twenty-two he had been made a member of the academy of fine arts at Bologna and he was evidently admired and liked by correspondents who addressed him as *illustrissimo signore,* sometimes as *carissimo*.[1] Yet Bruce does not mention his name in his book and has far less to say of him, even anonymously, than of many other people, Ethiopians, Arabs, Greeks and Sudanese, of whom he left lively portraits in words. He even misstates the date of Balugani's death at Gondar.

His critics found something very sinister in this. Perhaps, they suggested, Bruce simply could not draw and wished to claim Balugani's work as his own. It is, indeed, true that Balugani's drawings have an elegance which Bruce could not equal, but both men clearly took a part in this work, which was completed after the young Italian's death. Or perhaps, it was hinted, it was altogether too convenient that Balugani should not have come back from the journey. Perhaps, his death was no accident: perhaps he could have told that Bruce never got to Ethiopia, or at least never reached the Nile. This is flatly disproved by the fact that a detailed Italian record of the journey to the Nile in Balugani's handwriting still exists.[2]

Part of the truth may be that Balugani was an unassertive being, perhaps rather self-absorbed though obedient – a list of his own seems to show that he took a surprising variety of clothes, 'Turkish' and 'French', with him to Africa – for whom Bruce remained always *il mio principale*, a master who could be annoyed if one showed too much initiative, while to Bruce the young Italian was never more than a useful hand: so that throughout all their wanderings they never became friends. Warmth of feeling, strength of character, originality (for good or bad) were the qualities Bruce appreciated most easily: they were, indeed, his own.

With the arrival at Algiers of Balugani and his equipment the Consul-General was ready to begin his travels. He expected

[1] Broomhall MSS.
[2] At Broomhall. The draft of an unfinished letter by Balugani on the subject was printed by Alexander Murray in his edition of the *Travels*.

permission from London to leave the city and look for ruins, but it did not come. Instead he was ordered to remain in Algiers till a dispute over the rights of British shipping was settled.

This was the question of 'proper passes'. The Admiralty had been in the habit of giving sea-captains printed papers 'with a cheque, like a banknote' which were accepted by the Algerines as proof that their ships were, in fact, British, entitled to sail through the Mediterranean, and visit Algiers without interruption by the corsairs. But in 1756, when Port Mahon in Minorca, the chief British possession in the Mediterranean, was captured by the French, some of these passes were found there. To embarrass the British and disturb their trade these were sold by the French authorities to Spaniards and others with whom the Dey of Algiers considered himself at war. When a corsair boarded one of these vessels he found, in Bruce's words, that the crew 'were dark-coloured, wore moustachoes and spoke no English', and took the ship to Algiers, 'where the British consul detected this fraud and was under the disagreeable necessity of surrendering so many Christians into the hands of their enemies and slavery'.

The French stratagem was damaging to British merchants and sailors as well as enraging to the consuls, and its effects grew worse with time. For years British representatives in Algiers pressed their superiors in London to find some way of providing convincing passes again. But government offices were busy with other things, first war, then peace-making.

Algiers grew impatient. Its captains lived by piracy and slavery. To them it was an old grievance that British ships should be privileged to move freely. It was a loss to the Dey's Government, too – other European countries were prepared to pay heavily for the safety which British trade enjoyed under the treaty. A party among the Dey's councillors thought they saw a chance of ending the British exemption from attack either by seizing ships again or by extorting a regular tribute. Things were not improved when the governors of Minorca and Gibraltar began to issue written certificates to captains in place of printed passes.

'The British Government know that we can neither read or write, no, not even our own language,' declared the Dey, as Bruce reported an interview with him nearly thirty years later. 'We are ignorant soldiers and sailors, robbers if you will, though we do not wish to rob you: war is our trade and we live by that only. Tell me how my cruisers are to know that all these different writings and seals are Governor Mostyn's or Governor Johnston's and not the Duke of Medina Sidonia's or Barcelot's, captain of the King of Spain's cruisers.'

Both British shipping and Bruce himself were now in serious danger. Bruce had seen the French Consul, who displeased the Dey, arrested and harnessed with his staff to stone carts in the Algerian quarries. A ship from Minorca was seized in the port, its crew enslaved.

'I was just finishing my letter to your Lordship', wrote Bruce to Lord Halifax on July 20th, 1764, 'when word is brought me, that this morning early the master of the above-named vessel and the supercargo were carried before the Dey, and in order to extort a confession . . . were bastinadoed over the feet and loins till the blood gushed and then loaded with heavy chains. The captain, it is thought, cannot recover. I had likewise received from a friend some insinuations that I am in danger, and advice to fly: but as it was not the prospect of pay, or want of fortune, that induced me to accept of this employment, so I will not abandon it from fear or any motive unworthy of a gentleman.'

He was, in fact, attacked in the streets of Algiers. He succeeded in sending warnings to other ports that all British ships carrying written passes might be similarly treated. When this was known the Dey, who had already appointed a renegade slave to act as British Consul in his place, ordered him to leave Algiers within three days.

This would scarcely have been surprising if the Algerines had known of advice which he had already given to Lord Halifax (June 20th). The Navy should prepare for attack on the city, he suggested. A visiting British officer, Commodore Garrison, had advised him that two 74-gun ships would reduce it to the terms His Majesty would prescribe, or in two hours destroy it totally. I am satisfied that the opinion is well founded; but if to the two 74-gun ships two bombs were added for execution not on the batteries, but on the town, were they rash enough not to comply with His Majesty's requests (which they will not attempt) two hours would leave them in ruins, void of defence, without one vessel, and a prey to the Spaniards who would not fail to keep them under. There is, besides, an army of rebels, in number above 22,000 now in arms, within three days' march of Algiers, which would give His Majesty's representation weight, did they need it, which, with those ships, they would not.'

The mere rumour that a British fleet was gathering was enough to change the situation very suddenly. Bruce had his supporters, the chief of whom was the Dey's brother, the Aga, or general of the troops. Now the chief officers, military and naval, went in a body to the Dey, telling him that war with Great Britain would be a disaster and insisting that, to avoid it, the Consul-General must remain in Algiers. This was satisfactory, and so was a letter from Lord Halifax thanking him for what he had done. But no British fleet appeared and, for eight months, no further instructions came to Bruce from London. Algiers again grew threatening and Bruce elaborated his warlike advice.

To make a lasting impression of British power, he suggested to Lord Halifax, the Dey should be forced to pay reparations, including the cost of a naval expedition which, Bruce hopefully suggested, might be led by King George's brother, the Duke of York, already a vice-admiral at twenty-five.

'In the treasury in Algiers alone there are said to be contained thirty-five millions sterling in specie, besides an immense amount in jewels and plate.' There was also an island, Tabarca, which had been held by the Genoese and could become a British possession useful in both peace and war. Its annexation would make a naval demonstration against Algiers both gainful and 'perfectly proper for the first expedition of a prince'.

This was magnificent: quite possibly it would have been a useful way of showing the British flag in North Africa. But it was not the sort of advice which secretaries of state expected from consuls and it was not what Lord Halifax wanted. By this time the Dey had an agent in London, an English sea-captain, who also seems to have spoken for discontented British traders in Algiers and who was denouncing Bruce to Ministers and other influential people as a trouble-maker. Soon this man was telling the Algerines that the London Government would allow them to capture British ships even if these carried written passports.

Bruce was shocked. He had already offered to resign his post, and he now began to hint that if he came home he would find a seat in Parliament, the last resource of an eighteenth-century official in trouble. At last, in June 1765, a naval captain was sent to Algiers as Ambassador. Bruce was pointedly ignored. 'From your excellency having made me the only Christian in Algier to whom you have returned no visit', he wrote to Captain Cleveland, 'I am led to believe, if I could entertain such a suspicion, that your inquiry is rather pointed at me than at the grievances of the nation.' The unbelievable suspicion was too well justified. The erring Simon Peter Cruise became temporary Vice-Consul again.

This was a final humiliation to the Consul-General. His days in Algiers were over. They had ended in something like ignominious dismissal, though the fact that Bruce had offered to resign made it unnecessary to use this term, and though he and the Dey between them had at last forced the British Government to deal with the famous problem of 'proper passes'. They had not given Bruce the glory of bringing a royal prince to Algiers to settle accounts with the Dey. Much worse, from his point of view, they had not given him the leisure to look for ruins, except a few within easy reach of Algiers which he and Balugani had succeeded in drawing. But they had taught him a great deal – not only languages and Arab ways of life but the habits of half-civilized governments and a manner of approach to their rulers. He had made a friend of the Aga, but it is clear that he had also impressed the Dey, partly by boldness, partly by a sort of ceremonious tact, through all their repeated disputes. He had a friendly farewell and was given letters of recommendation to other North Africans in authority, including the Bey of Tunis and the Pasha of Tripoli, who were influenced by the Dey, though they were not his subjects. Letters of this sort could be very useful to a traveller, and Bruce never failed to gather as many as possible and make the utmost use of them.

For travel and discovery were still his aim. Nothing is heard of the project of getting into Parliament – if, indeed, this had ever been more than an ineffective threat. Bruce would scarcely have admitted that there was anything in human life which did not interest him, but he was not a political being. As he left Algiers for Minorca he was free, at last, to begin the work for which he had come to Africa.

First, for his reputation's sake, he must seek out the remains of Roman buildings and make those drawings he had promised to the King. Something was known about them chiefly from the work of Dr Thomas Shaw, who had been chaplain to the Algiers Consulate and had gone back to Oxford to become Principal of St Edmund Hall. Shaw's book, *Travels or Observations relating to Several Parts of Barbary and the Levant* (1738), had made a remarkable beginning, though James Bruce was inclined to be critical of some of his descriptions. But North Africa was scattered with ancient cities and shrines which no European had examined. After visiting some ancient sites on the coast, Bruce came to Tunis, where the Bey received him well, and then followed a route of Shaw's up the Medjerda valley towards the border between Tunisia and Algeria, drawing, measuring and recording ruins as he went. It was here that he met the lion-eaters with whom he was to shock Oxford and London.

'These Arabs', he wrote, 'are immensely rich, paying no tribute to Tunis or Algiers. . . . By the institution of their founder, they are obliged to live upon lions' flesh for their daily food as far as they can procure it: with this they strictly comply, and in consideration of the utility of their vow, they are not taxed, like other Arabs, with payments to the state.'

Dr Shaw had met with this tribe and had spoken about them at Oxford before his book was published. His fellow dons would not believe him. 'They thought it a subversion of the natural order of things that a man should eat a lion, when it had long passed as almost the peculiar province of the lion to eat men.'

The prudent doctor left the matter out of his book 'and only hinted at it after in his appendix'. Bruce was bolder. Faced by the critics – including such an enthusiast for Oxford as Samuel Johnson – he turned to the lion-eaters as a proof that literary Europeans could be wrong about Africa.

'With all submission to that learned university, I will not dispute the lion's title to eating men; but since it is not founded upon patent, no consideration will make me stifle the merit of the Welled Sidi Boogannim, who have turned the chace upon the enemy. . . . On the contrary, I do aver, in the face of these fantastic prejudices, that I have eat the flesh of lions, that is part of three lions, in the tents of Welled Sidi Boogannim. . . . I confess I have no desire of being again served with such a morsel, but the Arabs, a brutish and ignorant folk, will, I fear, notwithstanding the disbelief of the University of Oxford, continue to eat lions as long as they exist.'

Bruce passed on from Hydra, in the country of his lion-eaters, to the great ruins of Tebessa, to Constantine, the ancient Cirta, on its romantic height; to Setif, where the Bey of Constantine was making war against rebels: to the Medrassen, burying-place of the old kings of Numidia; and then into the Aures mountains, where walls and seven gates of Lambessa still stood around a mass of other ruins.

War turned him back to Sbeitla in the Regency of Tunis, where he arrived and recorded the remaining temples. Here he was surrounded by plundering tribesmen. He had with him ten Tunisian spahis, well armed and 'excellent horsemen . . . as eminent for cowardice, at least, as for horsemanship'.

'It was a fair match between coward and coward. With my company I was enclosed in a square in which the three temples stood, where there yet remained a precinct of high walls. These plunderers would have come in to me, but were afraid of my fire-arms; and I would have run away from them, had I not been afraid of meeting their horse in the plain. I was almost starved to death. A friendly tribe . . . came to my assistance and brought me at once, both safety and provision.'

Other Tunisian sites were then visited, the last of them the great amphitheatre at El Djem. Bruce concluded that 'there is not, either in the territories of Algiers or Tunis, a fragment of good taste of which I have not brought a drawing to Britain'.

The claim was not modest, but it was almost a century before the antiquities of the eastern Maghreb were more thoroughly explored and he was able to record buildings which have since been destroyed. Now he had to make a perilous crossing of the Libyan desert to Tripoli. The Bey of Tunis, who gave him all possible help in his own country, had quarrelled with his neighbour, the Pasha of Tripoli, and could do nothing for him there. The Pasha was also on bad terms with the British Consul in his city, 'the Hon Mr Frazer of Lovat', grandson of the Lord Lovat who, after complicated treacheries, was executed as a Jacobite in 1746. Bruce had written to young Lovat for an escort through the desert, which the Pasha promised but did not send. He waited for a month in the fruitful island of Jerba, a place of cave-dwellers who shared their food with snakes.

'These are so many in every habitation, and so familiar, that at each meal they come and pick up what falls from the dish like dogs . . . it being universally believed that they are a kind of good angels, whom it would be the highest impropriety, and of the worst consequence to the community, to remove from their dwellings.'

Impatiently, he decided to cross the desert 'inhabited only by ruffians and assassins' – Arab tribes not controlled by the Turkish governors – though his party 'was now reduced to nine men in all, seven of whom, though indeed resolute people, and well armed, were encumbered with the mules and camels, which carried our tents and provisions. . . . Nor did we escape; for the night of the third day we were attacked by a number of horsemen, and four of our men killed upon the spot. Providence, the prodigious resolution of our little company, and the night, saved the remainder, and we arrived at Tripoly when given over by everyone for lost. The Consul complained heavily to the Pasha, who excused himself poorly. I am persuaded he would have laid the blame upon Mr Frazer, if any accident had befallen us.'[1]

In fact, he had to return to Tunis until the visit of a British warship obtained the Pasha's formal consent to travel in Libya. Now from Tripoli he sailed to Benghazi to examine the relics of the ancient Pentapolis. But Cyrenaica was in the wildest confusion. There was war between two tribes and the defeated had taken refuge in Benghazi itself, which had been suffering from famine for many months so that ten or twelve people were found dead every night in the streets.

Bruce managed to make a journey to various sites, which ended at Tolmeita still surrounded by its ancient walls and gates. War, plague and famine made it impossible to go farther. He decided to turn his back on Africa for the moment and set out for Crete in a small Greek vessel which was soon crowded with refugees.

His next experience was shipwreck. A storm blew up. It proved to be the inexperienced captain's first voyage. Presumably it was also his last. The ship struck a rock. Bruce and two of his servants managed to get into a boat, which was still in tow . . .

'followed by a multitude of people whom we could not hinder, and there was, indeed, something that bordered on cruelty in preventing poor people from using the same means that we had done for preserving their lives. I had stript myself to a short under-waistcoat and linen drawers; a silk sash or girdle was wrapt round me; a pencil, small pocket-book, and watch, were in the breast-pocket of my waistcoat.

'We were not twice the length of the boat from the vessel before a wave very nearly filled it. A howl of despair from those that were in her shewed their helpless state . . . I saw the fate of all was to be decided by the very next wave that was rolling in; and apprehensive that some woman, child, or helpless man would lay hold of

[1] Letter to Robert Wood, from Tunis, April 2nd, 1766.

me, and entangle my arms or legs and weigh me down, I cried to my servants, both in Arabic and English, "We are all lost; if you can swim, follow me." I then let myself down in the face of the wave . . .

'I was a good, strong and practised swimmer, in the flower of life, trained to exercise and fatigue of every kind. All this, however, which might have availed much in deep water, was not sufficient when I came to the surf. I received a blow upon my chest from the eddy wave and reflux, which seemed as given me by a large branch of a tree, a thick cord, or some elastic weapon.'

Bruce blamed this blow and another that followed, for a good deal of ill health in the next year or two. He managed to fight his way ashore and fainted on the beach.

He was brought to himself by a heavy stroke on his shoulder from the butt-end of a lance. Arabs who had seen the shipwreck had come to plunder the survivors. 'It was a mere accident the blow was not with the point, for the small, short waistcoat, which had been made in Algier, the sash and drawers, all in the Turkish fashion made the Arabs believe that I was a Turk; and after many blows, kicks and curses, they stript me of the little clothing I had and left me naked.'

Once he could convince the Arabs that he was not a Turk, but 'a poor Christian physician, a dervish that went about the world seeking to do good for God's sake', Bruce was kindly treated and sent back to Benghazi with his servants, all of whom had escaped drowning. It was, of course, a return to famine, but they kept themselves alive by catching fish, which the starving population would not attempt to get for themselves. Bruce had lost almost all his possessions, including his instruments and his latest sketches; but, very luckily, he had sent one of his men from Tripoli to Izmir with his books, finished sketches, his camera obscura and other equipment. He found a French sloop at Benghazi whose captain he had helped at Algiers, and was offered not only a passage to Crete but the loan of money as well.

North Africa was behind him. He was very ill. But still he did not think seriously of going home. There was the transit of Venus to be observed. More immediately, there were remains of classical architecture in Anatolia which had never been properly described. From Crete he wrote to friends in London and Paris, 'desiring them to send me a moveable quadrant or sextant, as near as possible to two feet radius more or less, a time keeper, a stop watch, a reflecting telescope and one of Dollond's achromatic ones, as near as possible to three feet reflectors, with several other articles which I then wanted'. With this he would be ready for every sort of observation and mensuration.

But he learned that there were no instruments to be had. Foreign astronomers interested in the transit of Venus had ordered all that were likely to be available. And he was too ill to attempt a journey in unexplored districts of Asia Minor. He went, instead, to Syria, where he was well received by the consuls and merchants, more particularly the French. He had made up his mind that he must not try to rival other living travellers who had described classical sites. Baalbek and Palmyra were the territory of his friend Robert Wood but he felt drawn to visit them, though he could not plan to write about them.

At Aleppo, from which he hoped to find a route to Palmyra, he fell dangerously sick again, presumably with malaria, in the house of a hospitable Frenchman, one of those merchants from whom, through his arrangement with his London bankers, he was able to draw money. 'Never was a more lucky address, never was there a soul so congenial to my own than that of Mr Belville: to say more would be praising myself.' A British physician, Dr Patrick Russel, was called in. He was a specialist in Eastern diseases, and through him, during a slow convalescence, Bruce added a great deal to the knowledge of treatments and medicines that he had gained from Dr Bell at Algiers. This was to make it possible for him to win his way through Africa as a doctor. 'Perhaps my escaping the fever at Aleppo', he wrote, 'was not the only time in which I owed [Dr Russel] my life'.

Recovered, Bruce set out for Palmyra, almost drowning in the Orontes when he was misdirected at a ford. With Balugani he made elaborate drawings of the desert city. But this was not the great work which could make his name. It was five years since he had left home. His apprenticeship in travel was complete and still he was without the equipment either for astronomical observation or for the scientific surveying of new lands.

He began to think that the most rewarding thing for him would be an architectural exploration of Egypt. There were, indeed, European accounts of the ancient Egyptian temples, but they had never been thoroughly examined by a man of correct taste who would be able to recognize how Greek and Roman styles of building had developed from Egyptian models. He believed that he had seen 'the greatest part of the good architecture in the world, in all its degrees of perfection down to its decline.' 'Good architecture', of course, was classical architecture. It only remained 'to see it in its origins' and for this it was necessary to go to Egypt. There he could sketch and measure buildings, statues and paintings, and spend the rest of his life in evaluating and explaining the material he had collected for his own satisfaction and that of the educated world in general.

This was certainly work that needed to be done. It was done thirty years later by the corps of scientists, scholars and artists whom Napoleon took with him to Egypt: the result was an aesthetic revolution which did much to form the Empire and Regency styles in France and Britain.

But Bruce was scarcely the man to work such a revolution by himself in the 1770s. His taste was altogether too 'correct'. He knew well the orders and proportions of classical architecture as the authorities of his own day understood them. Of ancient buildings in North Africa which failed to conform to these patterns he would write that they 'did not merit the attention of any architect'. In Ethiopia he could mistake the extraordinary steles of Axum, belonging to what is, apparently, a South Arabian tradition, for obelisks in what he thought to be the style of the Ptolemies.

'Quantity and solidity are two principal requisites that are seen here, with a vengeance', was his comment on the elegant Ptolemaic temple at Dendera when he did pass through Upper Egypt. Though he noted that to record this one building and its hieroglyphics thoroughly would have taken him six months, though his eyes were sharp and his interest keen, he did not have the width of aesthetic sympathy that would have been needed to interpret an ancient civilization still little known, though it had been a legend in the West since Europe began – a civilization which must speak through buildings and pictures, because its language would remain unreadable till long after Bruce's day.

It was lucky, then, that this latest plan was blown away by messages from London and Paris which now came to him in the French Consulate at Sidon. First, most of the instruments he wanted had been found for him. This seems to have suggested to him that when he had seen the ruins of Egypt he might, after all, make his astronomical observations in Armenia, coming home through Asia Minor and Constantinople, and perhaps visiting Sicily to examine classical ruins there – surely a programme for a lifetime rather than for a lover who was still hoping to marry his Margaret. Then he learned that astronomers had begun to doubt whether, after all, the transit of Venus was likely to give them the sort of information that they had hoped to get from it.

This disposed of the idea of travelling to Armenia to look for Venus. But, almost at once, the dream which excited him most was revived by another letter from France. Some savants there, including the Comte de Buffon, the most famous of all, had heard of his ambition to find the source of the Nile. This, they thought, was something that must be done, and Bruce was the man to do it. They knew about the loss of his instruments and had suggested to Louis XV through his minister, Choiseul, that 'one most unlucky accident at a most unlucky time' should not be allowed to frustrate this most promising endeavour. King Louis had ordered that a quadrant from the military academy at Marseilles should be sent to Bruce. It was waiting for him at Alexandria.

Here was a decisive challenge which could not be refused. From the ship that carried him out of Sidon he saw very high thin white clouds moving north towards Asia Minor against the course of the Etesian winds which blew below them. Surely, he thought, these came from the Ethiopian mountains to be recharged with moisture and return to feed the Nile. It was a sign in the sky. His long apprenticeship to exploration was over at last. On June 20th, 1768, he reached Alexandria. His life work had properly begun.

5

River and Sea

It was El Hakim Yagoube who landed at Alexandria – Doctor James
– a physician and an inquiring philosopher. He went about in Arab
clothes, speaking Arabic, and was pleased to find that a casual
passer-by could mistake him and his servants for peasants. But he
carried with him a Firman of the Sultan, 'magnificently written and
titled, and the inscription powdered with gold dust', which he had
obtained through the Ambassador at Constantinople, a fellow Scot.
This described him as a noble Englishman, a servant of the British
King. Throughout the Turkish Empire and neighbouring countries
it was, or should have been, the most powerful of passports.

He had other letters of recommendation to important people in
Egypt and beyond: to these he was constantly adding. He had
letters of credit that allowed him to draw money from merchant
bankers in Cairo, the Governor of Jidda in Arabia, the Sherif of
Mecca's chief minister and a number of lesser figures from the
Mediterranean to the Sudan. He had, of course, his cases of instruments, particularly impressive because they showed that he could
observe the stars – and so was, presumably, an astrologer able to
foretell the future. He had his medicines. He had a formidable
armoury of weapons; pistols, guns and blunderbusses. He had presents suitable for princes, officials, even ladies. He had a travelling
library consisting of the pages from books dealing with the Nile,

the Red Sea, Ethiopia – their geography, history, languages, animals, plants, minerals – which he had torn from the works of ancient and modern authors. And he had, of course, paper to write and draw on.

In fact, on an expedition which was bound to be full of surprises and unknown dangers James Bruce was leaving as little as possible to chance. He was a scientific explorer, anxious to understand anything he could see.

To begin with he settled down in the French quarter of Cairo to find his bearings. 'It is one long street,' he wrote, 'where all the merchants of the nation dwell together. It is shut at one end by large gates, where there is a guard, and these are kept constantly close in the time of the plague', which returned every spring.

'All the enjoyment that Christians can hope for among this vile people, reduces itself to peace, and quiet: nobody seeks for more. There are, however, wicked emissaries who are constantly employed, by threats and extravagent demands, to torment them, and keep them from enjoying that repose which would content them instead of freedom, and more solid happiness, in their own country. . . .

'A more brutal, unjust, tyrannical, oppressive, avaricious set of infernal miscreants there is not on earth then are the members of the government of Cairo.'

Egypt, where Mediterranean history was believed to have begun, was indeed far gone in decay. Reduced by centuries of misgovernment and disease, the population was not more than a tenth of what it is now – in the long ribbon of the Nile valley where the great river makes it's way between deserts it was perhaps less than three million. Here, as in the other parts of the Turkish Empire which Bruce visited, the Ottoman Government had lost almost all control. There was endemic civil war between Turks and Arabs, and between the desert tribes themselves.

But Egypt had peculiar weaknesses of its own. For two thousand years the oldest of the nations had scarcely ever had a ruler of native blood. For five hundred years its masters had actually been slaves – the Mamelukes, from the Balkans or the Caucasus, bought to be soldiers, whose leaders fought their way to power. For a while Ottoman conquest had reduced the anarchy, but soon the Mameluke beys, governors of the provinces, were in command again. In Bruce's day Egyptian politics actually had rather more shape and meaning than usual. A single Mameluke chief, Ali Bey, had made himself the (more or less) effective ruler. Like other ambitious heads of the Egyptian State, from the Pharaohs to President Nasser, he wished to rule Syria and part of Arabia as well. He aimed to make himself completely independent of the Turkish Sultan.

Turkey and the Russia of Catherine II were at war. For the first time a Russian fleet had forced its way into the Mediterranean and had practically destroyed the Turkish Navy near Izmir. Bruce found this news hopeful and exciting. Perhaps the incompetent Ottoman Empire was going to collapse. Perhaps the long decline of the Near East might be ending. Perhaps the Russian Empress would revive it and give it freedom. Given a chance, he thought, all the discontented peoples would rally to her.

In fact, Ali Bey was reaching out for Russian help toward securing his independence. If the Russians had understood what they were doing, Bruce thought, 'Egypt and Syria would possibly have fallen dismembered from the Ottoman empire. But it was very plain that the Russian commanders were not provided with instructions, and had no idea how far their victory might have carried them, or how to manage those they had conquered. They had no confidential correspondence with Ali Bey, though they might have trusted him as he would have trusted them.'

Meanwhile Bruce was anxious to have Ali's protection on his journey, so far as the Bey's influence could help him. A Coptic Christian, Risk, was Ali's secretary and chief adviser. 'Risk professed astrology, and the Bey, like all other Turks, believed in it implicitly and to this folly [Ali] sacrificed his own good understanding. Risk, probably in pay to Constantinople, led him from one wild scheme to another, till he undid him – by the stars.'

However traitorous the secretary may have been, he was at least a half-believer in the astrology which he used in his intrigues. He had heard from the customs house at Alexandria of Bruce's astronomical instruments and thought at once that the traveller might be able to give him some prophetic hints about the future. Soon he visited Bruce and told him that the Bey would protect him. To prevent the curious citizens from guessing at their dealings, he proposed that Bruce should go to the convent of St George, outside Cairo, which was the headquarters of the Greek Orthodox Patriarch of Alexandria.

This was an unexpectedly happy arrangement for the explorer. In the convent he found an old friend, Father Christopher, who had been his unofficial chaplain at Algiers, and was now an archimandrite and the Patriarch's deputy. In Cairo, Bruce had been able to say nothing about his plans for visiting Ethiopia, except to his French hosts, for such journeys were forbidden by the Turkish Government: but he could talk freely to Christopher, who told him that there were a number of Greeks in Ethiopia who corresponded with the Patriarch. They were refugees who had fled from Turkey, but were influential, since the Ethiopians welcomed and valued foreigners so long as they could not leave the country again or act for governments that might try to interfere in Ethiopian affairs.

The Patriarch's will was almost law to these men. For them he was both their chief authority in religion and their best link with the world they had left. Bruce obtained letters from him, notably one 'in form of a bull' ordering the Greeks of Ethiopia not only to help him wherever they could but also to declare to the Ethiopian Emperor that he was their superior, 'a free citizen of a powerful nation and servant of a great king, not like them, born a slave to the Turks'.

This was to be of great use in Ethiopia. So, more immediately, was Father Christopher's advice about the Bey and his household, which contained many Greek slaves whom the archimandrite visited. Soon Bruce himself was summoned to the Bey – by night, so that his visit would not be seen.

He found Ali 'sitting upon a large sofa, covered with crimson-cloth of gold: his turban, his girdle, and the head of his dagger covered with fine brilliants; one in his turban that served to support a sprig of brilliants also, was among the largest I had ever seen'. At once the Bey asked him what the result of the Russo-Turkish war would be.

'I said the Turks would be beaten by sea and land wherever they presented themselves.' Istanbul would not be taken, however, 'but peace would be made after much bloodshed, with little advantage to either side'.

'That will be sad indeed,' commented the Bey, rather cryptically, 'but truth is truth, and God is merciful.'

Bruce's prophecy was evidently found satisfactory. He was promised the Bey's protection and was called back again a few nights later to give medical advice on a fit of indigestion. Among other things he suggested 'a good glass of spirits'.

'He looked surprised at this proposal,' Bruce reports, 'and said very calmly:

' "Spirits! do you know I am a Mussulman?"

' "But I, sir," said I, "am none. I tell you what is good for your body, and have nothing to do with your religion, or your soul."

'He seemed vastly diverted and pleased with my frankness, and only said, "He speaks like a man." '

Bruce had had enough of Cairo, in spite of the Pyramids, which disappointed him. Through Risk he obtained letters from the Bey to the Arab sheikh who was governor of a large part of Upper Egypt; to the Sherif of Mecca; the ruler of Massawa, the port for Ethiopia; and the King of Sennar, in the Sudan. Then he hired a ship for the long voyage up the Nile to Aswan.

The Nile! It was his first real contact with the great river, rolling northward for 1,700 rainless miles without a tributary, whose source he had promised to reach. *Quaerere fontes Nili*: to seek the springs of the Nile – since Roman times this had been a proverbial description of a hopeless quest. Yet, like nearly all men of his time interested in geography, Bruce had no real doubt where those sources were to be found.

He knew, of course, that a river came out of the unknown heart of black Africa to join that from the Ethiopian Highlands, and when he finally saw this Bahr el Abiad – the White Nile, the true Nile for us – he recognized that it was actually bigger than the Ethiopian Nile, the Blue Nile. Ancient writers had guessed at the truth that it came through great lakes from legendary Mountains of the Moon. But these could be the Ethiopian mountains, and it was known that the Blue Nile flowed through, or from, a great lake. It was known, too, that it was the Ethiopian waters which provided the annual floods that made possible the irrigation of Egyptian fields – floods without which Egypt would have starved. More than once rulers of Ethiopia had threatened to ruin Egypt by diverting their flood waters to the Red Sea; and this threat was taken seriously, though such an operation was far beyond the power of any Ethiopian government, in the eighteenth century at least. Clearly the Blue Nile was the river that mattered, the life-giving stream which ancient Egyptians had worshipped. It was entirely natural that Bruce, like other travellers before him, should be searching for the source of what, geographically speaking, was the wrong river.

He might reach it by following the stream through Egypt and the Sudan, but the last important European mission which had attempted this route had perished miserably at Sennar. The alternative was the route used by the Portuguese in the sixteenth century, when they first made contact with Prester John and then rescued Christian Ethiopia in the worst crisis of its history; the route which was still used for trade and (usually) by each Coptic bishop from Egypt who was sent to Ethiopia to be the nominal head of its national church. This was by the Red Sea to Massawa, which had been Ethiopia's chief port before the Turks took it in 1557. Bruce's voyage up the Egyptian Nile was a first step towards Massawa. He would have to cross the desert to the Red Sea, visit Jidda, the Arabian port where he could make contact with Ethiopia, and climb the mountains behind Massawa to the Ethiopian plateau.

*   *   *

His journey began in more comfort than he was to know for almost five years. His ship had a dining-room twenty feet long and a bedroom half that size. It was blown southwards by the regular Etesian winds. Its raïs (or captain) was a humorous being, reliable because he was obeying the commands of Ali Bey, whom Cairenes had every reason to fear. Bruce liked to call him a saint because he claimed to be a descendant of the Prophet and had made the pilgrimage to Mecca – the Protestant Scot could never take saints seriously. But this saint was no puritan Moslem; his chief weakness was a love of brandy, and he argued that though Mohammed had forbidden wine (a drink the raïs did not enjoy) the Koran said nothing about spirits.

There were, indeed, some dangers even on the Egyptian Nile – from extortionate local officials, from swimming thieves by night, from little wars between villages, between desert tribesmen and peasants, between Turks and Arabs. But, on the whole, they travelled smoothly, with occasional halts to examine temples or to fix by scientific observation the precise longitude of towns and ancient sites.

Bruce was most interested (and puzzled) by the remains of Thebes, the ancient capital of Upper Egypt. Life had shrunk so badly in the wasted Egypt of his day that he could not believe that anything so great as the 'hundred-gated' city described by Homer and other ancient writers could ever have existed in the narrow strip of the river valley between the desert hills to the east and west. He concluded that the ruins and tombs near Medinet Habu, west of the Nile, were the only remains of Thebes itself, and that Luxor and Karnak, on the other bank, had been a separate town, Diospolis, 'built by the Greeks long after the ancient Thebes was destroyed'. He could find no traces of houses among the temples, and decided that the old Egyptians must have been cave-dwellers, and that the pylons and temples themselves, with their sloping walls, were an architectural representation of mountain caves, 'a remnant of the partiality of the builders for their first domiciles'.

In his day outlaws, 'punishable by death if elsewhere found', did live in some of the cave tombs above Medinet Habu. But he recognized the tombs of the Valley of the Kings for what they were. Timorous guides from the remaining villages were not at all anxious to give him time to examine these tombs, from fear of the robbers around them and, possibly, of the ghosts of dead Pharaohs; but in the first that he entered[1] he found 'a prodigious sarcophagus . . . sixteen feet high, and six broad, of one piece of red granite . . . I suppose the finest vase in the world.'

He was fascinated by the paintings on the walls of the tomb, still lively in their original colours. Three frescoes of harps and the men playing them fixed his attention, and he set out to copy one of them, while Balugani dealt with another.

'Those harps', he wrote, '. . . are altogether an incontestable proof, stronger than a thousand Greek quotations, that geometry, drawing, mechanics, and music, were at the greatest perfection when this instrument was made.' He quoted King Solomon, 'a writer who lived at the time when this harp was painted' – certainly a dubious dating for the author of Ecclesiastes. 'Is there a thing whereof it can be said, See, this is new? It hath been already of old time which was before us.'[2] Bruce wished to copy all the paintings in this tomb and perhaps in others. He was disappointed.

'Upon seeing the preparations I was making to proceed farther in my research, my conductors lost all sort of subordination. They were afraid my intention was to sit in this cave all night (as it really was) and to visit the rest next morning. With great clamour and marks of discontent, they dashed their torches against the largest harp, and made the best of their way out of the cave, leaving me and my people in the dark; and all the way as they went they made dreadful denunciations of tragical events that were to follow.'

For fear of the outlaws they would not be bribed to come back.

[1] It is now identified as the tomb of Rameses III.
[2] Eccles. i. 10. Oddly enough, Bruce's critics in London were to find his account of these harps particularly incredible.

1. Old Kinnaird House, with James Bruce's additions from *Ancient Castles and Mansions of the Stirling Nobility* by J. S. Fleming

2. Roman Arch at Tripoli, from a drawing by Luigi Balugani (at Broomhall)

These fears, it proved, were natural enough. As Bruce rode through the dark valley towards his ship he heard voices on both sides of him, 'and in an instant a number of large stones were rolled down upon me, which, though I heard in motion, I could not see, on account of the darkness.

'Nevertheless, I was resolved upon revenge before leaving these banditti, and listened till I heard voices, on the right side of the hill. I accordingly levelled my gun as near as possible, by the ear and fired one barrel among them. A moment's silence ensued, and then a loud howl, which seemed to have come from thirty or forty persons. I took my servant's blunderbuss and discharged it where I heard the howl, and violent confusion of tongues followed, but no more stones. As I found this was the time to escape, I kept along the dark side of the hill, as expeditiously as possible, till I came to the mouth of the plain, when we reloaded our firelocks, expecting some interruption before we reached the boat; and then we made the best of our way to the river.'

In the ship they found an anxious raïs. 'We thought, since our enemy had left us tonight, it would be our fault if they found us in the morning. Therefore without noise we cast off our rope which fastened us and let ourselves over to the other side' – and the magnificent ruins of Luxor.

Bruce went on to Aswan to see the first cataract of the Nile, below the modern dam. On the way he stopped to treat the illness of the Sheikh of the Ababdeh, one of the great desert tribes, whose people solemnly swore to help and protect the traveller so long as one male child among them remained alive. From Aswan he turned north again to Kena to begin his journey across the desert.

He travelled with a caravan carrying corn for Mecca, whose members were in terror of the desert tribes, and with a group of Turkish pilgrims, 'all of them neatly and cleanly dressed, all on camels, armed with swords, a pair of pistols at their girdle, and a short neat gun, each of them with his little cloak bag very neatly packed up', who attached themselves to him not from fear of the tribesmen but for protection against thieves in the caravan itself. Their suspicion was justified: but for the oath of the Ababdeh, Bruce's party might have been in real danger when they reached Koseir on the Red Sea, after passing through plains of sand and gravel where 'there are not even traces of a living creature' and between mountains of green, red and white marble, granite, porphyry and jasper, which the ancients had quarried, and which, Bruce believed, could have yielded stone enough to 'build Rome, Athens, Corinth, Syracuse, Memphis, Alexandria and half a dozen such cities'.

Koseir was a miserable port, but busy with little undecked ships carrying wheat to Arabia – constantly overloaded and often sunk. Here Bruce met a Mameluke Bey returning to Egypt from exile, who arrived in 'a small but tight vessel' belonging to the Yemen which had proved its seaworthiness by voyages in the Indian Ocean. Its captain was known as Sidi Ali the Ape, 'for though he was a saint, yet, being in figure more like a monkey they thought it proper to distinguish him by that to which he bore the greatest resemblance . . . a very active, vigorous little man, and to the full as good a sailor as he was a saint', even though his claim to be able to make rocks remove themselves or become as soft as sponges when his ship was in danger of running on them was scarcely justified in Bruce's experience.

On April 5th, 1769, Bruce was glad enough to leave Koseir in the little ship of Sidi Ali the Ape. But still he wished to know more of the Red Sea, to look into the Gulf of Suez and judge for himself how the Children of Israel had passed from Egypt into Sinai – inevitably he had a theory on this subject. Much more important, he set himself to learn more about the navigation of the Red Sea, where ships were often lost. For British traders from India the route to Suez could be valuable and he was anxious to open it to them: in his day they were not allowed to go beyond Jidda, where, every year, a fleet of Indiamen brought goods which passed on to the market of Mecca, the Moslem Holy City, closed to all Christians. His book at this point almost becomes a sort of Red Sea Pilot, full of descrip-

tions of harbours, channels and islands with new calculations of
their latitude and longitude. He was, in fact, providing the first
scientifically reliable guidance to an important part of what has
since become one of the world's chief sea routes.

He had the lowest opinion of existing charts. 'God forgive those
who have taken upon themselves, very lately, to ingraft a number of
new soundings on that miserable bundle of errors', he wrote of one
chart. A copy had been sent to him 'new drest like a bride, with all
its original and mortal sins upon its head. I would beg leave to be
understood, that there is not in the world a man more averse than
I am to give offense even to a child. . . . But where the lives and
properties of so many men are at stake yearly, it is a species of
treason to conceal one's sentiments, if the publishing of them can
any way contribute to safety, whatever offence it may give to
individuals.'

From Sinai he passed down the east coast to Yanbo, a port with
a garrison of janissaries, where he arrived to the sound of gun-shots.
These Turks were engaged in a little war with the Arab townsmen.
However, Bruce found that he was expected and respectfully
received as the physician of Ali Bey. And the war was soon over:
both sides had exhausted their ammunition. The old men of
the place then agreed that nobody had been to blame for the
fighting.

'The whole wrong was the work of a camel.' The unfortunate
beast was solemnly denounced to its face. 'The camel had killed
men, he had threatened to set the town on fire; the camel had
threatened to burn down the Aga's house and the castle: he had
cursed the Grand Signor [the Turkish Sultan] and the Sherif of
Mecca; and (the only thing the poor animal was interested in) he
had threatened to destroy the wheat that was going to Mecca.
After having spent great part of the afternoon upbraiding the camel,
whose measure of iniquity, it seemed, was nearly full, each man
thrust him through with a lance . . . with a thousand curses upon
his head', and peace was restored to Yanbo.

Five days later Bruce sailed into Jidda. This was an important step in his travels. For the first time it could bring him into contact with Ethiopia. Through the desert port passed a large part of the trade of the Red Sea, and most Ethiopian trade in particular. Yet the place itself remained poor, isolated and comfortless – so poor that its men, as Bruce noted, could not afford to marry more than one wife because of the difficulty of feeding a polygamous household. It was controlled by the Sherif of Mecca, a descendant of the Prophet and a much more powerful figure in the Hejaz than any Turkish pasha: all its imports and the customs paid for them, besides the annual stream of pilgrims, passed on to the Holy City. Nine British ships from India lay in the harbour. Bruce was able to see the ingenious and complicated system of trade whereby sales were made without words by native Indian agents – neutral arbiters between Turks and Europeans because they were neither Moslem nor Christian – and payments were guaranteed, quite reliably, by Arab brokers who might have no funds of their own.

The Sherif's chief adviser was his sword-bearer, an Ethiopian slave whom Bruce knew as Metical Aga. This man was 'the great friend and protector of the English at Jidda', receiving large presents from their captains. He had great influence in his native country, particularly with the most powerful and formidable of its chieftains, Michael Suhul, Governor of Tigre, the northern province. Ethiopian exports came to Jidda, chiefly slaves and gold. In return Michael received through Metical Aga supplies of firearms which made his troops the best equipped in Ethiopia. The Aga also had contacts with the Moslems of Ethiopia, for whom his master, the Sherif, was the most important of Islamic princes, controlling the Holy City to which they might hope to make pilgrimage. The names of the Sherif and his minister carried weight beyond Ethiopia in the Moslem Sudan.

Bruce was anxious to have the strongest possible letters of recommendation from Metical Aga and the Sherif. He had to introduce himself to the British captains at Jidda. His reception, to begin with, was not too encouraging. He arrived tired and ill, looking so like a Turkish seaman that the port official he met first could hardly believe he was a European. He asked to be taken to a Scotsman, a relative of his own, whom he expected to find at the Bengal House, where the East India Company's men had their headquarters. This was a Captain Boswell.[1]

The captain was standing on a staircase, looking over a rail into the courtyard below.

'I saluted him by his name; he fell into a violent rage, calling me villain, thief, cheat and renegade rascal; and declared if I offered to proceed a step further he would throw me over the stairs. I went away without reply; his curses and abuse followed me long afterwards.

'The servant, my conductor, screwed his mouth and shrugged up his shoulders. "Never fear," says he, "I will carry you to the best of them all." We went up an opposite stair-case, whilst I thought within myself, if those are their India manners I shall keep my name and situation to myself while I am at Jidda.'

The traveller was then presented to Captain Thornhill, of the ship *Bengal Merchant*, 'sitting in a white calico waistcoat, a very high pointed white cotton night-cap, with a large tumbler of water before him, seemingly very deep in thought'. Though Bruce could scarcely bring himself to speak, and the captain evidently took him for a starving wanderer, this was a friendly meeting. He was offered a passage to India and a meal. When he had eaten he collapsed into sleep on a mat in the courtyard, though he was among British sailors who told one another that he was 'a very thief-life fellow and certainly a Turk'.

Meanwhile the Turkish Governor of Jidda, to whom Bruce had a letter of credit, had begun to force open his baggage at the custom

---

[1] James Boswell himself supplies the family name in his account of his interview with Bruce on August 9th, 1774 – *Boswell for the Defence*. The India Office records show that his cousin, Bruce Boswell, was the only East India captain of the name. When James Bruce was in Jidda, however, Bruce Boswell appears to have been on a voyage to China. (Information kindly supplied by Mr A. J. Farrington, Commonwealth Office.)

house. The first trunk revealed the Sultan's firman, a green and gold silk bag containing letters for the Sherif of Mecca, a plain crimson satin bag with letters for Metical Aga, and, finally, a letter from Ali Bey to himself threatening to 'punish the affront at the very gates of Mecca' if Bruce was not properly treated.

For the Governor this was alarming. He set off at once to look for 'the English nobleman' to whom these documents belonged. Nobody had seen him, he was told, but one of his servants was in the Bengal House. Bruce was asked where his master was. The reply (he says) was 'In Heaven'. But the Governor and the British community were finally convinced that Bruce was, in fact, himself. An explanation was made to Captain Thornhill, Bruce's friendly host during his stay at Jidda. English and Moslems combined to get the desired letters from Metical Aga, 'a very good man, but no great head-piece', whom Bruce wooed, successfully, with a present of pistols. The Aga also agreed to send a servant of his own with Bruce, an Ethiopian Moslem who would help to guide him and smooth his way and could report, if necessary, on his reception. This man, whom Bruce calls Mahomet Gibberti (Jabartis are people of Ethiopian race and Mohammedan faith), was to be immensely useful to the traveller.

Though Bruce's business at Jidda was complete, Mahomet Gibberti was not yet ready to leave Arabia. The southern part of the Red Sea was still to be seen, and on July 8th, 1769, Sidi Ali the Ape's small ship left once more, this time for the coast of the Yemen and the Straits of Bab el Mandeb.

'The wind was fair, and we sailed through the English fleet at their anchors. . . . The raïs was surprised to see the respect paid to his little vessel as it passed under their huge sterns, every one hoisting his colours, and saluting it with eleven guns except, the ship belonging to my Scotch friend, who shewed his colours, indeed, but did not fire a gun, only standing upon deck he cried with a trumpet "Captain [Boswell] wishes Mr Bruce a good voyage".

I stood upon deck, took my trumpet and answered, "Mr Bruce wishes Captain [Boswell] a perfect return of his understanding"; a wish, poor man, that has not yet been accomplished, and, very much to my regret, it does not appear possible that it ever will.'

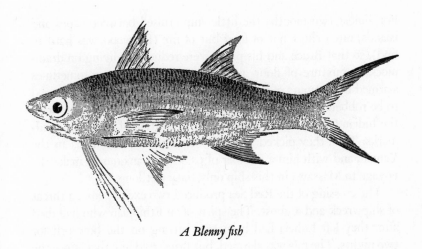

A Blenny fish

6

⊂—●○◎○●—⊃

Into Ethiopia

For almost two months the little ship cruised between capes and islands, often short not of food but of fire (for wood was hard to find), so that Bruce and his party were reduced to living on drammock, a mixture of flour and cold water. They were sometimes alarmed by rumours of pirates at sea and the sight of what seemed to be robbers and murderers on land. But Bruce had his glimpse of the Indian Ocean and he duly fixed the position of ports and landmarks. Then they picked up Mahomet Gibberti at Luheia in the Yemen, and with him a number of passengers anxious to make the voyage to Massawa in this ship only sixty feet long.

The crossing of the Red Sea produced two excitements, a threat of shipwreck and a ghost. The spirit of an Ethiopian who had died after they left Luheia had been seen sitting on the bowsprit for two nights. The raïs was alarmed, but Bruce told him that, since the man had paid for his passage and would scarcely overload the ship as a spectre, he should not be disturbed, but was entitled to ride on the bowsprit till he grew tired.

Five days later – for the passage was slow, largely because of the number of islands encountered – the ship struck on a coral reef. It was night. Some proposed to escape in a dinghy which was Bruce's private property, others to break up the ship itself and make a raft. Bruce reminded them that he and his party were well armed: 'therefore, do not imagine that we shall suffer you to enter that boat and save your lives at the expense of ours'. They must get the ship off the rock while the sea was calm. In organizing this work the

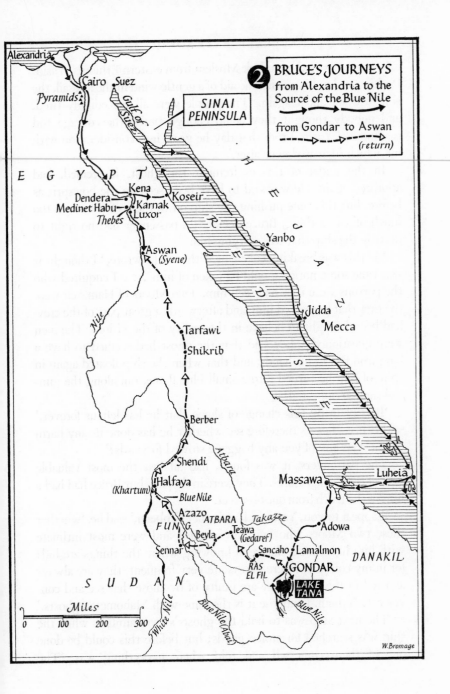

BRUCE'S JOURNEYS
from Alexandria to the
Source of the Blue Nile

from Gondar to Aswan
(return)

Alexandria

Cairo Suez

Pyramids

SINAI PENINSULA

Gulf of Suez

E G Y P T

Kena

Dendera
Medinet Habu
Thebes Karnak
Luxor Koseir

Aswan
(Syene)

Nile

H E J A Z

Yanbo

Jidda
Mecca

Tarfawi

Shikrib

R E D   S E A

Berber

Atbara

Shendi

Halfaya
(Khartum)

Blue Nile

Azazo

F U N G ATBARA

Beyla Teawa
(Gedaref)

Sennar

Sancaho

Takazze

Luheia

Massawa

Adowa

Lamalmon

DANAKIL

RAS
EL FIL

GONDAR

**LAKE
TANA**

S U D A N

White Nile

Blue Nile (Abai)

Blue Nile

Miles

0   100   200   300

W. Bromage

raïs was supported by a dark Moslem from eastern Ethiopia, Yasin. Pushing and pulling, with the aid of a gentle wind in the foresail, the ship was set afloat again. 'The people were all exceedingly tired, and nobody thought they could enough praise the courage and readiness of Yasin. From that day he grew into consideration with me which increased ever after.'

In the midst of this excitement the ghost, it seemed, had appeared again. He was said to have been seen on the bowsprit as before, but this time pushing the ship on to the reef. This was too much of a bad thing, Bruce decided; a passenger had no right to destroy the ship that was carrying him.

'As this was breaking covenant with me,' he wrote, ' I thought it was time some notice should be taken of him . . . I enquired who the persons were that had seen him. Two Moors of Hamazen were the first that perceived him, and afterwards a great part of the crew had been brought to believe in the reality of the vision.' The men were questioned. They said that the ghost had seemed to have a long iron rod in his hands, and that when the ship floated again in spite of him he turned into a small blue flame, ran along the gunwale and disappeared.

'It is plain by this change of shape that he has left us forever,' said Bruce. 'Let us therefore see whether he has done us any harm or not. Has any of you any baggage stowed forwards?'

The passengers, it was found, had all lost the most valuable part of their small stores. They were in despair, but Bruce had had a hint of the truth from one observer.

'I appeal to you, Yasin and Mahomet Gibberti,' said he, 'whether these two Moors who saw him oftenest and were most intimate with him have not a chance of knowing where the things are hid: for in my country, where ghosts are very frequent, they are always assisted in the thefts they are guilty of by those that see and converse with them. I suppose it is the same with Mahometan ghosts.'

The next step was to hold the ghosts's two familiars while the ship was searched for stolen goods; but before this could be done one of them confessed and told where everything was. 'The ghost, finding his associates discovered, never was seen any more.'

On September 19th, Bruce sailed into the bay of Massawa. The voyage was over. He was at the end of the world that Europe knew.

Massawa was no-man's-land. For the travellers it was to be a place of fears and frustration. This waterless island had been the chief port of Ethiopia when the Empire had a sea-coast of its own. Then, in the days of Ottoman conquest it had become the seat of a Turkish Pasha – the remotest outpost of the great Moslem Empire. But here Ottoman decay had reached its last stage. Though Massawa still had its garrison, descendants of the Turkish troops, they were scarcely distinguishable from the local tribesmen. The province behind the island port had shrunk to a strip of more or less desert plain sweltering beneath the Ethiopian hills. The Pasha had been withdrawn. A tribal chief had the Ottoman titles of 'Naib' and 'Aga', but the Sultan's Government had no real control over him, his exactions on the trade that still passed through his harbour, or his treatment of travellers whom he could hold to ransom.

The only authorities whom he feared were Michael, the Governor of Tigre and now Ras and Bitwaded (chief minister of the Ethiopian Empire) and the Sherif of Mecca, or his minister, Metical Aga. Either could have cut off Massawa's trade. Under an agreement between them some tribute was extracted from the Naib: indeed, the Ethiopians could easily have recaptured their port if it had not suited Michael to work through this foreign official whose misdeeds he could disown. Bruce's only safeguards against extortion, theft, or even murder, in Massawa were the interest which Metical Aga and Ras Michael showed in him, his own readiness to put up a fight if necessary, and the protection of the Naib's nephew and heir, Ahmed, with whom Metical Aga was friendly.

The news of Bruce's coming had reached Massawa before him. He was said to be a prince, nearly related to the British King, not a trader, but, no doubt, enormously rich. There had been long discussions over this between the Naib and his counsellors. 'Some were for the most expeditious, and what has long been the customary method of treating strangers in Masuah, to put them to death, and divide everything they had among the garrison.' Ahmed had other ideas. There had been too many murders in Massawa, he thought, and, in any case, a prince should be respected. The British ships which had fired salutes when Bruce left Jidda could destroy Massawa in an afternoon – the clay-built castle there possessed one small cannon, 'fired always with great trepidation and some danger'.

Ahmed persuaded his uncle and the troops to wait and see. Bruce, on his arrival, was equally cautious. He let Mahomet Gibberti land before him to make contact with a spy whom Michael of Tigre and Metical Aga kept to observe the Naib's doings, and this man sent off secretly a message to a notable Greek, Janni, who was in charge of Michael's financial affairs at his provincial capital, Adowa, telling him of Bruce's arrival and the letters he carried. With the message went a copy of the Patriarch's letter commanding all Greeks in Ethiopia to support the traveller, and Janni was asked to send 'some men of confidence' to Massawa to keep an eye on the Naib.

Next day Bruce had a formal interview with Ahmed, who had come to Massawa from Arkiko, a larger town on the mainland, to receive customs dues. He was not an impressive figure. 'His stature near five feet four, he was feebly made, a little bent forward or stooping, thin, long-faced, long-necked. . . . He was dressed all in white, in a long Banian habit of muslin and a close-bodied frock reaching to his ancles. . . . This species of dress did not in any way suit his shape or size, but it seems he meant to be in gala.' To such a figure the enormous Scot must have seemed an overwhelming being. Ahmed was a bold man, however, friendly but full of questions. When Bruce rose to leave he 'was presently wet to the skin by deluges of orange flower water showered . . . by two of his attendants from silver bottles. A very decent house had been provided; and I had no sooner entered than a large dinner was sent us, with a profusion of lemons and good fresh water, now become one of the greatest delicacies in life; and, instantly after, our baggage was all sent unopened: with which I was very well-pleased,

being afraid they might break something in my clock, telescopes
or quadrant, by the violent manner in which they satisfy their
curiosity.'

Ahmed's curiosity was not satisfied, however. He appeared
again later at night, wearing, this time, only a rough cloak, a pair
of drawers and a cotton cap. Was Bruce really a prince? he asked.
Why should Metical Aga be concerned about a Christian traveller?

'I am neither son nor brother of a king,' Bruce reports his own
reply. 'If you saw my prince, the eldest or any other son of the
King of England, you would then be able to form a juster idea of
them and that would for ever hinder you from confounding them
with common man like me. If they should choose to appear in this
part of the world, this little sea would be too narrow for their
ships; your sun, now so hot, would be darkened by their sails; and
when they fixed the terrible wide-mouthed cannon, not an Arab
would think himself safe on the distant mountains, while the houses
on the shore would totter and fall to the ground, as if shaken to
pieces by an earthquake.

'I am a servant to that king, and an inferior one in rank. . . .
Yet my ancestors were the kings of the country in which I was born,
to be ranked among the greatest and most glorious that ever bore
the crown and title of king.'

Ahmed, it seems, was duly impressed and promised his protection, though prophesying destruction if Bruce went among the
Ethiopians, 'a people without faith, covetous, barbarous and in a
continual war, of which nobody yet has been able to discover the
reason'.

If this forecast was not encouraging, the interviews with Ahmed
seemed to make a good beginning so far as things in Massawa itself
were concerned. They ended with the flattering gift to him of a pair
of English pistols – such as his agent in Jidda (Bruce had learned)
had been trying in vain to buy for him. But the Naib himself had
still to be encountered. Bruce 'found him sitting on a large wooden
elbow-chair, at the head of two files of naked savages, who made an
avenue from his chair to the door. He had nothing upon him but a

coarse cotton shirt, so dirty that, it seemed, all pain to clean it again would be thrown away: and so short that it scarcely reached to his knees. He was very tall and lean; his colour black; had a large mouth and nose; in place of a beard, a very scanty tuft of grey hairs upon the point of his chin; large, dull and heavy eyes, a kind of malicious, contemptuous smile on his countenance; he was altogether of a most stupid, brutal appearance. His character perfectly corresponded to his figure, for he was a man of mean abilities, cruel to excess, avaricious, and a great drunkard.'

Bruce produced his firman from the Sultan, a document which, even in the decline of the Ottoman Empire, would be treated with reverence by the most powerful pasha. The Naib merely declared he never expected to be able to read Turkish. As for the Arabic letters from Ali Bey of Egypt, the Sherif of Mecca and Metical Aga, the surly chief laid them down unopened, saying that it would take him a month to read them. He took the present Bruce offered him without a word.

This was far from the ordinary good manners of the ceremonious East. Bruce was anxious to leave Massawa as quickly as possible. Smallpox was raging so severely in the town that the living could not bury all the dead and bodies had to be thrown into the sea. It was impossible to begin the journey through the mountains into Ethiopia without a guide, or without the Naib's consent. The travellers were confined to the miserable sun-smitten island, 'infamous for the quantity of Christian blood shed there upon treacherous pretences'.

They heard nothing from Ahmed, who was at Arkiko, across the bay. He was lying ill there, though Bruce did not know it. The Naib, too, was usually absent. He came to Massawa, however, to clear Ali the Ape's ship for its return voyage to Arabia. Then when everyone who knew Bruce or could report what happened to him was out of Massawa, he began to make his demands. He must have three large presents, one as the Sultan's representative, one as ruler of Arkiko, and one for having passed Bruce's possessions without payment of customs – particularly his large quadrant, which inspired some puzzled awe. Bruce refused, saying that since he was under the Sultan's protection and was not a merchant he owed nothing. The reply was a threat to throw him into a dungeon without light, air or food, unless he produced 300 ounces of gold. Forty ounces more were demanded for the troops.

'You may do as you please with me,' said Bruce, 'but you may expect to see the English man-of-war, the *Lion*, before Arkiko some morning.' He explained that he had sent off with Sidi Ali a message explaining his position and that if another letter did not reach Jidda within twenty days action might be expected. He had letters for Ras Michael and the Ethiopian Emperor.

'What, Michael, too!' said the Naib. 'Then go your journey and think of the ill that is before you.' But all boatmen were forbidden to take Bruce out of the island, even to visit Ahmed at Arkiko. A week or two later the Naib summoned him before his divan, "all his janizaries and officers of state, all naked, assembled in parliament'. This time the questions were about a comet which Bruce had seen in the Yemen and which had appeared at Massawa a few days after his arrival. He had been observed watching it; and the large tubes of the telescopes had alarmed ignorant onlookers.

What did it mean? asked the Naib. The first time it was visible it had brought the smallpox, which had killed more than a thousand people in Massawa and Arkiko. It was known that Bruce talked to it every night at Luheia. It had followed him to finish off all that were still alive. Then he would take it into Ethiopia.

Before an answer could be given Bruce was accused of being an engineer going to teach the Ethiopians how to make cannon and gunpowder for an attack on Massawa. The Naib declared that, by the decision of the troops, Bruce must either accompany his brother to Hamazen in the mountains – a district leased from Ras Michael – or be sent in chains to Istanbul.

At this Bruce appealed to the soldiers' leader, a friend of Ahmed. 'I believe', he said, 'that to send me to Hamazen is to rob and murder me out of sight'.

'Dog of a Christian,' exclaimed the brother, 'if the Naib wished to kill you, could he not do it here, at once?'

'No,' said the garrison commander, 'I would not allow it. Ahmed asked me today to see that the Frank was not harmed. He is ill, or he would have been here himself.'

Bruce announced that he would go to Ahmed at Arkiko, but nowhere else. 'I then turned my back and went out without ceremony.

' "A brave man!" I heard a voice exclaim behind me. " *Wallah Englese!* True English, by G–d!" I went away exceedingly disturbed, as it was plain my affairs were now coming to a crisis.'

That night, indeed, an attempt was made to force the door of the house where he and his servants were living. A few days later a boat at last arrived, with four soldiers, to take him to Ahmed. Bruce had concealed his medical knowledge for fear that the smallpox epidemic might hold him at Massawa indefinitely, but he was able to deal with Ahmed's fever.

And now messengers arrived from Ethiopia, two of them in the Emperor's livery, 'a red short cloak lined and turned up with mazarin-blue'. The journey might begin. Even the Naib could no longer forbid it: the imperial messengers insisted that the Emperor needed his new physician, Yagoube, and the Ras needed themselves for a campaign against rebels.

But still the Naib had hopes of money, and of persuading Bruce to go no farther or at least of sending him along a route within his own power. For his dignity's sake, he said, he ought to have at least 1,000 patakas (Austrian thalers). He would, however, accept 300 if Bruce swore to tell no one of this shamefully meagre sum.

Bruce answered 'in the same grave tone' that it would be very wrong for the Naib to take less than was his honourable due. He could, if he felt so strongly about the matter, put down the 1,000 patakas as a debt in his accounts with Ras Michael. On the other hand, if Bruce was prevented from carrying out his mission to care for the Emperor's health, he himself would feel bound to claim 10,000 patakas for his trouble and loss of time, and no doubt Metical Aga

3. 'The Theban Lyre' version by Bruce or Balugani of the painting of an
ancient Egyptian harp and harpist from the tomb of Rameses III (at Broomhall)

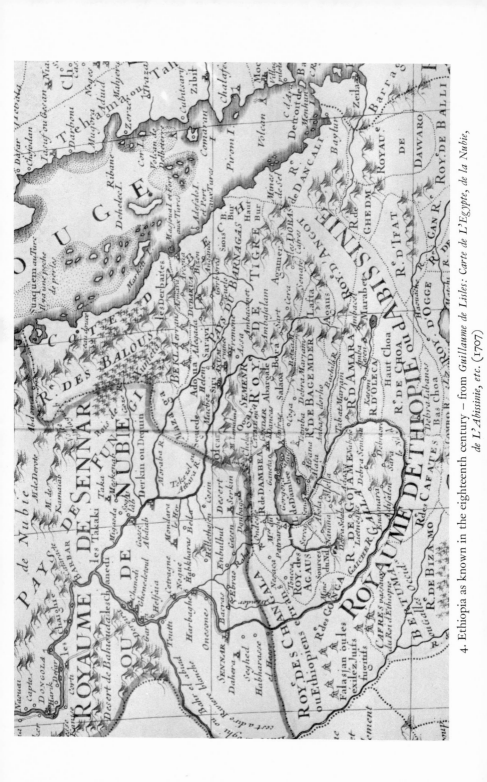

4. Ethiopia as known in the eighteenth century – from *Guillaume de Lisle: Carte de L'Egypte, de la Nubie, de L'Abissinie, etc.* (1707)

and the Ras would know how to extract this money from the Naib.

'The Devil!' was the Naib's only comment on this. He still had one device for delay, however. On November 15th, 1769, almost two months after his arrival at Massawa, Bruce called on him for the last time. Now all was friendship and helpfulness, though there were warnings of the dangers of the journey. But then a servant arrived, dusty and apparently weary with travel. The Naib opened the letter he brought and announced that the Saho tribes through whose territory Bruce would have to pass were in rebellion. 'Lifting up his eyes with great seeming devotion', he thanked God that Bruce's party were not already on their journey; for, innocent as he was, he would have been blamed if they had been murdered.

Bruce received this with angry laughter. He had seen two Saho messengers that morning who had come to tell Ahmed that all was peaceful. At once the Naib's face changed. He, too, laughed loudly. He had merely been trying Bruce's resolution, he explained. He would have liked to keep the explorer with him to complete Ahmed's cure. But the roads were safe and he would send a guide with the travellers.

In fact, the paths the travellers were to follow into Ethiopia could scarcely be called roads even by African standards. After the party had made their first march through the coastal plain, greening after the first rain for half a year, Ahmed caught up with them. He removed four of the men whom the Naib had provided to carry the baggage, substituted others, and gave new instructions to the guide in charge of them. They must not travel by the easiest way. It led to an Ethiopian town which was in the Naib's hands. 'I cannot answer,' he said, 'for the instructions he may have given to his servants.' Bruce might curse his adviser when he was sweating to cross Taranta, the highest of the mountains, but this climb would take him to Digsa, a town leased from Ras Michael where Ahmed himself was chief. His servants there would receive them well. 'As you are strong and robust, the best I can do for you is to send you by a rugged road, and a safe one.'

Strength was certainly to be needed. Before them rose three

ridges: in the foreground broken foothills; above these a range of barer, more rugged heights; beyond this, sharp mountains that appeared alpine. Far above all rose the summit they were to cross, wreathed in mist, 'the seat of lightning, thunder and of storm'. They followed the bed of a river through the foothills: it was still dry, since the coastal rains were just beginning. They passed numbers of Saho nomads who, with their cattle, were moving before the rain, which regularly ceases in Ethiopia when it begins on the eastern side of the mountains.

The travellers camped on a green hillock above the stony track of the stream they had been following. The sun still shone, though lightning flashed among the clouded hills.

'The river scarcely ran at our passing it: when all on a sudden we heard a noise on the mountains above, louder than the loudest thunder. Our guides, upon this, flew to the baggage, and removed it to the top of the green hill, which was no sooner done, than we saw the river coming down in a stream about the height of a man, and the breadth of the whole bed it used to occupy. The water was thick tinged with red earth and ran in the form of a deep river, and swelled a little above its banks, but did not reach our station on the hill.'

Next morning the torrent was not much more than a trickle, but the experience was a warning of what could happen in the Ethiopian rains, when villages, and indeed, whole provinces could be suddenly isolated by the swelling of streams in the deep gorges between them.

Bruce's party pressed on through thickets of thorn trees which tore their hands and faces and then came to an unexpectedly pleasant resting-place at the mouth of a narrow glen where a stream ran quickly over a pebbly bed. This was something precious; it was the first clear water Bruce and Balugani had seen since they left Syria. There was a tamarisk that cast a cooling shade. They halted, though there were armed nomads in sight.

Bruce decided to wash himself in a pool, taking his gun with him in case he was threatened: 'but none of the savages stirred . . . nor

seemed to regard me more than if I had lived among them all their
lives, though surely I was the most extraordinary thing they had
ever seen; whence I concluded that they are a people of small
talents or genius, having no curiosity'.

Two days later they emerged from the lower hills to the foot of
the crowning mountain. It was alarmingly steep. The surface below
them was broken by holes and gullies and by 'huge monstrous
fragments of rocks, which, loosened by the water, had been
tumbled down our way. It was with great difficulty we could creep
up, each man carrying his knapsack and arms; but it seemed beyond
possibility of human strength to carry our baggage and instruments. Our tent, indeed, suffered nothing by its falls: but our
telescope, time-keeper and quadrant were to be treated in a more
deliberate and tender manner.'

The heavy quadrant, in two pieces, had been carried by eight
men, but after a few hundred yards they gave up the effort. Yasin,
the Moslem who had taken the lead when their ship was in danger
on the way to Massawa, had joined the party with another Moslem
merchant. The two men had five donkeys, but these could not take
even their own loads up the daunting slope. Bruce himself with the
aid of Yasin now undertook to carry the head of the quadrant on
the worst part of the hill, and when that was done its tripod
also.

'Declaring ourselves now, without fear of contradiction, and by
the acknowledgment of all, upon fair proof, the two best men in the
company, we returned bearing very visibly the character of such an
exertion; our hands and knees were all cut, mangled and bleeding
with sliding down and clambering over the sharp points of the
rocks; our clothes torn to pieces; yet we professed our ability,
without any reproaches on our comrades, to carry the two telescopes and the time-keeper also.' At this the others were stung into
activity, and the baggage and instruments were placed half-way up
the mountain.

The worst of the climb was over. They had, to be sure, lost their
donkeys. Freed from their loads, the animals had refused to be

driven over the rocks and had cantered down towards a spot where they could find pasture. A party of servants discovered them eating bushes, massed together in a group, apparently for fear of the hyenas which were everywhere among the thickets. When the servants began to drive them up the hill the hyenas followed and could scarcely be held back with lances. One ass was actually pulled down and mauled by these creatures before the firing of a shot forced them away.

The party slept that night in caves, for there was not enough earth on the rocky hillside to hold a tent peg. In the morning Bruce gave his company a certain psychological stimulus. The injured donkey, whose owner was the poor Moslem merchant, Yasin's companion, could no longer carry his stock in trade. Bruce offered to buy another in its place at the first town they reached if each of the men would take a proportion of its load. This won the praise of the Moslems. Yasin, indeed, said that a Christian was setting them an example of charity which they should have thought of for themselves, and it was agreed that Bruce should bear only a third of the cost of a new beast, the Moslems making up between them what remained of the price when the injured donkey had been sold. Bruce offered an increase of pay for all his servants, and the party moved on in much better spirits.

The way was still hard. The mountain grew steeper and more slippery, though there were not so many holes or great stones to impede them. They had to force their way through thorny thickets and often fell as they toiled upwards. But by evening they reached the top, and emerged suddenly, through fine cedar trees, into a small cultivated plain with a village. It was Bruce's first sight of an Ethiopian settlement, though the district was still controlled by the Naib, or rather by his nephew.

On this mountain-top there were numbers of beautiful white cattle, large black silky-haired sheep, and goats. There were little wheat-fields, ready for harvest. The men were 'of a dark complexion, bordering very much upon yellow'. Their short hair was artificially curled. They wore sandals, a cotton cloth round their waists with a

long, crooked knife stuck into it, and each carried two lances with a
large shield of bull's hide.

Coming down the mountain, Bruce saw a hill before him 'perfectly in the form of a sugar-loaf', on which stood the town of
Digsa which was their objective, surrounded by a deep, moat-like
valley. The journey from Massawa had lasted a week. As it ended,
the guide whom the Naib had sent with them made a last attempt
to squeeze new payments from Bruce: he was foiled by Ahmed's
deputy.

There were, in fact, two towns – a Christian one on the lower
slopes of the hill, and a Moslem settlement above it, for in Ethiopia
people of the two religions did not live or eat together. The slave
trade, especially the sale of Christian children, was the mainstay of
the place. Bruce tells us that the priests of the province of Tigre
were deeply involved in this traffic – he was, of course, no lover of
priests either in Ethiopia or in Europe. To illustrate this he gives a
story which he heard from Ras Michael himself.

Two priests who lived not far from Digsa were intimate friends.
The younger was married and had two sons. His colleague told him
that he ought to be preparing the children for some work in life
instead of keeping them idle at home, but the father said he was too
poor to pay for any training and had no relatives who could help
them. The older man then offered to take one son to a rich friend
of his own, who had no children and would look after him. The
boy, about ten years old, was duly sent off. The old priest took him
to Digsa and sold him to a Moslem trader. Returning, he told the
father that the boy had had a fine reception and that his prospects
were glowing.

The second son was so excited by this story that he demanded to
be allowed to go and visit his brother. The old priest declared,
however, that he could not take charge of so young a boy unless
his mother came with him. He took them to Digsa and sold them
both.

The father was then told that his wife did not want to stay long
from home and expected that he would come to fetch her. The two

priests set off together, and when they reached Digsa the older sold his friend also. The price offered by two Moslem merchants for the entire family, which they were to divide between them, was the equivalent of £10 sterling.

The merchants, however, saw no reason why they should lose this money. They were afraid, they said, that the removal of this whole family might be questioned unless they had a responsible person with them when they left the town. They offered the old priest another ten shillings worth of cloth if he would go with them for a short distance.

It was at night that kidnapped children were removed from Digsa. When all were asleep the merchants and newly made slaves passed along the path towards the mountain, when 'the whole party fell upon the old priest, threw him down and bound him. The woman insisted that she might be allowed to cut, or tear off, the little beard he had, in order, as she said, to make him look younger; and this demand was reckoned too just to be denied her'.

At Massawa the two boys and their mother were sold to Arabs, but there was no demand for the two priests. The Naib wrote to Ras Michael offering to return the priests, but the Ras replied ironically that he might keep them to be his chaplains, since it was hoped that he might some day become a Christian. Bruce reckoned that two hundred kidnapped children were annually exported from Massawa, 'and in times of scarcity four times that number', besides pagans sent from the slave markets of the Ethiopian capital.

On November 25th, 1769, Bruce left Digsa with joy and crossed the river bed that was the boundary of the land cotrolled from Massawa. They encamped under a tree in Ethiopian territory. 'It will be to me a station ever memorable', he wrote, 'as the first where I recovered a portion of that tranquillity of mind to which I had been a stranger ever since my arrival at Masuah'. In spite of all the dangers that had been forecast for him in the Christian empire almost forgotten by Christendom he had won his way into the Ethiopian fortress. Through the mountains of the fantastic Tigrean landscape – 'some flat, thin and square, in the shape of a hearth-

stone or slab that scarce would seem to have been sufficient to
resist the winds; some like pyramids, others like obelisks or prisms;
and some, the extraordinary of all the rest, pyramids pitched upon
their points with their base uppermost' – lay the way to the
fountains of the Nile.

7

---◦◦◦◦◦---

The Fortress

Ethiopia was not, of course, completely unknown or forgotten in
Europe. Nearly three-quarters of a century before it had been visited
by a French doctor, Poncet, sent by Louis XIV as an ambassador to
the Emperor Jesus the Great whom he also treated for an illness,
and this man had left an account of his travels. From early in the
sixteenth century till 1633 or a little later, a number of Portuguese
and Spanish priests had worked in the country, which a tiny
Portuguese army saved from disaster. Some had left very full
records of what they had seen, part of which Bruce himself had
been able to read, though many of their manuscripts remained un-
printed till our own century. The learned Ludolf, too, had published
an important history and description of Ethiopia as well as his
accounts of its languages.

There were tenuous Ethiopian contacts with the outer world
even after the Jesuit missionaries were expelled. A few Ethiopian
pilgrims made their way to Jerusalem, where they had a little
chapel of their own at the Holy Sepulchre. A very few reached
Rome, where Santo Stefano dei Mori, a tiny hospice near St
Peter's, was maintained for them.

All this was known only to specialized scholars; Bruce's achievement was important not so much as a triumph of completely new
discovery, like the journeys of Captain Cook, as for giving the
Western world its first convincing and lively contemporary
picture of an ancient society far south of the Mediterranean – a
culture unique (for Africa) in possessing not only its own form of

Christianity but also its own written languages, literature, and records of the past.

He did, indeed, present innumerable facts that were entirely new. For a century after his day, and even later, his book remained the one essential document for those who wanted to follow him. It was the effective introduction of Abyssinia (as he and all his contemporaries normally called the country) to the Western world. His was also – and is always likely to remain – the fullest account of a crisis in Ethiopian history. One thing which was not new was precisely what Bruce valued most: the description of the source of the Nile.

The land of Ethiopia was a fortress. It is this fact which explains its history. Indeed, it was a whole series of natural fortresses – a great plateau, most of it more than 6,000 feet high, dissected by deep, narrow river valleys and divided by mountains, some of them flat-topped and concave-sided, forming almost impregnable castles in themselves. On the east its vast wall, which Bruce had climbed, fell to the half-desert coastlands of the Red Sea, on the west to the fringes of the Sudan, also largely desert. Broken mountain ranges gave it protection on the south also. To the north the plateau grew narrower till its walls converged. It was in the tropics, but so high above neighbouring lands that its people enjoyed an almost temperate climate.

Such a country was not easily invaded – though, in fact, it had known many invasions. It was not easily reached by peaceful travellers. It was also hard to rule, for almost all of its provinces were defended by their own mountain walls or river trenches. Nature tempted their governors to rebellion; indeed, some of them were apt to become almost independent princes. It was perhaps natural that its sovereign should have learned to call himself 'King of Kings'. It seems that the first Ethiopian ruler known to have used this title reigned in the second or third century A.D.

This was, in fact, a quite extraordinarily ancient nation whose kings could be allies or enemies of the later Roman Emperors, probably of the Ptolemies, Greek rulers of ancient Egypt, possibly of

Egyptian Pharaohs before them. Its people have kept a vivid sense of their antiquity and the continuity of their history in the claim that their emperors are descended from a son of Solomon and of the Queen of Sheba, who came to Jerusalem (from Southern Arabia, it is said) to learn his wisdom. Certainly the early Ethiopians spoke, and wrote, a Semitic tongue, from which Geez, Ethiopia's classical language, and the modern Tigrinya and Amharic developed.

These Semites must have come from Arabia, to mingle gradually with the Hamitic peoples of the plateau. They had strong links with Arabia and from their Red Sea ports traded with Egypt and perhaps as far as India. Their strength was in the north of modern Ethiopia and their capital was at Axum, a large and splendid city of palaces and temples whose remains are still to be fully examined. Through the centuries this was to remain the traditional crowning place of the emperors.

Somewhere about the year 330 two Syrian youths, Frumentius and Aedesius, were taken prisoner on the Ethiopian coast and brought to the court. The Ethiopians must have found them remarkably able and well educated, for they became first friends and servants of the Emperor; then, when he died, advisers to his widow and tutors to his young son. Probably Judaism was already influential in Ethiopia, as it was in Arabia, though the old religion was pagan – there are still native Ethiopians of Jewish faith, the Falashas, and Axum has claimed to have the Ark of the Covenant, brought there by the Queen of Sheba's son. The two young Syrians, however, were enthusiastic Christians. Through their influence their pupil was converted after he became King of Kings, and Frumentius was ordained the first bishop of the Ethiopian church by St Athanasius of Alexandria.

As the Christian Empire of Rome and Constantinople weakened the new African Christian Empire grew stronger on both sides of the Red Sea. Ethiopia can claim to have the oldest national church except Armenia's. But these two frontier peoples of Christendom were soon to be cut off from the rest of the Christian world. Arabia, Egypt and Syria were among the first conquests of Islam. Mohammed himself was well disposed to Ethiopia. He called it 'a land of justice' and declared that its people had 'nine-tenths of the courage of mankind'. But war on the Red Sea with the Empire of the Caliphs was unavoidable. Ethiopian ports were captured or destroyed.

The Ethiopians were thrown back into their fortress: their old wealth and trade were gone. Their one regular tie with other Christians was through the Coptic Church of Egypt, which, generation after generation, would always send a monk to be St Frumentius's successor, the one Bishop or Abuna of Ethiopia. But the Copts themselves were a conquered people, often persecuted by Egypt's Moslem rulers and they had separated themselves from the orthodox Christian Church by their monophysite heresy: the belief that Christ had only one nature – in effect (as it often seemed to others) that He was divine, but not properly human.

For almost eight centuries Ethiopia was an island between the seas of Islam and African paganism; a land full of monks and hermits, developing its own habits of worship, its own church architecture and art, using its own translations of the Bible and theological books. The very shape of the country and its habits of life were changed. With the collapse of overseas trade the Axumite north lost importance. Its cities shrank or died. The centre of government moved south.

In a fierce rebellion of the Jewish Falashas the ancient royal family was destroyed. Its one survivor (so we are told) took refuge in the southern sub-kingdom of Shoa, and a native dynasty from the mountain province of Lasta took over, quarrying extraordinary churches out of the living rock of hillsides.

But Moslem conquerors and missionaries were pressing in on the disorganized country. About the end of the thirteenth century a prince who claimed to be of the original Solomonic dynasty managed to displace the Zagwe Emperor. This began a national revival, something a little like the Middle Ages of contemporary Europe. There was a growth of new literature, chronicles, law-books and religious works – and also of theological controversies. The Moslem penetration was repelled and the power of successful emperors reached out over little states, partly Christianized or merely Moslem or Pagan, almost to the frontiers of modern Ethiopia. There was an elaborate organization of government in which each holder of high office – provincial governors, generals, church officials, judges – had his appointed place.

But it was a medievalism without cities. There were small towns and markets, but the chief permanent settlements were monasteries or groups of churches which grew rich with the golden gifts of centuries, and were often, for safety's sake, built on almost inaccessible mountain-tops or lake islands. The Emperor's court was a camp which moved with him during the dry season when he went to assert his authority in one region after another. This was the Ethiopia that Europe rediscovered in the fifteenth century and saved in the sixteenth.

For hundreds of years Europeans had dreamed of finding a powerful Christian ally beyond the lands of their Moslem enemies. They called this legendary figure 'Prester John' and first looked for him in Central Asia. Then, as the Portuguese began to push their voyages of discovery towards the Cape of Good Hope and thence to India, they recognized Prester John in what they learned from a distance of the Ethiopian emperor. The daring crews of Portugal's little ships, part plunderers, part merchants, part crusaders, swept the oceans and seized bases for themselves, but they needed an ally who would help them to strike at the heart of Islam in Mecca, and at Egypt, the eastern key to the Mediterranean.

The Ethiopians themselves were becoming vaguely aware of western Europe. Embassies were exchanged with Portugal, very slowly, and treaties planned. But Ethiopia, though glad enough to see foreign Christians, and usually very unwilling to let them go home again, felt too self-sufficient to carry these dealings very far, until she was suddenly faced by mortal danger.

A new wave of Moslem expansion rose from what is now Somalia and the Danakil coast north of it. It was a Holy War, led not by a prince but by an Imam or religious chief, Ahmed, called Grañ (the left-handed) by the Ethiopians. At the same time the Ottoman

Turks, who had conquered Egypt, were taking over the Red Sea ports. They had firearms, till then scarcely known in Africa, and Grañ could have the help of their musketeers.

Year after year the Somalis swept across Ethiopian provinces, massacring, burning, plundering the treasures of the monasteries. After Grañ's first victories the surviving Ethiopians withdrew into their fastnesses. The Emperor Lebna-Dengel could scarcely resist. He made a desperate appeal to Portugal, but he was dead, a hopeless fugitive in a mountain monastery, before help arrived in 1541.

It was an army of 400 men with eight little cannon and 100 muskets, commanded by Christopher da Gama, the youngest son of the great explorer. The feats of this band of heroes are more remarkable than those of the Spanish *conquistadores* who overthrew the empires of Mexico and Peru. The Aztec and Inca armies had never seen iron or horses, to say nothing of firearms, till the white men came: Ahmed Grañ had his tens of thousands of fully armed Somalis and Danakils. Eventually, his Turkish musketeers far outnumbered the whole Portuguese force.

Yet, with only a few hundred Ethiopians to help him, Christopher da Gama was victorious. Later he was captured and killed, but the young Emperor Claudius had been given time and encouragement to gather an army. In the next battle Grañ was shot down. With the aid of the remaining Portuguese (not more than 200) Ethiopia was cleared of the Somali invaders.

But the country was left in ruin, from which in some ways it had not fully recovered in Bruce's day. It is true that it drew from its contacts with Western men something like a shadow of the European Renaissance. Inevitably priests had accompanied the Portuguese ambassadors and soldiers, and though the great age of Portugal was passing, so that it could no longer send troops to Ethiopia, missionaries continued to come into the country. Their aim was to unite the Ethiopian Church with Rome in accordance with a promise made by Lebna-Dengal when he appealed to Lisbon for help, but they also brought with them some knowledge of the arts, particularly of building and of a rather more European style of painting. They were respected by successive Emperors, and since most of the survivors of Da Gama's army had settled and married in Ethiopia they had an influential nucleus of supporters. One of the missionaries, the beloved and indefatigable Jesuit Father, Pedro Paez, undoubtedly reached the source of the Blue Nile a century and a half before James Bruce.

But Portugal's decline and the Turkish grip on the Red Sea made communication with Europe increasingly difficult: and at the same time Rome's attitude towards the heresies, even the traditional customs, of the Ethiopian Church became more uncompromising. This was an offence to Ethiopian national feeling. If men like Paez had been able to work gradually and leniently the two churches might, perhaps, have grown together and the eighteenth century might have seen an African state, in no sense a colony, which was fully linked with Europe.

In their learning, the strictness of their lives, and their devotion, the Jesuits had great qualities. But when, in 1621, the Emperor Susenyos finally and publicly accepted Roman Catholicism for himself and his country the Spanish Patriarch Mendez insisted that Ethiopian religious usages should be completely discarded, that priests and churches should be reconsecrated, that even individual Ethiopians should be rebaptized.

This was too much to be borne. There was an immediate revolt, followed by eleven years of peculiarly bloody civil war. At last the Emperor gave way, recognizing that almost all Christian Ethiopians were against him. He proclaimed the restoration of the national church and abdicated in favour of his son Fasiladas, who forced the Patriarch and the Jesuits to leave the country in 1634.

The Ethiopian fortress cut itself off from the Western world again. 'Franks' – European Catholics, particularly clergy – were forbidden to enter the country. Agreements were made with the neighbouring Moslem rulers to prevent them from reaching the Ethiopian frontiers: repeatedly James Bruce had to insist that he himself was not a Frank. The impact of the Renaissance was not lost for a while. Fasiladas began to build himself a capital with a towered palace and fine new churches in the western country above Lake Tana. Gondar was the first true city that Ethiopia had seen for many centuries. His successors added palaces of their own. Wealth accumulated again. Books were written or translated. Trade increased, government was regularized. Life at Gondar even grew luxurious in a barbarous style.

But the national fortress had been breached in the wars of Grañ and was not fully restored. A primitive and ferocious pagan people, the Gallas, brown Hamites but far below their neighbours in civilization, had been pushing from the south into the devastated lands – first those of the defeated Somalis, then regions which had been Ethiopian. With every new disturbance in the Empire their tribes advanced farther, sometimes with the support of emperors who settled them in border districts to separate one rebellious province from another.

There were many disturbances, for in the Somali wars the Empire had lost a good deal of its coherence; and though, in their new palaces at Gondar, Fasiladas and his successors seemed more imposing than ever, their real authority over the provinces grew less.

In theory they were supreme in all things. The old kinglets who had ruled their districts under the King of Kings had disappeared, except in Shoa. Each governor had to be appointed to his province, though there were powerful local families from one of which he would generally be chosen. In theory the emperor could give land or office as he chose. Ethiopia was not a fully feudal country. Its nobles, or most of them, were descendants of imperial princesses.

As for the male members of the royal house, possible heirs of the throne, these had for centuries been segregated under guard, not in the Happy Valley of Samuel Johnson's *Rasselas*, but on a remote mountain-top. In other non-European countries rulers often safeguarded themselves against rivals by killing off their brothers. But the blood of Solomon was too sacred to be spilled in this way. Ethiopian princes lived on their mountain, where the State was supposed to provide for them, till an emperor died, when one of them would (in theory) be ceremoniously chosen and brought down to rule a country and court he had scarcely seen, and where, it could be hoped, he would have no favourites or rivals.

The system was too ideally neat to be very practical. In fact, many an emperor kept a favourite son or brother by him, ready to succeed, and many a prince managed to escape and get some experience of the world (and of war) before he was brought back to the mountain. When, after the murder of Jesus the Great (1682–1706) ambitious nobles or parties began to struggle for power, it was only too easy for them to find rival pretenders among the princes in waiting. One emperor after another reigned briefly and ended violently.

After its short period of national revival, the ancient Empire was beginning to slide towards dissolution. What Bruce found there was not the survival of a philosophical, classical world that Dr Johnson had imagined but something much more like the European Dark Ages of a thousand year earlier – a time of atrocious violence and confusion. The self-consciously rational eighteenth century, which had just discovered 'noble savages' in the South Pacific, splendidly innocent and comfortingly amoral, found such a state of society peculiarly hard to understand. Because Bruce described it as it was the London of George III refused to believe him.

There were, indeed, efforts to check the decay. The Ethiopia of Bruce's day was full of echoes of the last of them, made by the Emperor Bakaffa (1721–30), who set out to crush the ambitious nobles without mercy and avenge the murder of his predecessors. But to do this he had to use Galla tribes and chiefs – the very name by which he is remembered is a Galla word, meaning 'inexorable'.

Forty years later he was already the centre of legends. To learn what his people were thinking and saying, Bruce was told, he would disappear from the court and travel alone and unknown through the country. On one such journey he heard a prophecy that troubled him. It was that after his death a woman, by name Walatta-Giyorgis, would rule Ethiopia for many years. On another he fell ill in the western mountain province of Quara. Unrecognized, he was sheltered by a local noble and nursed back to health by a beautiful and intelligent daughter of the house, known as Berhan-Mugasa, 'Splendour of Light'. When he returned to Gondar he sent for her and she bore him a son who was to be his successor, Jesus II.

Ethiopian rulers could have many wives or concubines whose children were recognized as princes, but one alone could be crowned as Empress. This title gave her the right to act as regent for a young son or grandson if her husband died and to remain a chief figure at the court throughout her lifetime. The girl from Quara became Empress under the name Mentwab, meaning 'How beautiful thou art'. Her husband's fear of the fatal Walatta-Giyorgis who might displace her and her child revived. He had never told her of the prophecy. When he did so she reassured him by explaining that Walatta-Giyorgis was the first of her own baptismal names. Evidently the suspicious Bakaffa was not sorry to think that his wife would survive him and rule in the name of their son.

Still, in Bruce's day the Empress Mentwab was one of the three or four leading personalities in Ethiopia. Her prestige was immense. Her abbey-palace of Kusquam, close to Gondar, was a centre of what was most civilized in the country and of sympathy for the European traditions of the Portuguese, even, rather vaguely, for Roman Catholicism. The Empress had inherited Portuguese blood, and her beauty and that of her daughters – not children of Bakaffa – was almost European.

She had been regent of the Empire not once, but twice – for her son, and then for her grandson. But, because she was a woman who had to find men to fight for her, her influence had tended to divide the country rather than to hold it together. She had relied on her own relatives from Quara, who formed a party of which other nobles were jealous, and on one of Bakaffa's officers, a Galla who was known antithetically as Waranya – the rebel – because he was the one chieftain whose loyalty could always be relied on. To safeguard herself from the rivalry of a possibly more formidable Ethiopian queen, she had encouraged her son to put away his first wife and marry a Galla. When her grandson, the Emperor Joas, who grew up under her tutelage, wished to assert his independence he did so by calling his Galla uncles to power and putting some of the country's key provinces into their hands.

This was the root of the war and crisis which Bruce encountered in Ethiopia. The promotion of the Galla roused national feeling against the Emperor himself. It also gave an opportunity for rebellion to the most powerful and ambitious of the provincial governors, Michael Suhul of Tigre.

Michael had been the most formidable of rebels: to gain his support Joas was forced to give him the greatest office in the Empire, and the title of Ras and Bitwaded or Grand Vizier. But though Ras Michael made war for the Emperor he allowed it to be clearly understood that he was against Joas's policy of favouring the Galla. His first reward for his attitude was marriage to Princess Esther, a beautiful daughter of the Empress Mentwab, who gave herself to him in order to be able to avenge her previous husband, Maryam Barea, a hero killed for his resistance to the Galla. His second was to become a king-maker.

Joas resented Ras Michael's imperious control of himself and the country. He planned to raise against him the greatest of the Galla chiefs, Fasil, son of the loyal Waranya. The Emperor tried to have his Ras shot in Gondar as he sat in judgement close to the palace. When this failed he sent his own guards to support Fasil, in a battle with Michael. The Ras's reaction was to have Joas strangled. He brought an aged and infirm prince, a half-brother of Bakaffa, from the mountain and proclaimed him Emperor in the dead man's place.

Bruce was on his way to Jidda when this puppet-Emperor, John II, was raised to the throne. It was to safeguard his feeble health that Michael commanded the Naib of Massawa to allow the Hakim Yagoube to travel to Ethiopia. But, in fact, John was dead before Bruce left Massawa. Even as a puppet the old man was useless. He could not be persuaded to march with Michael in an attack on the Ras's rival, Fasil. The reluctant Emperor was poisoned, and his son, Takla Haymanot, a youth of fifteen, who had been brought with him from the princes' mountain, took his place and advanced with the Ras against Fasil's horde of savage Galla.

When Bruce crossed the hills into Michael's own province of Tigre all he met were still waiting to learn what the result of the campaign might be – whether their master was, in fact, master of Ethiopia or whether, perhaps, a Galla army was ravaging Gondar and all the rival provincial rulers and brigand chiefs could begin to shatter the Ethiopian fortress in an outburst of lawless confusion.

8

---◦◦◦◦---

The Road to Gondar

In spite of the optimistic spirit in which James Bruce crossed the
Ethiopian border he knew enough to realize that his chances of
reaching the source of the Blue Nile quickly were extremely
doubtful. There was the possibility of hopeless anarchy if Ras
Michael and his Emperor were defeated. Short of this, it was prob-
able enough that the way to the Nile would still be barred to him
unless their enemy, Fasil, was totally destroyed. Fasil was governor
of the provinces where the river rose and around which it flowed
to the Sudan – Agaumeder, Damot and Gojam. So long as he held
these lands and was in any way rebellious he might be able to prevent a traveller from entering them. Even if he fell, they might be
so disturbed and ruined by war that they could be reached only
with great difficulty.

Yet the first days in Ethiopia were, indeed, cheerful enough. To
be sure, Bruce could not move very fast on feet still torn by the
mountain rocks, but he was well received on his way. He was now
leading not only his small party, which included Yasin and the
Emperor's messengers, but also a number of traders who had joined
him for protection with thirty laden donkeys.

Yasin was his deputy in managing the caravan. Bruce learned
that this able young Moslem had ambitions of his own. He came
from Ras el Fil, on the borders of the Sudan, where he had married
the deputy governor's daughter and had become so much more
popular than his father-in-law that he had been driven into exile.
He hoped now that Ras Michael or the Emperor would be persuaded

to give him power in his own province and believed that Bruce might be able to help him at court.

To the Scot this seemed unlikely, but he was in high spirits when he met the first notable Ethiopian on his way. This was the Bahrnagash, or sea king, successor of the provincial chiefs who had welcomed Portuguese embassies and warriors. In the sixteenth century, the Bahrnagash had been a great personage of the Empire, governing most of what, 80 years ago, became the Italian colony of Eritrea. But in 1770 the status of this once powerful office was very much reduced.

The Bahrnagash, says Bruce, 'was the first Abyssinian I had seen on horseback: he had seven horsemen with him, and about a dozen on foot, all of a beggarly appearance, and very ill-armed and equipped. He was a little man of an olive complexion, or rather darker; his head was shaved close, with a cowl, or covering, upon it: he had a pair of short trousers; his feet and legs were bare: the usual coarse girdle was wrapped several times about him, in which he stuck his knife; and the ordinary web of cotton cloth, neither new nor clean, was wrapped about him. . . .'

This was not an impressive figure. On the other hand, Bruce, with his worn clothes and broken feet, evidently did not strike the Governor as a notably civilized being. The Bahrnagash asked if he had ever seen horses before.

'Very seldom,' said the traveller, amused.

'He then described their qualities in such a manner as would never have given me any idea of the animal.'

However, Bruce had noticed among the horses a black one from the Sudan which he admired. After some negotiation it was bought. 'I acquired that day a companion that contributed always to my pleasure, and more than once to my safety.' The black steed and his management of it was, indeed, to win him the interest of the Ethiopian Emperor.

The Bahrnagash was so pleased with his bargain that he followed Bruce to talk with him again. This time he had two drums beating and two trumpets sounding a charge before him – the traditional insignia of a provincial governor. His ancient 'kingdom' was indeed very shrunken. Most of its best lands had been taken by Ras Michael and either added to Michael's own province or leased to the Naib; but as a personality he proved more notable than he had seemed – 'a very simple, good-natured man, indeed remarkably so: a character rarely found in any degree of men in this country'. He was also a soldier of great bravery and loyalty.

He asked Bruce how he liked the horse, saying that he hoped he would not take the risk of mounting it himself.

'God forbid,' said the Scot, 'I am keeping it as a curiosity.'

By this time, however, the saddle, bridle and stirrups that Bruce had brought with him had been seen by the servants and his horsemanship had been praised to them. They told this to the Bahrnagash, who was not offended, but laughed heartily at Bruce's pretence of ignorance. He confessed that he was really poor: otherwise he would have taken no money for the horse. The meeting ended with an exchange of gifts and a carouse on the mead of the country, a drink which gave Bruce 'such a pain in my head that I scarce could raise it next day'.

A lasting friendship had been made, and the party moved on with a guard of twenty armed horsemen provided by the Bahrnagash to protect them against possible negro raiders. They were halted three days later at a mountain pass near the ancient mountain monastery of Debra Damo. This was one of the posts where local tax-farmers levied customs on all goods, fixing the rate of duty themselves and calling in the country people to attack any who resisted payment. As usual Bruce argued that, since he was travelling on the orders of the Emperor and Ras Michael and was not a merchant, he should pass freely. But the traders who were with him could plead no such protection and in this case the whole caravan was in need of provisions which had to be bought. Food was not to be got for money, however: it could be obtained only in exchange for goods.

'So we began to open shop by spreading a cloth upon the ground, at the sight of which hundreds of young women poured down upon us on every side, from villages behind the mountains which we could not see . . . Beads and antimony [kohl, to be used as a cosmetic] are the standard in this way-faring commerce; but beads are a dangerous speculation . . . for all depends upon fashion, and the fancies of a brown or black beauty, there, give the *ton* as decisively as does the example of the fairest in England.'

Unluckily the merchant in Jidda from whom Bruce had bought beads had been out of touch with the current Ethiopian fashion. He had supplied 'a quantity beautifully flowered, with red and green and yellow ones; whereas the *ton* now among the beauties of Tigre were small, sky-coloured blue beads, about the size of small lead shot or seed pearls . . . and large yellow glass, flat in the sides like the amber beads formerly used by the better sort of old women-peasants in England. All our beads were then rejected, by six or seven dozen of the shrillest tongues I ever heard.'

Here a good deed had its reward. Only one man in the caravan had a stock of small blue beads or large yellow ones. He was the poor Moslem whose mule had been savaged by a hyena on the way to Digsa and whom Bruce had helped to provide with a new animal. 'That fellow had felt the obligation in silence, and not a word but good-day or good-e'en had passed between us since conferring the favour.' Now the man handed Yasin a package full of the beads that were in fashion.

When it was opened, 'a great shout was set up by the women-purchasers, and a violent scramble followed. Twenty, or thirty, threw themselves upon the parcel, tearing and breaking all the strings as if they intended to plunder us.' This onslaught did not end till Yasin, 'who knew the country well, fired one of the ship-blunderbusses into the air behind their backs'.

Serious and careful trading now began. The Ethiopian men took no part in it. They 'seemed to have no talent for marketing; nor do they, in this country, either buy or sell.' Small quantities of beads, kohl, needles, scissors, razors and other goods, were exchanged for honey, flour, butter and pumpkins, till the caravan was fully victualled and the market 'seemingly savoured more of gallantry than of gain'. Bruce was amused by three or four of the women, 'most distinguished for beauty and for tongue. I made them a present of a few beads, and asked them how many kisses they would give for each. They answered very readily with one accord: "Poh! We don't sell kisses in this country, who would buy them? We will give you as many as you wish for nothing." And there was no appearance but, in that bargain, they meant to be very fair and liberal.'

Three days had been spent in marketing. Then the party passed down into a pleasant country, full of flowering trees and fresh with running streams, though lions lurked in some places and in others there were burned villages, destroyed by Ras Michael in a campaign against bandits. On December 6th, 1769, they saw before them the mountains of Adowa, 'nothing resembling in shape those of Europe, or, indeed, any other country. Their sides were all perpendicular rocks, high, like steeples, or obelisks, and broken into a thousand different forms.'

Ras Michael's house in the little town from which he ruled Tigre was more a prison than a palace. In and about it, were more than three hundred people in chains. Some had been there for twenty years. In the hope that money could be extorted from them many were kept in cages like wild beasts, 'and treated every way in the same manner'.

So far as Bruce and his men were concerned, however, Adowa town was a kindly place; for they were welcomed by Janni, the Greek who was Michael's steward and, like other Greeks in Ethiopia, was well disposed towards the travellers because of the letters of the Patriarch in Cairo. He met them at his door, a most respectable figure, Bruce says, with a well-trimmed white beard flowing to his waist and a red and gold sash setting off his white robe.

'He conducted us through a courtyard planted with jessamin to a very neat, and at the same time very large, room, furnished with a silk sofa; the floor was covered with Persian carpets and cushions. All round, flowers and green leaves were strewed upon the outer yard; and the windows and sides of the room stuck full of evergreens, in commemoration of the Christmas festival that was at hand.

'I stopt at the entrance to this room: my feet were both dirty and bloody; and it is not good manners to show or speak of your feet in Abyssinia, especially if anything ails them.'

Janni was so shocked that he burst into tears when he learned that they had made the terrible journey over the mountains from Massawa on foot instead of on mules provided by the Naib, as he had expected. He wished to wash his guest's feet personally, but Bruce would not allow this. He found that Janni had taken great pains to prepare the way for him by sending friendly messages about him to the Empress and her daughters and especially to Ras Michael. 'He had raised their curiosity to a great pitch.'

The smallpox epidemic which had devastated Massawa had now reached Adowa, and Bruce treated some of the sick there. But since the country was still unusually peaceful as its people waited to learn what had happened to Michael and the Emperor in their war with Fasil, he was anxious to move on as quickly as possible towards Gondar. He came next to Axum, the ancient capital with its little cathedral and the stone thrones, perhaps two thousand years old, where emperors were still crowned. The great area strewn with ruins and particularly the carved standing stones impressed him profoundly, but, unluckily for later writers about Ethiopia, he convinced himself that the buildings had been Egyptian, mostly of the time of the Ptolemies. He imagined avenues of sphinxes and of statues of the dog-headed god Anubis. The remains of great palaces and tombs which modern archeologists have traced were not visible to him.

It was just beyond Axum, in a country full of sweet-scented flowers, that he came on a sight his reporting of which was to give him endless trouble when he came back to Britain. He overtook three soldiers who were driving a cow before them. This seemed to give his party a chance of buying some beef, all the more promising when the drivers were seen to trip up the animal and hold it on the ground, one of them with a knife in his hand.

Bruce suggested to his servants that they should bargain for part of the cow, but his men, who had been talking to the soldiers, explained that the cow was not to be killed and could not be sold, since it did not belong entirely to the soldiers.

'This awakened my curiosity: I let my people go forward and staid myself till I saw, with the utmost astonishment, two pieces, thicker and larger than our ordinary beef steaks, cut out of the higher part of the buttock of the beast . . . The two pieces were spread upon the outside of one of the shields.

'One of them still continued holding the head while the other two were busy in curing the wound. This too was done not in an ordinary manner; the skin which had covered the flesh that was taken away was left entire, and flapped over the wound, and was fastened to the corresponding part by two or more small skewers or pins. Whether they had put any thing under the skin, between that and the wounded flesh, I cannot say: but at the riverside where they were they had prepared a cataplasm of clay, with which they covered the wound; they then forced the animal to rise, and drove it on before them, to furnish them with a fuller meal when they should meet their companions in the evening.

'I could not but admire a device so truly soldier-like, nor did I ever see so commodious a manner of carrying provisions along the road. . . . I could not as yet conceive that this was the ordinary banquet of citizens, and even of priests, throughout this country. In the hospitable, humane house of Janni these living feasts never appeared. . . .

'When first I mentioned this in England, as one of the singularities which prevailed in that barbarous country, I was told by my friends it was not believed. I asked the reasons for this disbelief, and was answered, that people who had never been out of their own country, and others well acquainted with the manners of the world, for they had travelled as far as France, had agreed the thing was impossible, and therefore it was so.'

However he persisted in telling his story and for this, above all else, was denounced as a Munchausen.

They went on through the province of Sire to the deep trench of the Takazze river, the boundary of the northern region where

Michael and his family had complete dominion. Bruce found it 'shaded with fine lofty trees, its banks covered with bushes inferior in fragrance to no garden in the universe: its stream most limpid, its water excellent, and full of good fish of great variety, as its coverts are full of all sorts of game'. But it was also full of crocodiles and noisy with the snorting of hippopotami. Its banks were haunted by lions and hyenas which alarmed the company's beasts at night. In the rainy season, when its water rolled at least three fathoms deep, it became an impassible barrier.

At the ford of the Takazze they met a deserter from Ras Michael's army 'with his firelock upon his shoulder, driving before him two miserable girls, about ten years old, stark naked and almost famished to death, the part of the booty which had fallen to his share' in ravaging the country near Lake Tana. The man could not tell whether Michael had won a decisive victory or not. Bruce had to press forward into a region which might be hostile.

As they passed through wild, uncultivated, mountainous country devastated by civil war they had, in fact, some trouble with a *shum*, or local governor, who declared that the Emperor and Michael had been defeated, but a display of Bruce's blunderbusses cleared the way for them.

From these hills they looked down into the deep, fever-ridden valley of Waldubba, a district chiefly peopled by monks, who withdrew there for solitary meditation. It was a refuge, too, for courtiers in disgrace or disappointment. 'They first shave their hair and put on a cowl like the monks, renouncing the world for solitude, and taking vows which they resolve to keep no longer than exigencies require; after which they return to the world again, leaving their cowl and sanctity in Waldubba.'

Bruce hints, scandalously, at periodic visits to the region by nuns 'who think living in community with their holy fraternity has not in it perfection enough', but 'retire, one of each sex, a hermit and a nun, sequestering themselves together upon the top of the mountains. These, on their return, are shown as miracles of holiness – lean, enervated, and exhausted. Whether this is wholly to be laid to the charge of the herbs, is more than I will take upon myself to decide.' In fact, his Protestant prejudices would seldom allow him to decide any question in favour of monks or priests. The self-mortification of the Waldubba hermits, 'all of the colour of a corpse', was undoubtedly genuine enough.

He was now coming to the great mountain barrier of Semien, the last to be crossed before reaching Gondar. Here was the high pass of Lamalmon, with a customs post, 'always the place where the first robberies and murders are committed in unsettled times'. He 'submitted every thing to the will of the robber of the place and gave him his present'. But though he and his own party were given permission to go forward it seemed likely that Yasin and the other Moslem traders would have to bear delays and extortion from the father and son who levied contribution and 'professed a violent hatred to all Mahometans'.

The son, however, was a soldier. He had served Ras Michael as a musketeer and insisted on a shooting match with Bruce – a lucky event, since the descriptions of it helped to raise the traveller's reputation at Gondar.

Bruce used a rifle which had a far greater range than the young man's musket.

'I then showed him the manner we shot flying, there being quails in abundance, and wild pigeons, of which I killed several on wing, which left him in the utmost astonishment. Having got on horse-back, I next went through the exercise of the Arabs, with a long spear and short javelin. This was more within his comprehension . . . but he was wonderfully taken with the fierce and fiery appearance of my horse, and at the same time with his docility, the form of his saddle, bridle and accoutrements. . . . I put Mirza to a gallop, and with one of the barrels of my gun, shot a pigeon, and immediately fired the other into the ground. There was nothing after this that could have surprised him, and it was repeated several times at his desire. . . . He invited himself to my house at Gondar. There I was to teach him everything he had seen.'

After this there was no attempt to hold up Yasin and his

companions. News came, too, of a victory by Ras Michael which had driven the Galla chief, Fasil, back beyond the Blue Nile. It seemed that the way would be open for Bruce to reach the source of the river. They moved on into a countryside full of people and cattle, but also of villages burned by Ras Michael in his last march southward; and on February 14, 1770, 'after having suffered with infinite patience and perseverance the hardships and danger of the long and painful journey, at forty minutes past ten we were gratified at last with the sight of Gondar'.

The towers of the Emperor's palace rose above the trees which masked the hill city 'like one thick black wood'. But when he reached the Angareb river above which Gondar rose Bruce found that all the men to whom he had letters of introduction were still absent with the army, among them the Greek Petros, Janni's brother, on whom he had counted for a welcome. He was afraid that the priests of Gondar would denounce him as a Frank. However Moslems welcomed Yasin and his companions. They had a town of their own, separated from the Christian capital, into which no priest would penetrate. Bruce carried a letter for their chief, the Negade Ras, head of the Ethiopian customs service, and though he, too, was with the army, one of his friends offered a house. Bruce was still wearing his Arab dress, and it was proposed that he should pass as a Moslem till someone in authority who could give him protection returned to Gondar.

At night a group of armed men came, rather alarmingly, to his door, as the traveller was sitting surrounded by Ethiopian books and Ludolf's dictionaries. Their leader bared his head and shoulders, according to the custom of Ethiopians when they came into the presence of people of high rank. This was a remarkable gesture for the Moslem town which was very seldom visited by Christian nobles or princes.

Ato Aylo (Lord Aylo) was almost a prince. He was a relative and intimate adviser of the Empress Mentwab. His standing was so high that he could afford eccentricities which would have ruined any lesser chieftain. One was an unconcealed hatred of war. In his youth he had been a famous horseman and hunter, but when he followed the Emperor Jesus II on a campaign against the King of Sennar, in the Sudan, he had been so horrified by what he saw that he declared himself a monk and would not fight again. A second was his liking for Europeans, not only the Greeks in Ethiopia, whom he protected, but even the hated Franks and their Roman Church.

His profession of monk did not prevent him from living as and where he chose.

'Though no man professed greater veneration for the priesthood, no one privately detested more [the priests] of his own country than he did; and he always pretended that, if a proper way of going to Jerusalem could be found, he would leave the large estates and the rank he held in Abyssinia, and with the little money he could muster, live the remaining part of his life among the monks in the convent of the Holy Sepulchre. This, perhaps was, great part of it, imagination; but as he had talked himself into a belief that he was to end his days in Jerusalem, which was a pretence, or at Rome, which was his inclination, he willingly took charge of white people of all communions who had hitherto been unhappy enough to stray into Abyssinia.'

Janni had written from Adowa to tell Aylo of Bruce's arrival and of his success in saving lives from smallpox. Now the epidemic had spread south and Ras Michael's son, Welled Hawaryat, was lying ill in the Empress's palace. Aylo had come to inspect the distinguished stranger and to ask him to go to the Empress next day.

The two men talked freely after a 'contention of civilities' to decide which should sit down first. Aylo was surprised to see Bruce's Ethiopian books and to find that he could speak both Tigrinya, the language of the north, and Amharic. 'Come, come, he'll do if he can speak,' he said to the bystanders. 'He'll make his way.'

Before Bruce had seen the Empress, Petros, the Greek, had returned from his visit to the army and Bruce found that he and

Aylo were shaken and afraid. Petros had seen a sight that shocked them both. It was the stuffed skin of Watchaka, a Galla chief well known to them, which was hanging near the Ras's tent.

'This is Esther, this is Esther,' said Aylo. 'Nobody knows her as I do.'

An African Rhinoceros

9

Courtier

For Bruce, Princess Esther was a key to Ethiopia. Her constant friendship was to support him through war and revolution and to help to open the way to the source of the Blue Nile: daughter of the Empress, wife of Ras Michael, a friend of the Emperor, she had influence with most of the rival powers in the distracted country, except, perhaps, with the Galla chief, Fasil, for whose people she felt an unappeasable hatred.

It was impossible to see her or talk to her, Bruce declared, 'without being attached to her for ever'. This sounds like part of a love story; and so, in a sense, it was – the expression of his feeling not only for this one woman but for the country which she symbolized for him. Esther was unmistakably a great lady, charming, intelligent and devoted to her children and her friends, but she was also capable of relentless ferocity towards her enemies. Her insistence on revenge for the murder of her second husband, Mariam Barea, helped to push Ethiopia into a century of anarchy.

It was her influence on Ras Michael which led to the flaying of Watchaka. This man had been the Galla chief best liked by the Ethiopian leaders. When he was taken prisoner in Michael's battle with Fasil the Ras's chief allies, Gusho, Governor of Amhara, and Powussen, soon to be Governor of Begemder, had both begged that his life should be spared. But it was he who had captured Maryam Barea in the previous war. For this he was exposed to Esther's vengeance, though he had no hand in her husband's murder and had actually saved the lives of some of his followers. When he was condemned by Michael in spite of their pleas, Gusho and Powussen began to fear for themselves, and the seeds of a new rebellion were sown in the very moment of the Ras's victory.

This was Ethiopia and this was Esther, a compound of savagery and romance. Bruce recognized and described all the Ethiopian barbarities: sometimes, perhaps, even with exaggeration. But he also enjoyed his Ethiopian friendships: he saw the people of the country not as 'natives', an inevitably inferior race, but as human beings, as individual and interesting, sometimes as sympathetic, as any he knew in Europe. Often they reduced him to depression, almost to despair, but to the end of his life he looked back on Esther and Ethiopia with a lasting nostalgia.

When Aylo came to find Bruce in the Moslem town below Gondar, Esther was with her mother, the Empress, in the palace of Kusquam, near by – a place of safety in difficult times both because of Mentwab's prestige and because the abbey beside it gave it a quality of sanctuary. For the Scot, the presence of monks was not at all reassuring, particularly when he heard that the chief of the court clergy, Abba Salama, had been speaking of him as a Frank, who should not be tolerated in Gondar. However, the Empress had summoned him to give advice on the treatment of smallpox and Aylo and he rode to Kusquam together.

Aylo, who had been a famous rider in his day and had the slight figure of a jockey, was anxious to see how the huge foreigner managed his mount, 'but he was an absolute stranger to the great advantage of Moorish furniture, bridles, spurs and stirrups, in the management of a violent, strong, high-mettled horse. It was with the utmost satisfaction, when we arrived in the plain called Aylo Meydan, that I showed him the different paces of the horse. He cried out with fear when he saw him stand upright upon his legs and jump forward, or aside, with all four feet off the ground.' Bruce's horsemanship was duly reported to Ras Michael and the Emperor, who could see in him a possible trainer of cavalry.

At the Empress's palace, however, it seemed at first that he would not be needed. A cure had been found for the chief invalid there, Welled Hawaryat. A respected hermit had written a charm on a tin plate, the ink was washed off and drunk by the patient, who thereupon developed an appetite for raw beef. Next day he was no better, but it was proposed to defeat the disease by laying a holy picture on his body. Bruce commented that a miracle would be the best of all cures, but that it would indeed be a miracle if the invalid survived.

During this visit Aylo was able to present him to the Empress. She was friendly, still handsome, and 'whiter than most Portuguese'. They talked of Jerusalem, which she longed to visit. Then she asked if, indeed, he was not a Frank. Coming from Mentwab this was a trying question. She was proud of her Portuguese ancestry and (says Bruce) 'had a warm attachment to the Catholic religion in her heart, as far as she could ever learn it'. But her visitor does not seem to have hesitated.

A large Bible was lying on the table beside her. Bruce laid his hand on it and answered:

'I declare to you, by all those truths contained in this book, that my religion is more different from the Catholic than yours is: that there has been more blood shed between the Catholics and us, on account of the differences of religion, than ever was between you and the Catholics in this country; even at this day, when men are becoming wiser and cooler in many parts of the world, it would be full as safe for a Jesuit to preach in the market-place of Gondar as for any priest of my religion to present himself as a teacher in the most civilized of Frank, or Catholic countries.'

This reply, and even a sceptical reference to the miracles of Ethiopian saints, do not seem to have prejudiced Mentwab against Bruce. Next morning Aylo came again to tell him that Welled Hawaryat and his daughter, a grandchild of the Empress, were dead, and that the disease was spreading at Kusquam. Many children of the Empress's daughters were in the palace under Princess Esther's care. He must come and treat them.

Bruce had been attending patients in the Moslem town. He got himself a new suit of Ethiopian clothes which would not carry infection from these sickrooms. His hair was 'cut round, curled and perfumed in the Amharic fashion', and he went to Kusquam 'thenceforward, in all outward appearance, a perfect Abyssinian'.

He found the sick children stewing in closed and heated rooms, loaded with bedclothes and without a breath of fresh air. He demanded absolute control of their treatment, saying that any interference with his orders might be fatal, 'and I saw that the more scrupulous and particular I was, the more the confidence of the ladies increased.'

'I set all the servants to work. There were apartments enough. I opened all the doors and windows, fumigating them with incense and myrrh in abundance, washed them with warm water and vinegar, and adhered strictly to the rules which my worthy and skilled friend, Doctor Russel, had given me at Aleppo.'

This régime was remarkably successful. Only one child died. But the smallpox found new victims. Esther's son by her second husband, the heroic Maryam Barea, was beginning to recover, but Confu, the son of her first husband, was infected, and after him her youngest child, the baby son of Ras Michael.

The Princess was almost in despair. 'She did not eat, or sleep, herself; and the ends of her fingers all broke out into pustules, from touching the several sick persons. I removed my bed to the outer door of Confu's chamber, to be ready whenever he should call; but his mother's anxiety kept her awake in his room all night, and propriety did not permit me to go to bed.' They talked together through the hours of watching and, 'from this frequent communication began a friendship which ever after subsisted without any interruption'.

Soon Esther's three sons and the rest of the Empress's family at Kusquam were out of danger. Bruce had won the lasting gratitude of Ras Michael, the most powerful man in Ethiopia, and of Mentwab, the greatest of its women. As for Esther, 'If I am not as good a friend to Yagoube, who has saved my children', she declared to Aylo, 'as I am an enemy to the Galla, who murdered my husband, you may say I am no Christian.'

But the Scot was still confined to Kusquam till he could be given the formal protection of the Ras and the Emperor. Within the circle of walls that enclosed the palace and the monastery were houses built for Mentwab's relatives and chief supporters. One of these, standing against the wall itself, was given to Bruce as a reward for his doctoring. He was offered gold as well, but refused this – a rash demonstration of independence as he found afterwards, since Ethiopians concluded that he must be enormously rich and would be worth plundering when he began his travels again.

Meanwhile he studied in his new home and mounted his instruments, telescopes, quadrant, thermometer and barometer. As usual, this raised rumours of magic. Morning and evening he was with Esther, 'where I seldom met with any'; each day he saw the Empress, and the priests who attended her grew used to tolerating him.

His fear of these churchmen was genuine and vivid. He had seen at Gondar the cairns that covered the bodies of the last three Roman Catholic missionaries to reach the city; they had been stoned to death and the same fate could come to any 'Frank' if the people were roused against him. He came to believe that Abba Salama was his most dangerous enemy in Ethiopia. This handsome, eloquent, bold little man was third in rank in the Ethiopian Church as 'Guardian of the Hour' in the Emperor's palace; he was, surely, the first in vigour and in hatred of white foreigners. He had also an insatiable appetite for women and fine food and was said to have recruited seventy mistresses partly by threatening them with excommunication if they refused him.

Bruce had an interview with this personage, who tried to entangle him in theological discussions.

'I am a physician in the town, a horseman and soldier in the field,' the Scot declared. 'This I was bred to; as for disputes on matters of religion, they are the province of priests. When I have doubts I bring them to some holy man like you.'

'By St Michael, prince of angels, that is right!' Abba Salama exclaimed. But it soon became clear that his suspicious enmity was not really dulled.

On the whole the interlude at Kusquam was a happy one, but Bruce was anxious to press on towards the Blue Nile, which the Ethiopians called Abai, 'the father of waters'. It was now within a few days' journey. Yet, though the rebel Fasil had been defeated he still held or threatened the country through which Bruce had to travel to reach the source of the river. Nothing could be done without the help of Michael.

This remarkable man was as nearly master of Ethiopia as any recent emperor had been. He was far-seeing, very intelligent, daring and unscrupulous, and still an active and able general, though he was well over seventy and limped from an old wound. By force and careful treasons he had built up his power till he was the dreaded ruler of the north. As Ras and Bitwadet he was the Emperor's deputy for almost all purposes, commander in war, prime minister and chief judge in peace; and the Emperor was his nominee and pupil.

But he himself could not become sovereign of Ethiopia. As a boy, indeed, he had been an emperor's nephew. Yostas was the one man not of the sacred Solomonic line to reach the Ethiopian throne in five centuries. He had been an able ruler, but after him, the country had turned back with relief to the old dynasty.

Though the Ras claimed to have a supernatural guide, the Archangel Michael, he could not hope, at his age, to establish a new royal line. Yet he knew his country's danger and seems to have cared, in his own way, for law and order. Probably his hope was to leave a strong legitimate ruler behind him – he seemed to have found a youth who could become such a ruler in Takla Haymanot. In his latest campaign he had had the support of all the most powerful men in Ethiopia but one, Fasil. One more victory and the whole country might be properly at peace.

The Ras showed his years when Bruce first saw him as he rode with the returning army, stooping over his mule, lean, white-haired, red-eyed, weary, and wrapped in a dirty coarse cloth like a blanket. But still Bruce must wait till the Emperor and his army had marched into Gondar in triumph – with the stuffed skin of Watchaka carried on a pole behind them – and till their victory had been publicly celebrated. Some things in this victorious display were shocking enough. It was the Ethiopians' custom to castrate the bodies of the men they killed. Their sexual trophies were laid in heaps before their chiefs. On this day, too, forty-four captive Galla leaders were publicly blinded. These helpless beings were abandoned on the riverside below the city. Bruce's good nature – and also, perhaps, a politic wish to earn favour with people of all kinds in Ethiopia – led him to take three of them into his house, where they were nursed back to health.

Meanwhile Esther, Aylo and the chief of the Moslem merchants had been pressing Michael to see the traveller and reward him for his medical work. The letter from Metical Aga, of Mecca, asking the Ras to ensure Bruce's safety, was read.

'Safety!' Michael exclaimed. 'Where is that to be found? I am obliged to fight for my own life every day. All I can do is to keep him beside me.'

At this Aylo declared that Bruce was well able to look after himself. 'He is a devil on horseback. He rides and shoots better than any man that ever came into the country.' He should be given an appointment in the Emperor's household. He was a sober, religious man and would do Takla Haymanot good.

At last Bruce was presented to the Ras, who this time made an impressive figure.

'He appeared to be thoughtful, but not displeased: his face was lean, his eyes quick and vivid. . . . He seemed to be about six feet high, though his lameness made it difficult to judge with accuracy. His air was perfectly free from constraint, what the French call *degagée*. In face and person he was liker my learned friend, the Count de Buffon, than any two men I ever saw in the world. They must have been poor physiognomists that did not discern his capacity and understanding by his very countenance. Every look conveyed a sentiment with it.'

His words to Bruce were interrupted from time to time by a sort of chorus or commentary from a priestly figure in a corner of the room.

'You are', Michael said, 'a man who makes it his business to wander in the fields in search of trees and grass in lonely places and to sit up all night looking at the stars.' But Ethiopia, he declared, was not like other countries. The people hated strangers and would murder for mere mischief.

'The Devil is strong in them,' said the Voice from the corner.

The Ras continued that, after consulting with Aylo, 'whose advice I hear you happily take, as indeed, we all do', he had decided that a post must be found for Bruce which would give him some freedom to do as he wanted and would ensure him respect that would help to protect him, so that he might not be troubled by monks about their religious matters or be in danger from rascals who may seek to murder him for money.

'What are monks?' said the Voice. 'They will not meddle with a man like this.'

Michael explained that the Emperor had agreed to appoint Bruce one of his *Baalomaals*, or Lords of the Bedchamber, and to make him commander of a body of his black horse-guards, whose captains were always foreigners. He must go to the Emperor and kiss the ground before him. Aylo would go with him and also the Voice, who, it appeared, was the Emperor's chief scribe and historiographer royal. This man became one of Bruce's chief friends in Ethiopia.

The Emperor's palace was a great walled square, rising from the hill-top on which the city stood, with a tower at its centre which contained the state rooms. Some of these were already half-ruined, but the finest of them were still in use. Here Takla Haymanot sat in an alcove, silent, his head and mouth veiled in white muslin.

When Bruce came to know the young Emperor he found him tall for his age, graceful and intelligent. Though it was only a few months since he had been brought from the mountain where he

was born 'his manners and carriage were those of a prince that had
sat from his infancy on a hereditary throne. He was not so dark in
complexion as a Neapolitan or Portuguese, had a remarkably fine
forehead, large black eyes but which had something very stern in
them, a straight nose, rather of the largest. . . . His features, even
in Europe, would have been thought fine'. His long hair was elab-
orately dressed. He was prudent, his naturally hot temper very
carefully controlled. He accepted the guidance of Ras Michael, who
had murdered his father, without ceasing to command respect.

All this was not to be seen when Bruce was first presented to
him. At a public audience the Emperor spoke not directly but
through an official who was called his Voice. When Aylo introduced
Bruce there was no comment on what he said. Instead there came
an endless string of questions. What could the traveller tell about
Jerusalem? – the Ethiopians' favourite topic. Where was his
country? Why had he come so far from it? Were the moon and stars
the same in Britain as in Africa?

Hours passed while Bruce and his companions, who had been
invited to supper by the Emperor's Treasurer at his house within
the palace walls, grew weak with weariness and hunger as they
stood. Probably Takla Haymanot was rather suspicious of the
stranger whom Michael had introduced into his household and,
boyishly, had decided to test this giant's endurance. When only
the small group of Lords of the Bedchamber remained in the room
the Emperor unveiled himself and spoke directly. But still the
questioning went on 'sometimes about horses, at other times about
shooting; how far I could look into the heavens with my telescopes:
and all these were deliberately and circumstantially repeated if
they were not pointedly answered.

'I was absolutely in despair, and scarcely able to speak a word,
inwardly mourning the hardness of my lot in this my first prefer-
ment, and sincerely praying that it might be my last promotion in
this court.' At last one man stepped forward, pretending to have a
message from the Empress, and whispered something to the
Emperor – probably that Ras Michael would be annoyed if Bruce

were made too uncomfortable. 'He then laughed, said he thought
we had supped, and dismissed us.'

As it turned out, this unpromising beginning laid the foundation
of friendship between the new courtier and his royal master.
Bruce and some of his fellow *baalomaals* went off to eat in the
Treasurer's house 'in violent rage, such as is usual with hungry
men'. With them was a nephew of Michael's, Gebra Maskal, the
commander of the Ras's musketeers. He was an able though vain-
glorious soldier.

The supper soon developed into a drinking bout, though Bruce
declares that he kept sober, since the Treasurer's wine was soon
finished and he would not drink mead like the others. Gebra
Maskal boasted of his knowledge of firearms. A Greek suggested
that he could learn a great deal from Yagoube. The musketeer
captain was contemptuous. Bruce, provoked, declared that even
in his servants' hands a bullet from any of his guns could reach
twice as far as any of Gebra Maskal's. As for himself, 'the end of a
tallow candle in my gun shall do more execution than an iron ball
in the best of yours'.

This produced a violent quarrel. The Ethiopian drew his knife.
Bruce snatched it from him, but not before he had been slightly
wounded in the head, so that his face streamed with blood. Bruce
was striking back, luckily with the haft of the knife, not with the
blade, when the party suddenly came to their senses. The use of
arms in the palace precincts was a capital crime. If Bruce was
seriously wounded, as his companions thought, Gebra Maskal
could scarcely escape and the rest of the company – indeed, the
whole city – might be in trouble.

Next morning Gebra Maskal was lying, fettered, in Ras Michael's
house and Bruce, whose scratch was almost healed, was discussing
with Aylo, prudent but agitated, what was to be done. The Ras
did not love his nephew; though he valued him as a soldier he
suspected him of adultery with one of his wives. Now he might be
very ready to do justice on Gebra Maskal. But Gondar was full of
troops from Tigre to whom the commander of the musketeers was

a hero. If he was condemned, they might mutiny. If he was executed, all the Tigreans would feel that they had a lasting blood-feud with Bruce as the cause of his death.

With Aylo, Bruce rode through the city to make it clear that he was not badly hurt. First Esther, who was greatly concerned about his wound, and then the Ras had to be convinced that, for the sake of the traveller's safety, Gebra Maskal ought to be forgiven. Michael was, indeed, full of rage.

'What sort of behaviour is this my men have adopted with strangers?' he exclaimed, looking, Bruce says, like a fiend. 'My stranger, too, and in the palace. What! Am I dead or incapable of governing any longer?'

However, he was persuaded to be merciful. Gebra Maskal was sent off with some of his soldiers to gather revenue. The Emperor began to treat his new Lord of the Bedchamber very kindly. Like Michael and most of the court, he was evidently ashamed that a foreigner should have been treated in this way: foreigners were rarities to be cherished and, if possible, impressed by life in Gondar, so long as they did not interfere with Ethiopian affairs – particularly Ethiopian religion.

Takla Haymanot still had doubts on one point. He asked whether it was really true that Bruce had not been drunk when the quarrel with Gebra Maskal began.

The Scot insisted that he had been perfectly sober.

'Then', said the Emperor, 'did you soberly say that the end of a tallow candle in your gun would do more than a bullet in his? You will not persuade me that you can kill a man or a horse with a candle.'

Bruce declared that he had simply been telling the truth. He did not think he ought to be asked to show that he could kill a man. But some other experiment might be equally convincing. 'Will piercing the table on which your dinner is served at the length of this room be deemed a sufficient proof of what I advance?'

'Ah, Yagoube, Yagoube', answered the Emperor, 'take care what you say. You don't know the Ethiopians. They will tell lies all day – their whole life is one lie. But they expect better from you, or would be glad to find worse. Take care!'

Engedan, a warrior chief who was Bruce's friend and a relative of the Empress, suggested that the attempt should be made to pierce his great leather shield with a candle. The Emperor was anxious that the demonstration should take place at once, before a crowd could gather which might report Bruce's failure. The gun was brought. Bruce demanded two more shields and the three were placed against a post outside the palace window through which Takla Haymanot could watch unseen.

'I loaded the gun before them,' Bruce tells, 'first with powder, then upon it slid down half of what we call a farthing candle'.

' "Now, Engedan," said I, "Will you please say – Fire! but mind you have taken leave of your good shield for ever".

'The word was given and the gun fired. . . . The candle went through the three shields with such violence that it dashed itself into a thousand pieces against a stone wall behind.'

Bruce then proposed that the other half of the candle should be tried against the Emperor's table, which was three-quarters of an inch thick. It, too, was pierced. This demonstration of the effect of concentrated explosive force, familiar enough in Europe at the time, made an immense impression. Some priests who saw it decided that it had been done by magic, and this was generally accepted as the most rational explanation of what had happened. But it was not so with the Emperor.

'It made the most favourable and lasting impression upon his mind; nor did I ever after see, in his countenance, any marks either of doubt or diffidence, but always, on the contrary, the most decisive proofs of friendship, confidence and attention, and the most implicit belief of everything I advanced on any subject from my own knowledge.'

Bruce was now firmly established at court – too firmly established for his own peace of mind. He was no nearer the Abai and the prospect of getting there had grown very little brighter. As often happened when he grew depressed he began to feel physically ill.

For a while Gondar had been enlivened by a great wedding. Princess Ayabdar, a granddaughter both of the Empress and of Ras Michael, was married to Powussen, newly made the Governor of Begemder, a province of special importance both because it produced the best Ethiopian cavalry and because its herds and crops gave food to the capital. Bruce was to argue in his book that marriage in what was then the Western sense of the word did not exist, properly speaking, in Ethiopia, since couples could part by consent and polygamy was common among the rich. But this was an exaggeration. There could be a religious ceremony which was legally indissoluble, and marriages made for political reasons could certainly be important.

In this case 'all Gondar was one scene of festivity'. Michael, Esther and her sister, Princess Altash, the bride's mother, gave repeated entertainments.

'A vast number of cattle was slaughtered every day, and the whole town looked like one great market; the common people in every street appearing loaded with pieces of raw beef, while drink circulated in the same proportion.

'The Ras insisted upon my dining with him every day, when he was sure to give me a headache with the quantity of mead, or hydromel, he forced me to swallow. . . . After dinner we slipt away to parties of ladies, where anarchy prevailed as completely as at the house of the Ras. All the married women ate, drank and smoaked, like the men; and it is impossible to give the reader any idea of this bacchanalian scene in terms of common decency.'

Impossible or not, Bruce wrote an account of an Ethiopian feast vivid enough to shock eighteenth-century London, which was not famous for abstinence or a squeamish morality. Wherever there was security, he tells us – 'in the capital where one is safe from surprise at all times' or in the country during the rainy season when the rivers were flooded and sudden raids were impossible – men and women 'of the best fashion' would meet for dinner soon after midday.

A long table was set up in a large room, with benches beside it for the guests. A cow or bull – or several animals if the gathering was big enough – would be tied beside the door. A shallow cut was made in the fat of the creature's throat and a few drops of blood spilled on the ground to satisfy the law of Moses. Flesh was then systematically stripped from the still-living beast 'in solid square pieces, without bones, or much effusion of blood; and the prodigious noise the animal makes is a signal for the company to sit down at table'.

Several large round cakes of unleavened bread made from *teff*, a favourite grain, were placed before each guest, men and women sitting alternately, and servants brought in square pieces of raw beef to be laid on the cakes, which served as plates.

'The man with his long knife cuts a thin piece, which would be thought a good beef-steak in England, while you see the motion of the fibres yet perfectly distinct and alive in the flesh. No man, of any fashion whatever, feeds himself. The women take the steak, and cut it length-ways like strings, about the thickness of your little finger, then cross-ways into square pieces, something smaller than dice. This they lay upon a piece of teff bread, strongly powdered with pepper and fossil salt; they then wrap it up in the teff bread like a cartridge.

'In the mean time, the man, with each hand resting upon his neighbour's knee, his body stooping, his head low and forward, and mouth open, very like an idiot, turns to the one whose cartridge is first ready, who stuffs the whole of it into his mouth, which is so full that he is in constant danger of being choked. This is a mark of grandeur. The greater the man would seem to be, the larger piece he takes in his mouth; and the more noise he makes in chewing it, the more polite he is thought to be.'

When this was quickly chewed and swallowed a second cartridge was received from the woman on his other side, and the process continued till the man could eat no more.

'He never drinks till he has finished eating; and before he begins, in gratitude to the fair ones that fed him, he makes up two small rolls of the same kind and form; each of his neighbours open their mouths at the same time, while with each hand he puts their portion into their mouths. He then falls to drinking out of a large handsome horn; the ladies eat till they are satisfied, and then all drink together. *Vive la Joye et la Jeunesse!* A great deal of mirth and joke goes round, very seldom with any mixture of acrimony or ill-humour.'

By this time the butchers at the door had probably reached a point where they must cut the great arteries of their unlucky victim, which at last bled to death. What was left of the meat quickly became so tough that the servants and others to whom it was given found it 'very hard work to separate the flesh from the bones with their teeth like dogs'.

The diners, meanwhile, were merry with drink.

'Love lights all its fires, and everything is permitted with absolute freedom. There is no coyness, no delays, no need of appointments or retirement to gratify their wishes; there are no rooms but one, in which they sacrifice both to Bacchus and to Venus. The two men nearest the vacuum a pair have made on the bench by leaving their seats, hold their upper garments like a screen before the two that have left the bench; and, if one may judge by sound, they seem to think it as great a shame to make love in silence as to eat.

'Replaced in their seats again, the company drink the happy couple's health; and their example is followed at different ends of the table, as each couple is disposed. All this passes without remark or scandal, not a licentious word is uttered, nor the most distant joke upon the transaction. These ladies are, for the most part, women of family and character.'

This picture of barbarism was to be too much for Bruce's readers, who refused to believe that such things were possible in the land of *Rasselas*. At Gondar it was soon too much for Bruce himself.

'I found it necessary to quit this riot for a short time, and get leave to breathe the fresh air of the country, at such a distance as that, once a day, or once in two days, I might be at the palace, and avoid the constant succession of those violent scenes of debauchery.'

IO

To the Cataract

As Ras Michael sat at his table during one of the last carousals for the marriage of Powussen, which was to symbolize the union of the Ethiopian factions, Bruce saw a weary youth in torn clothes come suddenly into the room. He was a messenger from the Damot Agaus, who lived in the hill country beyond Lake Tana round the source of the Blue Nile.

The Agau people are sometimes said to represent the original Hamitic race that occupied most of Ethiopia before the coming of the Semites from Arabia. They had a language, customs and clan organization of their own. Their land was, in Bruce's day, the most productive in the Empire. Like Begemder it fed the city of Gondar. Because their country was attached to Fasil's province they had been forced to follow him in the late war, but at the first chance they had rallied to Michael and the Emperor. Now Fasil had attacked them, hoping to exterminate them and give their fields to his own Gallas. Seven of their chiefs had been killed in battle, announced the messenger, who was a son of one of them.

Michael had a gold wine-cup in his hand: it was the special privilege of the Governor of Tigre to drink from gold. He threw down the cup, so that the wine ran on the floor. 'I am guilty of the death of these people,' he cried.

The table was removed, the boy told his story, and Michael held a council of war with his chief guests. The rainy season, when movement would be impossible because of swollen rivers, was not far away, but it was decided to strike at Fasil as soon as the largest

possible force could be collected. Gusho and Powussen were to go
to their provinces and bring out all their men. The Emperor and the
Ras would re-equip their army and march to the spot where the
Blue Nile flows out of Lake Tana. The two Governors would join
them there. They would cross the river together and make for
Burie, which was Fasil's chief town.

'No resolution was ever embraced with more alacrity; the cause
of the Agaus was the cause of Gondar,' which might starve if their
country was devastated.

This seemed a hopeful state of things for Bruce. The armies
were going where he wanted to go. It had even been agreed that if
Fasil withdrew into the heart of the Galla country before he was
defeated, Michael and the Emperor should settle down for the
rainy season close to the Blue Nile source, so as to be able to pursue
the rebel as soon as the rivers became passable again. Following
them, he would no doubt have to pass through scenes of blood and
pillage, but the main purpose of his African journey could probably
be accomplished fairly safely within a few months.

He was still feeling ill after the orgies of Gondar and got the
Emperor's permission to move twenty miles out of the city to
Emfras, near Lake Tana, while the army was preparing to march
again. It was a town of tent-makers and he wanted to have a tent
made to his own design, with a slit in the roof through which he
could make observations of the sky without being disturbed
by curious visitors.

He was a little surprised to find that some of his friends did not
seem to approve of his plan. Though the Empress gave him gold
and supplies for his journey to the Nile, she wanted him to stay at
Kusquam till it could be seen whether the Emperor and Michael
would return from a campaign which, to Bruce and themselves,
seemed bound to be successful.

It was strange, she said, that he should come from Jerusalem
(which, in fact, he had not visited) 'through vile Turkish governments, and hot unwholesome climates, to see a river and a bog, no
part of which you can carry away were it ever so valuable'. He

5. The Imperial Palace of Gondar, a modern photograph

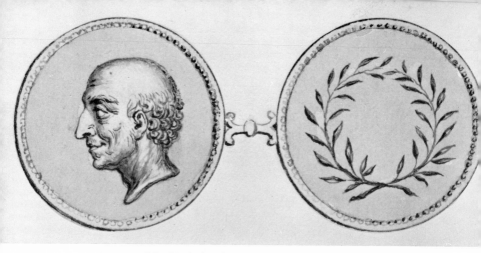

6a. Ras Michael Suhul – sketch for a medallion by James Bruce
(at Broomhall)

6b. Princess Esther and Takla Mariam sketched by James Bruce
(at Broomhall)

might die on the way, 'his friends at home never knowing when or where.' Yet she, the mother of kings, had no wish but to go to Jerusalem and beg her bread there if only she could be buried within sight of the Temple where Christ had once been. 'This was said in the most melancholy tone possible; an unusual gloom hanging upon her countenance.'

Gusho, too, though ready to lend Bruce a house he had at Emfras, urged that it would be wiser to go with himself into his province, Amhara, where the Scot could stay safely till he was well again.

However, Bruce would not change his mind. Emfras was a pleasant place, built half-way up a steep hill looking over the great lake, which stretched forty-nine miles from north to south and thirty-five from east to west. Here he could collect plants and make observations in peace while he got back his massive good health again.

It took Michael more than a month to mount his new campaign. At least twice in this time Bruce was back in Gondar, called to advise his patients there. The most grateful of these was Esther's eldest son, Confu. Though he was still only a boy of fourteen, Michael had made him Governor of the small province of Ras el Fil. This strip of low-lying country on the border of the Sudan was the homeland of Yasin, who had been so useful to Bruce on his journey from Arabia to Gondar. Its people were Mohammedans, and they always had a deputy governor of their own religion. The reigning deputy, who was Yasin's father-in-law and had expelled him as a rival to himself, had failed to join Michael in the war with Fasil and had also quarrelled with the Sudanese, whose trade with Ras el Fil gave the province most of its revenue.

Bruce had been asked by Moslems in Gondar to try to have Yasin appointed to replace him. Since the Scot had made up his mind to go home by way of the Sudanese kingdom of Sennar rather than risk any further dealings with the rascally Naib of Massawa, it might be very useful to him to have a reliable friend on the frontier. Though he was anxious to keep himself clear of court intrigues, he did try to push Yasin's claim. But it seemed that if affairs in Ras el Fil were to be cleared up Confu himself might have to go there and deal with them. The boy was still weak from his smallpox, and Bruce believed that a journey into the tropical lowlands might kill him. He gave this warning to Confu, who explained that he had resigned the governorship, but believed his successor might appoint Yasin.

Rather mysteriously he would say no more, but when Bruce went to seek out this new Governor he found that, by Confu's and Esther's influence, the province had been given to himself. The appointment would bring him money, he was told, and he need not actually go to Ras el Fil unless he wanted to. The Empress gave a dinner for him. Yasin was sent for and invested as deputy. All this, Bruce says, 'gave me the first real pleasure I had received since landing at Masuah'. With his friends he 'abandoned himself to joy'.

The celebration was too much for him and he went back to Emfras in a fever to live for a while on boiled rice and cold water.

He was called to court again by the news that the Emperor's secretary, who had been one of his supporters in the matter of Ras el Fil, was ill and needed his medical help. This time the road to Gondar was full of monks going to take part in a great religious controversy. As usual, Bruce was afraid that this might develop into an attack on himself as a dangerous Frank, but he shrouded his face, as great men in Ethiopia normally did, and rode to the capital without opposition.

There he met his friend Aylo and asked him what the trouble was about – 'I hope not the old story of the Franks?'

'No, no,' replied Aylo, shaking with laughter, 'a great deal worse than that; it is about Nebuchadnezzar'. The whole country might be convulsed by this. A monk who was a favourite of the Empress and the Emperor had declared that the Biblical King of Babylon was a saint, while Abba Salama, chief of the court chaplains maintained 'that he was a Pagan, Idolater and a Turk, and that he is burning in hell fire with Dathan and Abiram.'

Next day Bruce presented himself before Takla Haymanot, who insisted on asking him whether Nebuchadnezzar was a saint or not. Bruce did not want to answer. It was dangerous for him to speak about religion, he said. But the young Emperor insisted. He had been studying the Bible and had learned the case for the pagan king's sainthood, whether he believed it or not. Bruce, too, knew his Old Testament.

'I never thought, sir,' he said, 'that Nebuchadnezzar had any pretensions to be a saint. He was a scourge in God's hand, as is famine, or the plague, but that does not make either of them a wholesome visitation'.

'What!' said the Emperor. 'Does not God call him His servant? Does He not say he did His bidding about Tyre, and that He gave him Egypt to plunder for His vengeance? Was it not by God's command that he led His people into captivity? And did he not believe in God when Shadrach, Meshach and Abednego escaped from the fiery furnace? Surely such a man must be a saint?'

Bruce answered that he was quite prepared to accept Nebuchadnezzar as a saint rather than risk excommunication by Abba Salama. At this the Emperor broke into laughter.

It was said that Ras Michael would decide this point of hagiology by a statement in the great courtyard of the palace; but Michael did not come. Instead a large drum called the Lion was beaten there and it was proclaimed that if the disorderly and wild people who had come into the city without bringing food for themselves were not out of sight by noon next day they would be punished 'like robbers and rebels'. This was followed by the announcement that the Emperor was sending out 400 Galla troops to patrol the streets by night. The Galla, being pagans, could, of course, be expected to show no favour to Christian clergy. There were, in fact, no Galla soldiers in Gondar, but the monks understood the hint quickly enough. They dispersed without waiting to hear more about St Nebuchadnezzar, and Bruce returned to Emfras in peace.

It was at daybreak on May 13th, 1770, that the advance guards of the army passed below the town. At this 'every one hid what was best in his house, or fled to the mountains with it. Emfras was left in a few hours quite empty. Ras Michael, advancing at the head of an army spread as much terror as would the approach of the day of judgement. For, strict and just as he was in time of peace, or in preserving the poor from the tyranny of the rich, he was most licentious and cruel the moment he took the field.'

It was late in the evening when they heard the Emperor's kettle-drums. Forty-five of these instruments were carried before him, beaten continuously while he was on the march. His *fitauraris*, or commander of the advance guard, had left a man to protect Bruce from plunder: this precaution was very necessary.

'The Mahometan town, near the water, was plundered in a minute; but the inhabitants, long before, had removed every thing valuable. Twenty different parties of stragglers came up the hill to do the same by Emfras. Some of the inhabitants were known, others not so, but their houses had nothing in them; at last these plunderers united in mine, demanding meat and drink, and all sorts of accommodation. Our guard, left with us by the Fit-Auraris, resisted as much as one man could do with sticks and whips, and it was a scuffle till mid-night: at last, having cleared ourselves of them, luckily without their setting fire to the town, we remained quiet for the rest of the night.'

Taking all his men servants with him Bruce rode off next morning to the Emperor's headquarters. A council with Ras Michael was beginning and he decided to go to Princess Esther's tent. Though she was pregnant, Esther was making the campaign with her husband: Bruce found her lying on a sofa.

'There is Yagoube! There is the man I wanted!' she exclaimed as soon as he appeared.

'The tent was cleared of all but her women, and she then began to enumerate several complaints, which she thought, before the end of the campaign, would carry her to her grave. It was easy to see they were of the slightest kind, though it would not have been agreeable to have told her so, for she loved to be thought ill, to be attended, condoled with, and flattered; she was, however, in these circumstances, so perfectly good, so conversable, so elegant in all her manners, that her physician would have been tempted to wish never to see her well.'

When the medical advice had been given 'the doors of the tent were thrown open; all our friends came flocking round us'. Breakfast appeared, served in wooden platters on the carpet.

'There were excellent stewed fowls, but so inflamed with cayenne pepper as almost to blister the mouth; fowls dressed with boiled wheat, just once broken in the middle, in the manner they are prepared in India, with rice called *pillaw*, this, too, abundantly charged with pepper; Guinea hens, roasted hard without butter or any sort of sauce, very white, but as tough as leather; above all the never-failing *brind*, for so they call the collops of raw beef, without which nobody could have been satisfied; but, what was more agreeable to me, a large quantity of wheat-bread, equal in all its quality to the best in London or Paris.'

'Plant first and then water' was the Ethiopian proverb. When eating was done 'the glass went cheerfully about; there was excellent red wine, but strong, of the nature of côte-roti, brought from Karoota, which is the wine country about six miles south-east from where we were; good new brandy; honey-wine or hydromel, and a species of beer called bouza, both of which were fermented with herbs, or leaves of trees, and made very heady; they are disagreeable liquors to strangers'.

Still lying on her sofa, Esther 'pressed about the glass in the very briskest manner, reminding us that our time was short, and that the drum would presently give the signal for striking the tents.' Bruce remembered that he must see the Emperor and Ras Michael and began to wonder whether he was sober enough to get so far.

'I thought to put on my most sedate appearance that none of my companions should see that I was affected with liquor!' He was not very successful. Takla Haymanot's young brother, whom Bruce calls Prince George,[1] was standing beside the Emperor when Bruce came forward to kiss the ground according to custom. The boy came forward and held out a hand to prevent the massive Scot from kneeling.

[1] Takla Giyorgis. In the anarchy after Bruce left Ethiopia he was six times enthroned as Emperor and six times deposed.

'Sir,' he said to the Emperor, 'before you allow Yagoube to kneel you should provide two men to lift him up again. Princess Esther has given him so much wine that he will never be able to do it himself.'

The courtiers laughed and Bruce himself could not help smiling. He explains that 'the drink had really this good effect that it made me less abashed than I otherwise should have been at the unexpected sally of the young prince. I was, however, somewhat disconcerted, and made my prostration perhaps less gracefully than at another time, and this raised the merriment of those in waiting, as attributing it to intoxication'.

This was awkward. Bruce was fond enough of fun, but he could not afford to be thought of as a clown by the Ethiopian chiefs. The Emperor, however, would not allow himself to laugh. With proper ceremony he gave Bruce his hand to kiss and coldly told his brother that if he thought Yagoube was drunk it would have been wiser to say nothing.

'The prince was much abashed. I hastened across the carpet and took both his hands and kissed them; the laughers did not seem so much at their ease.' Bruce admitted that he had, in fact, drunk more that day than he had ever done at Gondar.

'Come, come!' said the Emperor. 'Giyorgis is your firm and true friend, and so he ought to be. He owes it to you that he is so able a horseman and so good a marksman, without which he could never be more than a common soldier. He commands a division of the army.' It was a body of 570 horse. 'Giyorgis', he concluded, 'is more drunk with the thoughts of his command today than any soldier in my army will be tonight with *bouza*.'

In spite of his illness and his absences from Gondar, Bruce seems somehow to have found time to teach the prince riding and shooting in the Arab style, perhaps even to begin the training of the body of negro guards he had been given to command. But in this campaign he was not marching with the army as a soldier. It had been accepted that his purpose was to reach the Blue Nile. He was to wait till the Emperor reached the place beyond the river where Powussen and

Gusho were to join him. Then Bruce was to visit the great Tissisat cataract which the Jesuits had described, and finally, when the way was clear for him, to make for the source itself.

When news of the army's advance reached him Bruce began to travel leisurely down the shore of Lake Tana, collecting botanical specimens and watching hippopotami swimming in the lake and feeding among the grass beside it. He had a new companion to take the place of Yasin in the management of his other servants. This was Strates, a Greek, who was sent forward with the baggage and tents. At the River Gomara, which flowed out of Begemder, Strates reappeared again, completely naked except for a cotton nightcap. He had been attacked and robbed by two wild young relatives of the Empress who were apparently leading the advance guard of the forces of Powussen. The other men of his party had escaped with him, and Bruce at first believed that this was a mere outburst of mischief, alarming enough but with no other object but plunder. Later he learned that the attack had been planned by Abba Salama, still anxious to destroy the Frankish stranger.

Much more discouraging was a report that the Governors of Begemder and Amhara, who had left Gondar as Michael's allies, had made a secret agreement with his enemy, Fasil, that all three would assail the Ras at the rendezvous beyond the Blue Nile where he and the Emperor could be caught between Lake Tana and a small lake south of it. The Ras would be destroyed and the three rebels would be able to occupy Gondar and, between them, rule the country.

This piece of treachery, typical enough of Ethiopia, explained the attempts of Gusho and the Empress to persuade Bruce not to travel till it was seen whether Michael and the Emperor would win their war against Fasil. The Empress, too, had known of the new conspiracy. Possibly she had helped to make it.

Bruce was horrified. It seemed now that his way to the source of the Blue Nile might be blocked and that, even if he himself escaped from the turmoil, his chief protectors in Ethiopia might lose their power and all the planning for the climax of his journey might have to begin again. However, when the party who had attacked Strates appeared beyond the Gomara – about a hundred horsemen, 'skirmishing, playing, pursuing one another, shrieking and whooping, like so many frantic people' – he was no longer unprotected; he had supporters who made him feel strong enough to challenge them. He had met with two chiefs who were his friends and who were bringing up men to join the Emperor. One of them, the District Governor of Karoota, the wine country, though not disloyal, had an old quarrel with Ras Michael. The other was sincerely anxious to join the Ras. But neither of them was at all ready to hand over Bruce to the raiders as they demanded. With these allies Bruce crossed the river and fired two rifle shots at the leader of his assailants. One wounded him, and he and his followers galloped away.

The *shum* of Karoota now turned back, but Bruce's other friend was prepared to press on, and Bruce could not bring himself to retreat now that the Nile was so near. He learned that Michael and the Emperor had heard of the traitors' plot against them, but had decided first to fight Fasil for protection of the Agaus and then to turn back and chasten Powussen and Gusho, whose lands were on the east side of Lake Tana. His informant was Mohammed, the Negade Ras or chief of the Ethiopian customs service, who was gathering revenue for Michael south of the lake.

Bruce felt that even if he could not reach the Nile's source on this expedition at least he must not miss his chance of seeing the great cataract, which was only fourteen miles away; he might never be so near it again.

He rode out the next morning with an escort provided by the Negade Ras to protect him from raiders, passing over rocky land, 'full of trees, mostly of unknown kinds, and all of the greatest beauty possible, having flowers of a hundred different colours and forms upon them'. The party came to a Moslem village where, perhaps for the first time in Ethiopia, Bruce heard English spoken.

A servant who led his horse towards the *shum*'s door exclaimed in Arabic, 'Good Lord! to see you here!' Bruce asked him to explain himself.

'Do you not know me?' the man said. 'I was with you at Jidda. I was the man who brought you letters from Metical Aga at Mecca.' He had been on board the Lion East Indiaman 'when your little vessel, all covered with sail, passed with such briskness through the English ships, which all fired their cannon; and everybody said, there is a poor man making great haste to be murdered among those wild people of Ethiopia; and so we all thought'.

Then he broke into all the English he knew, 'Drink! no force! English very good – God damn, drink!' crying as loudly as he could, with an air of triumph. This, Bruce reflected sourly, was the English language as it could be learned by listening to Englishmen.

The noise of the waterfall was clearly heard long before they came to a single-arched stone bridge, built a century and a half before under Portuguese guidance, which spanned the river half a mile downstream, where it roared through a narrow opening between two rocks. Here the Blue Nile plunged into a great canyon, three hundred miles long, which was impassable to travellers, except at rare crossing-places, and made the river valley useless as a link between Ethiopia and the Sudan.

'The cataract itself was the most magnificent sight that ever I beheld. The river had been considerably increased by rains, and fell in one sheet of water, above half an English mile in breadth, with a force and noise that was truly terrible, and which stunned and made me, for a time, perfectly dizzy. A thick fume, or haze, covered the fall all round, and hung over the course of the stream both above and below, marking its track, though the water was not seen . . .

'It was a most magnificent sight, that ages, added to the greatest length of human life, would not efface or eradicate from my memory; it struck me with a kind of stupor, and a total oblivion of where I was and of every other sublunary concern. It was one of the most magnificent, stupendous sights in the creation, though degraded and vilified by the lies of a grovelling fanatic priest.'

The 'fanatic priest' was Jeronimo Lobo, the Jesuit whose account of Ethiopia Samuel Johnson translated from the French

version of his travels. Bruce felt bound to prove to his own satisfaction that no missionary had reached the Nile source before them.
It does, indeed, seem more than likely that Father Lobo never did
visit the source: his description of it seems to be borrowed from
that of his great predecessor, Pedro Paez. But he may well have
been at the waterfall. Bruce discredits him mainly on two grounds.
Lobo wrote that the depth of the fall was fifty feet. After measuring
it as best he could Bruce decided that forty feet would be more
accurate, 'but', he adds with proper honesty, 'I confess I could at
no time in my life less promise upon precision; while in the sight
of the fall, I think I was under a temporary alienation of mind; it
seemed to me as if one element had broke loose from, and become
superior to, all laws of subordination; that the fountains of the great
deep were again extraordinarily opened, and the destruction of a
world was once more begun by the agency of water.'

In fact, it has since been shown that his own measurements were
in this case even farther out than Lobo's. His other reason for
scepticism was rather more serious. Lobo claimed to have been able
to get behind the wall of falling water and, resting on the rock of
the river bed, to admire 'a thousand rainbows' which the sunlight
raised in the cataract. Bruce convinced himself that even 'a very
robust man, in the prime and vigour of life, a hardy, practised,
indefatigable swimmer' like himself could not have found his way
through the pool at the bottom of the cataract so as to pass through
the curve of the plunging river. The rainy season was beginning
when he was at Alata, and the Abai may have been higher than
when Lobo visited it. In the 1920s R. E. Cheesman[1] was to find
that it was not difficult to reach a position behind the fall very like
that described by the Portuguese.

But for Bruce the great self-fostered illusion that he was the first
European at the headwater of the Nile had to be maintained at all
costs. The Jesuits must be liars if the whole effort of the Laird of
Kinnaird was not to lose most of its meaning.

[1] *Lake Tana and the Blue Nile.*

I I

Rain and Revolution

Ras Michael's plan of campaign had collapsed. Though he still
hoped to defeat Fasil, even without the two allies who had deserted
him, he could not hope to push into the Agau country, or to Burie,
the centre of Fasil's power; for the rains had come, the mountain
streams that poured into Lake Tana were rising and the lake itself
would soon be spreading over the low ground near it. The Ras and
the Emperor must move towards Gondar before they could be im-
mobilized by these annual floods. On the other hand, the rebels'
plans had also gone wrong. Powussen and Gusho failed to bring up
their forces to attack Michael in the rear as they had promised
Fasil they would do. What should have been a decisive campaign –
decisive for one side or the other – was becoming a scrambling con-
test with the Ethiopian weather.

After the excitement of his visit to the Nile cataract, Bruce was
in the deepest depression. He had decided to cross the Blue Nile
where it left Lake Tana and go forward to join the Emperor and Ras
Michael, but his hope of reaching what he believed to be the
river's source in the mountain lands fifty miles south of the lake
was practically lost for the present.

Modern geographers may argue that he passed the true beginning of the great river at the point where it flowed from the lake.
But this meant nothing to him. Like the Ethiopians themselves, he
believed that the stream, sometimes called the Little Abai, which
ran into the lake on its south-western side, was the true origin of
the Nile, and though he would actually cross this river as he skirted

Lake Tana with the Emperor's army its source was still far out of sight.

How rash he had been to push himself into so many unnecessary dangers, he thought, as he lay in his tent between sleeping and waking. There seemed to be very little chance that he could complete his discoveries and then return to Europe. If he did not, his fellow countrymen might never hear what had happened to him. How presumptuous it was of him to think that where so many travellers had failed he alone would succeed. 'All those reflections filled my imagination with what I have heard other people call the *horrors*, the most disagreeable sensation I ever was conscious of.'

He was passing through a deserted countryside: 'the houses uninhabited, the grass trodden down, the fields without cattle. Every thing that had life and strength fled before that terrible leader [Ras Michael] and his no less terrible army; a profound silence was in the fields around us . . . interrupted only at times by thunder, now become daily, and the rolling of torrents, produced by loud showers in the hills. As we advanced, we had seen a great number of dead mules and horses, and the hyaenas so bold as only to leave the carcass for a moment, and snarl, as if they had regretted at seeing any of us pass alive.' The party came up with stragglers from the army, searching the bushes for people who had taken refuge there. 'They had some of them three, some four women and girls, whom, though Christians, like themselves, they nevertheless were dragging away into slavery, to sell them to the Turks for a very small price.'

They heard gunfire and guessed that Fasil's troops had met Michael's. The shots seemed to be coming nearer: the army must surely be in retreat. They took their arms, mounted and prepared to join the Emperor: 'yet it was a thing appeared to us scarcely possible that Fasil should beat Ras Michael so easily, and with so short a resistance.'

Then, with relief, they saw the enemy. They were a vast herd of antelopes, so alarmed by the firing that 'they had every appearance of running us down.' The wild animals of the countryside, antelopes, buffaloes, boars and others, had fled from the troops till they were hemmed in between two rivers and the lake. Then, as the army advanced, they tried to break out of their corner, and the hungry musketeers began to shoot them down.

The rest of the army did not understand what was happening. The Emperor and Michael thought they were being attacked. 'The balls flew about in every direction, some few were killed, and many people and horses were hurt, still they fired, and Ras Michael, at the door of his tent, crying, threatening and tearing his grey locks, found, for a few minutes, the army was not under his command.'

At this point Netcho, the chief with whom Bruce was travelling, had his drums beaten, as was usual when a governor was approaching the Emperor. It was a new alarm: part of the army believed that the rebels, Gusho and Powussen, had come up against them. This confusion ceased when the young Emperor, who recognized the new-comers, gave the signal for forming an encampment. All was soon quiet again, but Bruce was convinced that if even five hundred rebels had, in fact, made an attack when the battle with the beasts was going on, the whole army would have fled without resistance.

It had been rumoured that the explorer and all those with him had been killed and he was received in the camp with joy and relief. At last he was able to join his own troop of black horseguards. The army was now close to the Little Abai. Its waters could be seen flowing through Lake Tana to the point where they left it again farther east. Rain had been falling heavily. The young river was growing deeper and broader and it was decided to cross it as soon as possible. 'Violent claps of thunder followed close on one another, almost without interval accompanied by sheets of lightning, which ran on the ground like water; the day was more than commonly dark, as in an eclipse; and every hollow or foot-path, collected a quantity of rain which fell into the Nile in torrents.' The enemy were thought to be close by when the army came to the river bank.

The current looked alarming to Bruce when he stationed himself and his men at the ford to prevent anyone from passing before the

Emperor's party and Ras Michael's. 'As soon as these were safely on shore, the household and black troops, and I with them, advanced cautiously into the river and swam happily over, in a deep stream of reddish-coloured water, which ran without violence almost upon a level.

'Each horseman had a mule in his hand, which swam after him, or by his side, with his coat of mail and head-piece tied upon it. My horse was a very strong one, and in good condition, and a servant took charge of my mule and coat of mail, so that, being unembarrassed, I had the happiness to get safe and soon over.'

But the approach to the ford was difficult and soon churned into mud. 'It is impossible to describe the confusion which followed; night was hard upon us, and though it increased our loss it in great measure concealed it; a thousand men had not yet passed, though on mules and horses; many, mired in the muddy landing-place, fell back into the stream and were carried away and drowned.' All night the troops, horse and foot, continued to cross. 'Those that could swim seemed best off', says Bruce, though the sky cleared and the level of the stream fell in the darkness.

It began to be suspected that the local guides who had taken Ras Michael to this ford had misled him – indeed, that it was not a customary ford at all. When dawn broke two-thirds of the army had crossed, but the rear, with the baggage and most of the ammunition, was still on the south bank of the river under the best of Michael's Tigrean generals, Kefla Yasus, a soldier whom Bruce admired and trusted. With him was a group of priests whom Michael had made prisoners because of a suspicion that they had had dealings with Fasil. These men now told Kefla Yasus that Fasil's forces were, indeed, in the neighbourhood and that the recognized passage of the river was eight miles downstream. One of the guides was forced to reveal the whole stratagem. Fasil had hoped that Michael's army would be divided and largely destroyed in attempts to cross through deep water. He had left a force to attack the rear-guard when it was struggling through, while he himself would fall on what remained of the disorganized main body north of the river.

Kefla Yasus sent due warning to Michael and then marched off to the lower ford, which he crossed successfully, with due precaution. Fasil's trap had failed. His cavalry did, indeed, face Michael's main force on high ground well beyond the river. Bruce, with his company of black horsemen, rode as part of the Emperor's guard. The troops, fresh from their plunge through the river, were very ready to fight. But nothing more than a skirmish followed. Fasil's horsemen turned and withdrew, and the army passed on to the narrow pass of Dingleber between a high rock and the lake, where they were secure.

Michael had escaped destruction, but his great force, which had set out confidently to make an end of the rebels, was in retreat. At Dingleber, where there was a royal fortress, Takla Haymanot held a feast. It began with an omen. As he sat down to dinner a black eagle was chased into his tent by inferior birds of prey. This proved, it was whispered, that he would be dethroned by rebels, 'and though,' says Bruce, 'we cannot but look upon the whole as an accident, it was but too soon fulfilled.'

For the moment, however, there was a promise of peace. Two envoys from Fasil rode into the camp. They announced that their master was retiring to the south. The Emperor would not be attacked on his way to Gondar. Indeed, Fasil's only wish was to live as his loyal subject – and Governor of the provinces he already held. The plot with Gusho and Powussen was acknowledged. Fasil declared that he would never trust them again. He proposed that, as a guarantee of friendship he should marry one of the Ras's granddaughters. But to the Emperor he sent a private message that Michael's promises were not to be relied on.

In fact, these assurances were not believed by anyone, but they had to be accepted. Bruce was astonished to hear a proclamation made at the door of the Emperor's tent: 'Fasil is Governor of the Agau country, Maitsha, Gojam and Damot; prosperity to him, and long may he live as a faithful servant of the Emperor.'

Never was so quick a political overturn, the Scotsman thought. 'It was scarce forty-three hours since Fasil had laid a scheme for drowning the greater part of the army in the Nile and cutting the throats of the residue on both sides of it; it was not twenty-four hours since he had met us to fight in the open field, and now he was become lieutenant-general in four of the most opulent provinces of Abyssinia.'

'The whole camp abandoned itself to joy.' In the evening Esther came to thank the Emperor for his gift to her of twenty oxen, twice as many as he had sent her husband to feed his warriors. Takla Haymanot declared that while Michael was feasting vigorous soldiers the princess was caring for the sick and wounded, 'for which reason I sent you a double portion so that you may be able to do double good'.

Bruce says he had thought for some time that Esther and the Emperor 'were not insensible to the merits of each other', in his discreet eighteenth-century phrase. Esther 'had been ill and alarmed, as well she might, at the passage of the Nile, which had given her a more delicate look than ordinary, she was dressed all in white, and I thought I seldom had seen so handsome a woman.'

The tent was cleared and they had half an hour alone together. It is unlikely, Bruce suggests, that they had anything to say to one another about Ras Michael. The Emperor was left in the gayest good humour. 'The Ras loved Esther, but was not jealous.'

By the 3rd June the army was at Gondar again. But it was not to stay there. Michael's best troops were from Tigre and he dared not let himself be cut off from his own provinces in the north. Their boundary, the great River Takazze, was rising. In a few days it would be quite impassable and the Ras learned that Gusho and Powussen were preparing to attack him in Gondar as soon as this happened.

For the moment a brave face was put on affairs. The proclamation giving Fasil his four provinces was repeated in Gondar and his envoys were given rich clothing and sent home to him ceremoniously. They had brought a special message to Bruce. Fasil's favourite

7a. Bruce's watercolour sketch of Leopards

7b. Bruce's watercolour of Feho Antelope

8. A battle scene
from an early
eighteenth-century
Ethiopian manuscript,
BM Oriental 533

Galla general was a sick man, suffering, apparently, from cancer of the lip. They were to ask for advice that would relieve him. Bruce gave them a pain-killer. 'To keep on the safe side, I prescribed small doses, being much more anxious to preserve myself from reproach than warmly solicitous about the care of my unknown patient!' He also gave advice about diet.

The messengers were overjoyed. Fasil, they said, would be even better pleased with a medicine that would help Wellata Yasus than with the Emperor's grant to him. At this Bruce said he would ask for two favours.

'And that's a rarity,' Takla Haymanot commented. There was only one thing he must not ask, to go home.

Bruce explained what he wanted. He asked the Emperor to give him the village of Gish and the source of the Nile, which was near it, and to order Fasil to confirm the grant, since it was in his territory of Agaumeder. And he sought an undertaking that when there was an opportunity Fasil would help him to reach the Nile source 'without fee or reward and without excuse or evasion'.

This was a small request, the Emperor said. He told the envoys to swear to the grant of Gish in the name of their master, 'upon which they took the two fore-fingers of my right hand, and, one after another, laid the two fore-fingers of their right hands across them, then kissed them; a form of swearing used there, at least among those that call themselves Christians'. Bruce went to bed happy, feeling that in spite of his disappointments and the general scepticism about Fasil's new-found loyalty, he had perhaps opened a way for himself to his chief objective.

But now Ras Michael, with his army and his Emperor, was to leave Gondar for the north. Bruce had to ask Takla Haymanot to leave him behind. He was ill, he said. His one purpose in Ethiopia was to reach the Nile source, 'without which I should return into my own country in disgrace'. He hoped now that Fasil would enable him to do this. In any case, he expected to see the Emperor return to Gondar soon, but he felt that if he himself went to Tigre he might never have courage enough to come south again.

The young Emperor took a surprisingly indulgent view of this request from his Lord of the Bedchamber, whose duty was to attend him everywhere. He was full of doubts about his own future. Though he might not believe that there was magic in Bruce's gun, he still thought that anyone who looked long at the stars must surely be an astrologer who could foresee what was to come, and the Scot's belief that they would meet again in the capital cheered him. He wanted a firmer prophecy, however.

'Those instruments and wheels with which you observe the stars can be of no use except for prying into futurity,' he said.

Bruce explained that his apparatus could help to guide ships at sea and fix positions for the use of travellers by land, 'but of the decrees of Providence for you or myself I know no more than your mule'. He believed the Emperor would return, because he had been almost miraculously lucky both in his first battle with Fasil and in his and the army's escape at the crossing of the Nile. These were special marks of the favour of an overruling Providence. God would not leave his work half finished. 'He it is who, governing the whole universe, has yet reserved specially to himself the department of War; he it is who has styled himself the God of Battles.'

This was the voice of a descendent of Scottish Covenanters. It seems to have comforted Takla Haymanot, who then advised him to live at Kusquam and never to leave the Empress's palace unless Fasil came to Gondar, giving him a chance to reach the Nile source. He was to report to the Emperor what happened to him.

'Upon this we parted with inexpressible reluctance. He was . . . worthy to rule over a better people; my heart was deeply penetrated with those marks of favour and condescension which I had uniformly received from him since I entered his palace'.

That evening Michael told his council that his familiar spirit, the archangel, had ordered him to seize the princes' mountain, Wechne, and to kill or carry off all the possible heirs to the throne who were confined there. This would have prevented the rebels from bringing a prince from Wechne and setting him up as a rival emperor, but Michael was persuaded to agree that the plan, arch-angelic or not, was altogether too shocking.

A second piece of heavenly advice was to burn Gondar to the ground before he left it. When the Emperor heard of this he exclaimed that he would rather stay in the city and be killed there than allow such an enormity. Gondar was spared, and Takla Haymanot's protest was remembered by the citizens when he needed their support.

Next morning Emperor, Ras and army marched away. Just before they left, Esther took refuge with her mother, the Empress. The gates of Kusquam were closed. 'Gondar was like a town which had been taken by an enemy; every one that had arms in his hands did just as he pleased.'

The city lay open to the first comer, and five days later the rebels, Gusho and Powussen, duly came. Michael had let them have false news of his movements and his army had crossed the Takazze without interruptions. Now they wanted to legitimatize their power in the capital.

They turned to the Empress Mentwab. Her prestige was still immense – she was the one figure in Ethiopia whom no one dared to attack violently – and, as Bruce soon discovered, her ambitions were not dead, in spite of her age and her longings for Jerusalem. She was still the Yatege who had twice been regent for boy emperors and could be regent again in another minority. She had never forgiven Michael for the murder of her grandson, the Emperor Joas, and she had not forgotten that Fasil had been faithful to Joas when Michael and the other chiefs turned against him. Gusho and Powussen asked her to come to the palace in Gondar and act as sovereign there. She refused to do this unless Fasil joined them. But the Galla chief would not trust them so far. He made public gestures which, in effect, defied both the rebels and Michael himself, though he still claimed to be loyal to the Emperor.

The two rebel chiefs in Gondar did not know what to do. When they had been there for some days Bruce decided that he should go to see them 'to avoid giving umbrage'. He found them lying on the floor in the house that had been Michael's, playing draughts 'with the figure of a draught-board drawn with chalk upon the carpet'. He was annoyed that they did not pay him the ceremonious respect he had come to expect at court. He insisted (he says) on speaking of Takla Haymanot and Michael as Emperor and Ras; this irritated them, but, fundamentally, they were not too unfriendly. Powussen had brought a gun and sword of Bruce's which Strates the Greek had been carrying when he was attacked at the Gomara river and he was prepared to give them back – in return for a present, which was duly produced.

A few days later the two chiefs left the city. They had received a warning message from Michael saying that he would soon bring the Emperor back to Gondar. But the rains still fell and the palace stood empty.

At the beginning of August the Empress went to the city 'and sat on the throne all day. She had not been there these three years, and I sincerely wished she had not gone then.' It was proposed that a new Emperor should be chosen. The Empress would have named a great-grandson of her own, the baby son of Joas's brother. This would have made her regent again, but no one else was prepared to confront Michael and Takla Haymanot with an infant sovereign, and when Mentwab returned to Kusquam the rest of the not very impressive council that had gathered in Gondar chose a still less impressive candidate, a reputed son of Jesus II, whose 'low life and manners had procured him safety and liberty by the contempt they had raised in Ras Michael'. This young man was proclaimed Emperor, taking the royal name of Susenyos. Next day he went in state to Kusquam, prostrated himself before the Empress and promised to govern only by her advice.

From its beginnings the royalty of Susenyos was a sordid charade built on deception and self-deception. Even those who made him a king, says Bruce, never made him a friend. He was loutish, drunken and stupid. His chief supporter, Sanuda, a nephew of the Empress whom he appointed Ras, was plotting with Michael and Fasil from the beginning. The other chiefs played with him so far as they dealt with him at all. They were waiting to see whether Michael would move south again when the rains ceased. Even the Empress only half believed in Susenyos, who claimed to be her grandson. And meanwhile a corpse was resurrected to trouble her and Gondar.

In the first days of the usurper a Galla was brought to the city under arrest. During a quarrel his wife had accused him of the murder of Joas. Officially that Emperor's fate was unknown. He had simply disappeared. There was no proof that he was not living still, though everyone believed that Ras Michael had ordered his death.

Bruce was there when the Galla – 'of small stature, thin and lightly made, his complexion a yellowish-black, and singularly ill-favoured' – was brought before the Empress and Susenyos. He confessed freely that Ras Michael had sent for him and offered a reward if he, with five nobles and a monk from Tigre, would murder the Emperor that night. Joas had been alone in his palace, all his court having deserted him after the defeat of Fasil and his other supporters. He tried to fight off the cord of two of the murderers who meant to strangle him, the meagre Galla struck him down with a bludgeon and the stranglers finished their work. They carried the body to St Raphael's Church beside the palace and shovelled it hastily into a hole that had been dug for it. Then they escaped and were not seen or heard of (except, presumably, by Michael, their paymaster) till the Galla quarrelled with his wife.

At once the Galla was taken out and hanged on a tree at the palace gate. His confession implicated too many people or families close to the Empress's to make a longer trial seem wise – one of the named murderers was a relation of Susenyos himself.

Joas's body was dug up and laid on the church floor. But no one dared to prepare it for reburial or even to look at it. The whole matter was too dangerous as well as horrifying – it touched both the Empress and Ras Michael. With his respect for everything that was royal, Bruce alone seems to have felt bound to visit this macabre tomb. He took with him a Greek merchant who had known Joas. They found the body lying on the floor. 'It affected me more than the murder itself, for it appeared as if it had been thrown on the ground, the head, arms and legs lying in all sorts of directions, and great part of his haunch and thigh bare . . . His features were easily distinguishable, but some animal had eaten part of his cheek.'

The Greek recognized the face immediately and ran off in terror crying 'It is he!' Bruce felt that something must be done to restore the decencies of royalty in death. He bought a Moslem prayer rug and a length of muslin from the trembling Greek and asked the monk who kept the church keys to place the body on the carpet, lay it out as well as he could and shroud it in the white cloth. Apparently it was allowed to lie in this way for weeks till the Empress received a brutal message from Ras Michael –

'Bury your boy now you have got him, or when I come I shall bury him and some of his relatives with him.'

Then there was a secret funeral. Not a word was said in public about the dead Emperor's fate, but Bruce found that his action had pleased almost all who heard of it. Both Takla Haymanot and Empress praised him for it, and one day Esther, though she had been Joas's enemy, called to him to take one of the upper seats in a gathering at Kusquam, saying, 'Sit there, Yagoube! God raised you above all in this country when he allowed you, a stranger, to give charity to its Emperor.'[1]

Michael's messenger had brought private news to Bruce. The Ras and Fasil had made an alliance. Takla Haymanot and Michael had rallied the Tigreans. They had remitted all taxes in the province for a year, and the men in the north were clamouring to be led to Gondar. The Ras was still besieging a rebel mountain fortress which once before had defied him for fifteen years, but he expected

---

[1] Considerable doubt has been thrown on Bruce's part in this happening. It is said to be incredible that a royal body, buried for more than a year and then disinterred, should have been allowed to be untended on a church floor for weeks. Bruce was certainly capable of imagining minor incidents that belonged more to dream than to reality, but scarcely anything so elaborate as this story. It is not the sort of event which would be likely to be described in Ethiopian annals.

its surrender soon. When the Takazze could be crossed again the Emperor and Ras would come to Gondar.

It was now October; the great rains were over and movement towards the source of the Nile would not be too difficult, though the last irregular downpour might still fill the streams again. Bruce decided that he must make an attempt before there was another warlike crisis in the country. He sent a message to the Emperor saying that he hoped to do this and to be back in time to meet his army before it reached the city. The Empress tried to hold him back. She warned him of the danger of attack on his way by bands of Fasil's pagan Galla or by the priests of Damot and Gojam, who hated white men and could raise the peasants against the traveller.

'This was all true,' writes Bruce, 'but then many reasons, which I had weighed well, concurred to show that this opportunity, dangerous as it was, might be the only time in which my enterprise might be practicable.'

On October 27th, 1770, he set out for his great object with his usual small company of attendants, Balugani among them. As he left news came from Tigre again. The mountain stronghold of Aramata had fallen and Michael and the Emperor would at once be moving again.

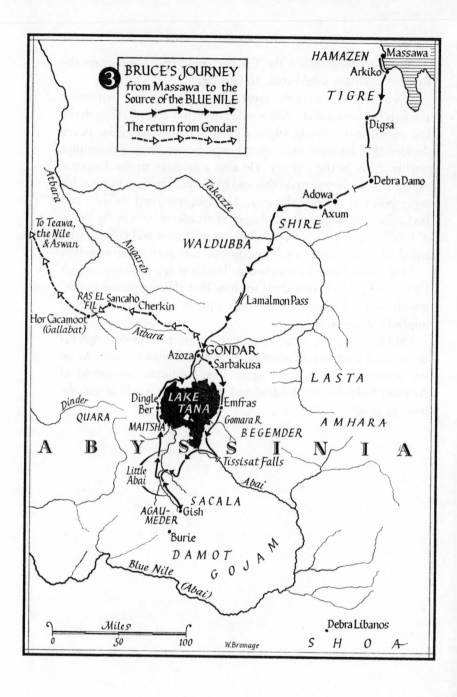

BRUCE'S JOURNEY
from Massawa to the
Source of the BLUE NILE

The return from Gondar

HAMAZEN
Massawa
Arkiko
TIGRE
Digsa
Debra Damo
Adowa
Axum
SHIRE
WALDUBBA
Takazze
Atbara
Angareb
To Teawa,
the Nile
& Aswan
RAS EL Sancaho
FIL Cherkin
Hor Cacamoot
(Gallabat)
Atbara
Lamalmon Pass
Azoza GONDAR
Sarbakusa
LASTA
Dinger
QUARA
Dingle
Ber
MAITSHA
LAKE
TANA
Emfras
Gomara R
BEGEMDER
AMHARA
ABYSSINIA
Tissisat Falls
Little
Abai
Abai
SACALA
AGAU-
MEDER Gish
Burie
DAMOT
GOJAM
Blue Nile
(Abai)
Miles
0 50 100
W. Bromage
Debra Libanos
SHOA

12

The Coy Fountains

If Michael was coming from the north-east, Fasil was also advancing from the region of Lake Tana. Throughout the troubled months of rain he had been expected in Gondar by the Empress, by Susenyos, by Gusho and Powussen. Repeatedly he had promised to come, but had held back while his messengers negotiated with the rival leaders. He had most of the Galla behind him, both the more or less settled part of this people to which he, like his father Waranya, belonged and the wild tribesmen of the south-west. Fasil's ambition was not merely for plunder, however. He wished to rule Ethiopia, as Ras, since he could not be Emperor. Parties of his wild Galla were raiding towards Gondar, while he gathered his forces, but he was preparing to send most of these savages home while he moved forward slowly with the better-organized troops of his four provinces.

To reach the source of the Little Abai, Bruce had to travel not much more than one hundred miles. The chief difficulty was to find a way through country full of men prepared for every sort of violence: for this he must have the protection of Fasil himself.

He found the Galla chief with his army in a valley not far from the north-west shore of Lake Tana. His reception was not encouraging. Fasil sat in his tent on a lion's skin, 'a cotton cloth something like a dirty towel' wrapped round his head and his cloak drawn tightly round him, so that when Bruce tried to kiss his hand he could only press his lips to the greasy cloth. The veiled head and figure were intended as a demonstration of superiority, almost of sovereignty. When Bruce spoke, saying that he had come, on Fasil's invitation to pay his respects to him and to ask to be allowed to go to the source of the Abai, the Governor pretended to be astonished. Of course, he knew well that Bruce had been given the district of Gish by the Emperor precisely to make it easier for him to visit the Nile source, but it seems that he resented this grant, though he had confirmed it when it was made.

'Do you know what you are saying?' he exclaimed. 'The source of the Abai! Why, it is God knows where in the country of the Galla, wild, terrible people. Are you mad? It might take you a year to get back.'

Bruce answered that everyone in Ethiopia knew that the source of the river was near Sacala and Gish, 'both villages of the Agaus and both in your government'.

All Ethiopia might know this, said Fasil, but all Ethiopia would not get him there. Bruce, whose temper was rising fast, replied that he certainly could not expect to reach the source if Fasil chose to prevent him. 'It was relying upon you alone I came so far, confident if all the rest of Abyssinia could not protect me, then your word alone could do it.'

This softened Fasil a little. He could do it, he said, but Abba Salama, that powerful priest, had asked him not to allow Bruce to go farther. It was against the law, the Guardian of the House had declared, to allow Franks to travel through the country and he had dreamed that misfortunes would come to Fasil if the traveller was not stopped.

'So,' exclaimed Bruce, 'the time of priests, prophets and dreamers is coming on again.'

Fasil laughed. 'I care as little for priests as Michael does,' he said, 'and for prophets, too, but remember the men of this country are not like yours: a boy of the Galla would think nothing of killing a man of your country. You white people are all effeminate; you are not fit to go into a province where all is war and the men are warriors from their cradles.'

At this the Scot boiled over. He had visited many barbarous

nations, he said, 'but the worst and lowest individual among the most uncivilized people never treated me as you have done today, under your own roof, where I have come so far for protection'. Fasil had falsely called him a Frank, meaning a Roman Catholic, 'the most odious name in this country and sufficient to occasion me to be stoned to death without further ceremony'. Without having seen anyone from Britain but Bruce himself, 'you have discovered, from that specimen that we are all cowards and effeminate people, like, or inferior to, your boys and women'.

The huge Scot declared that he was not a soldier, though he knew enough of war to see that Fasil's men were no models of soldierliness. 'As to myself, let me but be armed in my own country fashion, on horseback as I was yesterday, I should, without thinking myself overmatched, fight the best two horsemen you shall choose from this army of famous men who are warriors from their cradle.' If when the Emperor came back Fasil had not returned to his duty and they met again in war Bruce would remind him of this challenge and ask him to choose two men who, together, would be prepared to match him.

At this point Bruce's passion found another vent. 'My nose burst out into a stream of blood . . . Fasil seemed to be a good deal concerned.' Bruce was hurried out of the tent, and when he had recovered began to wonder whether he had made a fool of himself. 'I will confess', he comments, 'that I was from my infancy, of a sanguine, passionate disposition, very sensible of injuries that I had neither provoked nor deserved; but much reflection, from very early life, continued habits of suffering in long and dangerous travels where nothing but patience would do, had, I flattered myself, abundantly subdued my natural proneness to feel offences, which, common sense might teach me, I could only revenge upon myself.'

Now he was depressed not only by Fasil's insults but still more by the thought that he might be losing his last chance of reaching the Nile source. However, he soon found that his protest – or possibly his bleeding nose – had changed the Governor's mind. Fasil was preparing to send his wild Galla home. He thought it wise to start Bruce on his journey before these tribesmen set off, so that the traveller might not be attacked by them on his way. But first he proposed to make him a present of one of his own horses. A dozen of these were paraded for Bruce's choice. Bruce did not think much of them, but the groom urged him to take a bay pony, 'the fattest of the whole, but not strong enough in appearance to carry me; he assured me, however, the horse had excellent paces, was a great favourite of Fasil's, but too *dull* and *quiet* for him'.

Bruce was urged to mount it, and did so. 'For the first two minutes, I do not know whether I was most on the earth or in the air; he kicked behind, reared before, leaped like a deer, all four off the ground, and it was some time before I recollected myself.' The pony, in fact, was unbroken. Bruce soon began to get control of him, however, and by riding him up and down two opposite hillsides 'wrought him so that he had no longer breath or strength'.

When this was over, 'as my own horse was bridled and saddled, and I found myself violently irritated, I resolved to ride to compose myself a little before another interview; for I thought this last piece of treachery that might have cost me my legs and arms was worse than what happened in the tent; it seemed to be aimed at my life'.

In fact, he gave an exhibition of horsemanship on a slope above the camp which much impressed the Galla, who were horsemen themselves.

He had taken a double-barrelled shotgun with him. Many kites, the scavenger-birds of the country, were hovering over the camp. 'Choosing two gliding near me, I shot one on the right, then one on the left; they both fell dead on the ground; a great shout immediately followed from the spectators, to which I seemingly paid no attention, pretending absolute indifference, as if nothing extraordinary had been done. . . . Sitting down on a large stone, I began to apply some white paper to staunch a small scratch the first horse had given me on the leg by rubbing it against a thorn tree: as my trousers, indeed, were all stained with the blood of the first horse, much cut by the spur, it was generally thought I was wounded.'

Fasil had watched the show of riding and shooting. He had never seen or heard of small-shot and could not understand how the kites had been brought down. He seemed genuinely shocked to think that Bruce was wounded and protested that he had known nothing of the offer to him of an unbroken pony. He proposed to give him a horse not to ride but to drive before him on his journey. Any horse known to be Fasil's would be respected by the wild Galla – this was the best passport Bruce could take with him. The groom who had endangered his life would be executed.

'I wished to put an end to this disagreeable conversation,' writes the Scot. He claimed the right under Ethiopian law to decide how the groom should be treated.

'Take him, Yagoube', said Fasil. 'Cut him in a thousand pieces, if you please, and give his body to the kites.'

'I am a Christian,' Bruce declared; 'the way my religion teaches me to punish my enemies is by doing good for evil. . . . Set the man at liberty and put him in the place he held before, for he has not been unfaithful to you.'

Fasil was now very friendly indeed, though he was surprised and alarmed when Bruce told him that Ras Michael had disposed of his last enemies in the north and was actually moving towards Gondar.

'I cannot say but I enjoyed heartily the fright I had visibly given him,' writes the Scot. However, the shock was blunted when Bruce produced a present, for which the chieftain had apparently been hankering – four long silk sashes from Tunis and Cyprus, a Persian hubble-bubble pipe and two fine bowls of blue glass from Cairo. 'I saw that I had gained the ascendant; and, in the expectations of Ras Michael's speedily coming to Gondar, he was as willing to be on his journey the one way as I was the other.'

When Bruce came again to take his leave he was ceremoniously clothed in new garments by Fasil, his formal investiture as Lord of Gish. Seven men stood round the Governor – 'I never saw more thief-like fellows in my life', is the Scot's comment.

'You see those seven men,' said Fasil. 'They are all leaders and chiefs of the Galla – you may call them savages, but they are all your brethren. You may go through their country as if it were your own. You will soon be related to them all, for it is their custom that a stranger of distinction like yourself, when he is their guest, should sleep with the sister, daughter, or near relation of the chief man among them.' Bruce bowed, though the prospect did not seem very inviting.

Fasil praised him for saving three of the Galla prisoners whom Michael had blinded at Gondar. 'After such good care' he said, 'these Galla will die for you before they see you hurt!'

All then stood in a circle, raising their hands while Fasil and the Galla repeated what seemed to be a prayer in their own tongue.

'Now,' said the Governor, 'go in peace, you are a Galla; there is a curse on them and their children, their corn, grass and cattle, if they ever lift a hand against you or yours, or do not defend you if you are attacked, or fail to defend you against any plot they hear of.' Fasil explained that he had ordered one of his officers to guide Bruce to Gish and protect him. He presented him with a handsome grey horse which he was to drive before him. At last the traveller was free to move safely towards the springs of the Nile.

The guide Fasil had chosen, Shalaka (Colonel) Woldo, an Agau by birth, did not seem an impressive figure. His bush of black hair was uncovered. Though he sometimes wore a sort of cotton toga, this was generally carried by a mule: as he walked, the upper part of his body was naked, 'his shoulders only covered by a goat's skin in form of what women call a tippet'. He had a pair of very short cotton trousers and went barelegged and barefooted, never riding, but keeping up easily with those who rode. 'Sometimes he had a long pipe in his hand, being a great smoker; at other times, a stick of about three feet long, something thicker than one's thumb, with which he dealt about him very liberally, either to man, woman or beast, upon the slightest provocation.'

Woldo understood men, however, Bruce among the rest, and he had a sardonic outlook of his own. They spoke, by the way, about the three blinded Galla prisoners Bruce had saved at Gondar. Forty others, Fasil had said, were eaten by hyenas. Woldo explained that he and Fasil's other officers knew that they had been killed by his orders as they made their way home 'that none of them might be seen in their own provinces to terrify the rest of their clans by their mangled appearance, for this was Ras Michael's intention in disfiguring them, and yet leaving them alive.'

'What,' said Bruce, 'kill his own people taken prisoner while fighting for him! That is not credible.'

'But it is true' said Woldo. The Galla, he explained had what may be considered in a nuclear age a scientific military outlook. 'They do not talk about what is cruel and what is not. They do just what is for their own good, what seems to them reasonable, and think no more about it. Ras Michael,' he added, 'would make an excellent Galla.'

They were passing through the country where the Emperor and Michael had confronted Fasil in May, and wooden houses which Michael had burned down were being reconstructed. It was 'with a barbarous kind of smile' that Woldo replied to Bruce when he said he was glad to see this, 'Aye, and so am I, too, for if those villages had not been built again we should have had no firewood tonight.' Though the villagers of this province of Maitsha were Galla themselves, Fasil's disbanded wild Galla were pulling down the new huts to make their fires.

For greater safety Woldo led them to the camp of a partisan chief called 'the Jumper' explaining that there was not a greater thief or murderer in all the Galla country. This made him a reliable protector, it was said. His campfires were amply fed with the wood of the wrecked villages.

When Bruce went to see him the Jumper was embarrassed. He 'was naked, having only a towel about his loins, and had been washing himself in the Kelti [the river near by] to very little purpose, as I thought, for he was then rubbing his arms and body over with melted tallow. His hair had been abundantly anointed before and a man was then finishing his head-dress by plaiting it with some of the long and small guts of an ox, which I did not perceive had ever been cleaned; and he had already put about his neck two rounds of the same, in the manner of a necklace, or rather a solitaire, one end of them hanging down to the pit of his stomach.' This was the typical toilet of a Galla great man.

'The Jumper was tall and lean, very sharp faced, with a long nose, small eyes and prodigious large ears; he never looked you in the face, but was rolling his eyes constantly round and round, and never fixing them upon any thing: he resembled very much a lean keen greyhound. . . . He was allowed on all hands, to be the most cruel, merciless murderer and spoiler of all the Galla.'

As Bruce was leaving the warrior's tent he met a little group of men who had come from Gondar to find him. One was Strates the Greek, the clown of the Nile journey. After his grotesque misfortunes on the first expedition to Lake Tana he had refused to come with Bruce again, but, in the end, he could not reconcile himself to the idea of being left behind.

More important, at the moment, was a messenger from Esther. The Princess thought she was dying and begged Bruce 'by every claim of friendship she had upon me' to return and give her medical help before it was too late.

She was suffering, indeed, from an anxiety neurosis. Though she was in her mother's palace, she had a sense of total isolation. The Empress supported the usurper Susenyos, whose régime was obviously ending. Her husband, Michael, had sent a threat to Kusquam that he would hang Susenyos and Mentwab from the same tree when he returned to Gondar. Esther knew too well that his threats were seldom unfulfilled; the Empress for once was terror-stricken. The only counterweight to Michael in this anarchical welter was Fasil, who was well aware that since her second husband's murder Esther had been a relentless enemy of the Galla, and consequently of himself. Worn out by fever and anxiety, 'by want of sleep, exercise and nourishment', Esther had 'fallen into a very dangerous situation, and of a very difficult cure, even though the cause was perfectly known'.

For Bruce this was an agonizing summons. He was at least half in love with Esther, he owed a great deal of the success he had had in Ethiopia to her influence, her son Confu was his best friend in the country, her husband had been his chief protector. If he did not turn back he could be reproached for 'the foulest and basest of all sins, that of ingratitude'. If he died on the journey, the thought that this was so would be, he believed, 'one of the most bitter reflections of my last moment'.

All the same, he does not seem to have hesitated long. He was within a few days' journey of the Blue Nile's source, and he believed that this was likely to be his last chance of reaching it, since war was boiling up again in Ethiopia. He sent back a message that he could not return at once, but that he would move as quickly as possible. He sent, too, advice to a Greek priest at Kusquam who was 'a sort of physician' on the treatment he would approve. Then he pushed on towards the land of the Agaus.

Soon the party came to a market-place where Agaus, Ethiopians and Galla met to trade in the open under the shade of trees. Here a detachment of Galla who had been sent forward by Fasil to protect them was waiting. Its commander, a brother of the Jumper, was known as 'the Lamb' on account of his merciful character – when he raided the Ethiopians, Shalaka Woldo explained, he never killed women, even if they were pregnant.

This amiable chief and his men showed little obvious interest in the travellers, but they paid careful respect to Fasil's horse. 'The greatest part of them, one by one, gave him handfuls of barley, and the Lamb himself had a long and serious conversation with him. Woldo told me it was all spent in regretting the horse's misfortune and Fasil's cruelty in having bestowed him on a white man, who would not feed him, nor ever let him return to Bizamo' – a Galla region beyond the Abai.

As they travelled Bruce and his men looked for birds and beasts, not seen before, which could be added to his record of Ethiopian fauna. They were passing through a district beautifully shaded with acacia trees, the ground beneath them covered with flowering lupins. Strates the Greek shot a particularly striking bird among the acacias, and Bruce was making a sketch of it when wild cries were heard and a group of horsemen with their lances lifted charged towards them. 'The ground was woody and uneven, so they could not make the speed they seemed to desire, and we had just time to put ourselves upon our defence, with our firelocks, muskets and blunderbusses in our hands, behind our baggage.' But Woldo checked their fire. He had recognized the Lamb's company of Galla, who, hearing Strates's shot, had thought that enemies might be attacking Bruce and his men and had come up to defend them.

'Thus did we see that this man, who, according to our ideas, seemed in understanding inferior to most of the brute creation, had yet, in executing his orders, a discernment, punctuality, activity and sense of duty equal to any Christian officer.' In recognition of this Bruce offered the Lamb breakfast, for which a tablecloth was spread on the ground, and presented him with tobacco and other such gifts. 'All these he took with absolute indifference, as formerly, much as if they had been his own; he expressed no sort of thanks, either in his words or in his countenance; only, while at breakfast said that he was very much grieved it had been a false alarm, for he heartily desired that some robbers had really attacked us, that he might have shown us how quickly and dexterously he would have cut them to pieces.'

When the tablecloth was being folded up the Lamb did come to life. He asked Woldo if it could be given to him to cover his head, and keep his face from the sun. 'I could not help laughing within myself at this idea of preserving that beautiful complexion from sun-burning, but I gave him the cloth very readily, which he accordingly spread upon his head till it covered half his face; he then got upon his horse and rode quietly away.' He detached fifteen men to travel not with Bruce's party but near them, so that they could come to their help again if necessary. In fact as Bruce discovered later, the Lamb was protecting him not from casual attack but from an attempt to cut him off organized by Abba Salama.

The party went on towards the Little Abai, among 'trees and shrubs covered with flowers of every colour, all new and extraordinary in their shape, crowded with birds of many uncouth forms, all of them richly adorned with a variety of plumage'. But the flowers, except for roses and jasmine, had no scent, and the tropical birds no song.

'At two o'clock in the afternoon of the second of November', writes Bruce, 'we came to the banks of the Nile.'

At this point the highland river flowing to Lake Tana was already a sacred stream, the Father of Waters. Nearer the lake, where Michael's army had made its almost disastrous crossing, Bruce had found no trace of this veneration. There the district, Maitsha, was a Galla colony. Its Ethiopian inhabitants had been driven out or exterminated. But here the old native population remained, Agaus and Ethiopians.

'They crowded to us at the ford, and they were, after some struggle, of great use in passing us; but they protested immediately, with much vehemence, against any man's riding across the stream mounted either upon horse or mule. They, without any sort of ceremony, unloaded our mules, and laid our baggage upon the grass, insisting that we should take off our shoes, and making an appearance of stoning those who attempted to wash the dirt off their cloaks and trowsers.'

To ride through the ford or wash was evidently an insult to the majesty of the river. On Woldo's orders, however, the travellers were allowed to drink and water their beasts, and Bruce and Balugani were carefully conducted through the ford, though the sharp stones cut their feet.

The horses and mules were also driven through the stream, but Woldo, the servants and the baggage remained on the other bank, with twenty or thirty armed Agaus around them. Fasil's officer now gave an exhibition of his powers of management. Sitting down on a green hillock, with a stick in one hand and his lighted pipe in the other, he told the Agaus to carry the baggage across the ford on their shoulders, since they had insisted on unloading it.

'The poor people candidly declared, that they had done so, because none are permitted in any other manner to cross the Nile, but they would likewise carry out baggage safely and willingly for pay.' At this word Woldo laid down his pipe and jumped to his feet with every sign of fury. He told the Agaus that they were Fasil's slaves.

'You want payment, do you?' he shouted. 'Here is your payment.' Leaping in the air he belaboured heads and faces, seized a lance from one man and threatened to run him through. As the Agaus turned and fled he even demanded a gun. For Bruce, who had begun to fear that someone would actually be killed, this was reassuring. He knew well that Woldo was afraid to touch any kind of firearm. Obviously the display of rage was part of a manoeuvre. In fact, as soon as the Agaus were out of sight Woldo led Bruce's servants through the ford very calmly, leaving the baggage behind him.

As the party moved off with their unladen beasts on his instructions a group of Agaus suddenly reappeared beyond the river and began to carry the baggage across, begging Woldo to tell nothing to the terrible Fasil about their behaviour. He said sulkily that he was a merciful man. Then he pulled out a silk bag of tobacco Bruce had given him as if to fill his pipe. As his fingers thrust into it he exclaimed, with new fury, that his gold was gone – that the Agaus must have taken it. The travellers rode on and left them terror-stricken, but that night two of them came to the village where they halted and Bruce had no doubt that the gold Woldo had so suddenly invented had been brought to him in the solidest form.

The Agau country was a place of little plains and mountain-sides, well watered and temperate because of its height, and one of the most productive districts of Ethiopia. In spite of its natural riches and the ivory, gold, cotton and slaves which they obtained by trade (or raiding) from the negro lands below them, its people were poor, partly because of heavy taxation (in goods) which Gondar drew from them, partly because of defeats in war, most recently and disastrously at the hands of Fasil. They were nominally Christian, but had, in fact, kept their ancient religion as well as their language and their organization in clans. Since Bruce was anxious to learn all that he could about the source of the Nile, he was determined to be as friendly to the people as he could.

Woldo's talent for extortion alarmed him. He told the guide that as the Emperor had given him the district of Gish and he meant to stay there some days he proposed to remit all the taxes it should have paid that year.

'Stay,' said Woldo. 'Don't be in such a hurry. See first how they behave.'

'No,' Bruce reports his own reply, 'I wish to begin by teaching them how to behave; I will not wait till their present misery prompts them to receive ill (as they very naturally will do) a man who comes, as they may think, wantonly, for curiosity only, to take from them and their starved families the little Fasil had left them. You shall have money to buy every thing; you shall have money or presents, or both, to pay those that serve us or do us any kindness and you shall tell your master Fasil that I have received the Emperor's rent from the Agaus of Gish.'

As they advanced the villages they passed were empty. The peasants took them for a detachment of the Galla, and the sight of Fasil's horse confirmed their terror. But the landscape itself grew more attractive, to Bruce more exciting, because it foretold the Nile source. They were moving towards ranges of high mountains which curved before them into the shape of a crescent, and rose to 12,000 feet, or higher. Perhaps, Bruce thought, these were the Mountains of the Moon which, according to the ancient geographer Ptolemy, overhung the beginnings of the river.

'The climate seemed here most agreeably mild, the country covered with the most lively verdure, the mountains with beautiful trees and shrubs, loaded with extraordinary flowers and fruits. I found my spirits very much raised with these pleasing scenes, as were those of all my servants, who were, by our conversation, made geographers enough to know we were approaching to the end of our journey. Both Strates and I, out of the Lamb's hearing, had shot a variety of curious birds and beasts. All but Woldo seemed to have acquired new strength and vigour.'

Woldo was a puzzle; the tirelessly active humorist seemed to be growing more and more depressed, even physically weak. They climbed a steep mountain by a sort of sheep path among the thorny thickets, but moved cheerfully because this seemed to be the last obstacle between them and Gish. They passed a church, St Michael's Sacala, empty and unused – like other churches of the Agau country, it had been built by an Ethiopian invader anxious to force Christianity on the people, and was deserted now that neither Michael nor Fasil showed any interest in their religious state. From the hill-top 'we saw, immediately below us, the Nile itself, strangely diminished in size and now only a brook that had scarcely water to turn a mill. I could not satiate myself with the sight, revolving in my mind all those classical prophecies that had given the Nile up to perpetual obscurity and concealment. . . . I was awakened from this delightful reverie by an alarm that we had lost Woldo our guide.'

No one knew what had become of him. Strates the Greek, who had been shooting among the trees, had seen a group of baboons which, tail-less and walking on their hind legs, seemed to him peculiarly horrifying creatures. He thought that if Woldo had fallen in with them he would be totally devoured, clothes and all. Others suggested that he might have orders from Fasil to arrange for treacherous murder of the whole party in some lonely place like this one. Bruce feared that he might have collapsed on the hill path and sent back two servants to look for him. They soon found him creeping feebly towards them, but declaring that he was too ill to go farther. Bruce felt his pulse, cast a doctor's eye over him, and decided that he was as well as he ever had been, but had some curious plan of his own. He told him so, and the guide simply asked that they should halt for a while to let him gather strength to pass another hill between them and Gish.

The explorer was convinced that no such hill existed. He walked to the bank of infant Abai and sat down to sketch a rose while the others, Woldo included, walked through the quick-running mountain stream. They stopped at a second church, St Michael Gish, as forsaken as St Michael Sacala. Woldo asked to talk with Bruce privately along with Aylo's servant, who was accompanying them.

'You have told me one lie,' said Bruce; 'now I know by your face that you are going to tell me another. You will get nothing from me in that way.'

The man admitted that, in fact, he was not sick. But, he said, he was afraid. In Fasil's battle with the Agaus he had killed men from Gish, and now the villagers would want to take revenge on him. 'You know the usage of this country: blood must pay for blood.'

This story was as incredible as the last one, and Bruce said so. Clearly Fasil, who had been responsible for the death of more Agaus than any other man, could not control the people as he did if blood-guilt made it impossible for him to send one of his officers into one Agau village. At this point Aylo's servant thought it best to state matters plainly. Bruce was wearing a long sash of fine crimson silk wrapped several times round his waist: in it he carried his pistols and knife. Woldo had set his mind on having this garment. He had been promised a reward at the end of his travels, and this was what he wanted; but he did not believe that once Bruce had actually reached the Nile source he would be willing to give such a splendid thing away. The Nile springs were much less impressive than rivers and waterfalls they had passed already. Bruce would be disappointed by them and probably by his guide. Now, just before he saw what he was looking for, was the last moment for claiming the glorious wrapping.

'This rational discourse had pacified me a little; the sash was a handsome one; but it must have been fine indeed to have stood for a minute between me and the accomplishment of my wishes. I laid my hand then upon the pistols . . . and drew them out to give them to one of my suite, when Woldo, who apprehended it was for another purpose, ran some paces back and hid himself beyond Aylo's servant. We were all diverted at this fright, but none so much as Strates', who himself was easily scared. The sash was handed over, though with a stern warning of what Fasil would be asked to do if there were any more tricks of this sort, and Bruce demanded to be led at once to Gish.

Woldo took him to the other side of the church and pointed down into the valley.

'Look at that hillock of green sod in the middle of that watery spot,' he said. 'The two springs of the Nile are there. If you go to them, pull off your shoes as you did the other day, for the people here are all pagans, worse than those we met at the ford. They believe in nothing that you believe, but only in this river, to which they pray every day as if it were God – but perhaps you will do as much yourself?'

Here one must quote at length from the vigorous, emotional, sometimes deliberately grotesque and at one point certainly imaginary description of what he claimed to be his greatest triumph which Bruce set down twenty years later. He was at the climax of his ambition. He could not hold himself back from the springs for an instant.

'Half undressed as I was by loss of my sash, and throwing my shoes off, I ran down the hill towards the little island of green sods, which was about two hundred yards distant; the whole side of the hill was thickly grown over with flowers, the large bulbous roots of which appearing above the surface of the ground, and their skins coming off on treading upon them, occasioned me two very severe falls before I reached the brink of the marsh; I after this came to the island of green turf, which was in form of an altar . . . and I stood in rapture over the principal fountain which rises in the middle of it.'

His mind was full of glory.

'Kings had attempted this discovery at the head of armies, and each exhibition was distinguished from the last only by the difference of the numbers which had perished, and agreed only in the disappointment which had uniformly, and without exception, followed them all. Fame, riches and honour had been held out for a series of ages to every individual of those myriads . . . without having produced one man capable of gratifying the curiosity of his sovereign, or wiping off the stain upon the enterprise and abilities of mankind.'

But then the thought came to him that only half his journey was over, that there were as many dangers and difficulties ahead as those he had escaped on his way, 'the least of which would have overwhelmed me, but for the continual goodness and protection of Providence, I found a despondency gaining ground fast upon me, and blasting the crown of laurels I had too rashly woven myself.'

He felt the need for a little comedy. Strates was waiting for him on the hillside.

'Faithful squire,' he called, 'come and triumph with your Don Quixote at that island of Barataria where we have most wisely and fortunately brought ourselves! Come and triumph with me over all the kings of the earth, all their armies, all their philosophers and all their heroes!'

Not surprisingly, the Greek, who can never have heard of Cervantes, answered that he did not understand a word of what Bruce had been saying; but he was persuaded to advance, a little unwillingly, into the marsh.

' "Come" said I, "take a draught of this excellent water, and drink with me a health to his majesty King George III and a long line of princes." I had in my hand a large cup made of a coco-nut shell which I procured in Arabia and which was brimfull. He drank to the King speedily and cheerfully, and tossed up his cup with a loud huzza.

' "Now, friend," said I, "here is to a more humble, but still a sacred name, here is to – Maria!" He asked if that was the Virgin Mary? I answered, "In faith, I believe so, Strates." He did not speak, but only gave a humph of disapprobation.

' "Strates," said I, "here is to our happy return. Come, friend, you are yet two toasts behind me; can you ever be satiated with this excellent water?"

' "Look you, sir," says he very gravely, "as for King George, I drank to him with my heart, to his wife, to his children, to his brothers and sisters, God bless them all! Amen – but as for the Virgin Mary, as I am no Papist, I beg to be excused from drinking healths which my church does not drink. As for our happy return, God knows there is no one wishes it more sincerely than I do, for I have long been weary of this beggarly country. But you must forgive me if I refuse to drink any more water. They say these savages pray over that hole every morning to the devil and I am afraid I feel his horns in my belly already, from the great draught of that hellish water."

' "Come, come," said I, "don't be peevish. I have but one toast more to drink."

' "Peevish or not peevish," replied Strates, "a drop of it never again shall cross my throat. There is no joke in meddling with devil-worshippers, witchcraft and enchantments to bring some disease upon oneself here, so far from home. No, no! As many toasts in wine as you please, or better in brandy, but no more water for Strates."

' "Then," said I, "I will drink it alone, and you are henceforward unworthy of the name of Greek; you do not even deserve that of Christian. Here is to Catherine, Empress of all the Russias and success to her heroes at Paros; and hear my prediction from this altar today; ages shall not pass before this ground, whereon I now stand, shall be a flourishing part of her dominions."

'He leaped on this a yard from the ground. . . . Says he "Give the cup; I will drink that health though I should die." '

This is a strange account of what was for James Bruce the most seriously important event of his life. His whole purpose was to convince his readers of its importance, to enforce his claim to be the first discoverer of the Nile source for the Western world. Yet he not only turns the occasion to farce in describing Strates's unwilling toasts, he also adds a detail that must have shaken the faith of some well-informed readers. There can be no doubt that the second toast in Nile water was not to any 'Maria' but to the girl he had left behind him eight years before and still hoped to find and marry in Scotland, Margaret Murray. As, in fact, his Peggy did not wait for him, to have used her real name in his book twenty years later may have seemed tactless. But he embroiders this fiction by inventing Strates's reluctance to honour the Theotokos, a reluctance that no Greek Christian would be at all likely to show.

One wonders whether the elaboration of this comic episode at the 'coy fountains' of the Abai and the despondency which led

Bruce to force himself into such a display of high spirits may not have sprung, perhaps only half-consciously, from a painful doubt in his own mind. While he triumphs over the emperors, armies and learned men who have failed to reach these springs before him, he says nothing of the one European, the Jesuit Pedro Paez, who claimed to have been there. Certainly in a later chapter he does his best to demolish Paez's claim. Though he may have taken comfort from this criticism, it can convince no one else who looks twice at it. In spite of his courage, enterprise and endurance, his real achievements as an explorer of almost unknown lands and his unveiling of a unique African society, James Bruce was not the first Western man 'to discover the source of the Nile', and if he did not know this, he deceived himself.

Woldo was waiting for him on the hillside above the marsh and with him the headman of the village of Gish, who, to Bruce's delight, was also high priest of the Nile, an office his family had held 'from the beginning of the world, as he imagined'. Here was the best proof that the Little Abai had long been accepted not as one mountain river among many but as the headwater of the Nile itself.

The priest was a venerable figure, seventy years old, cloaked and hooded, with a long white beard, which was something rare in Ethiopia. His name, or title, was Kefla Abai – Servant of the Father of Waters. Woldo had already made it clear to him that Bruce would pay for everything he used and that the taxes of the district would be remitted.

Kefla Abai offered the traveller his own house, built of clay and straw, with others for his servants, and he insisted that three of his daughters, among the youngest of his eighty-five children, should act as housekeepers. One of these, Irepone, took charge of all their arrangements. 'She was about sixteen years of age, of a stature above the middle size, but she was remarkably genteel, and, colour apart, her features made her a beauty in any country in Europe.' Bruce gave her gold and small goods – beads, antimony, scissors, knives and needles – to pay for their needs and told her she could keep what she did not spend. 'I often thought the head of the little savage would have turned with the possession of so much riches, and so great confidence, and it was impossible to be so blinded as not to see that I had already made great progress in her affection.'

A messenger from Fasil arrived with a milk-white cow, two goats, two sheep, fifty wheaten loaves, mead, and 'excellent strong spirits'. 'Our hearts were now perfectly at ease, and we passed a very merry evening. Strates, above all, endeavoured, with many a bumper of the good hydromel, to subdue the devil which he had swallowed in the enchanted water.' The cow was killed, mead was distributed among the Agaus, and all was feasting and joy.

But the reaction which had followed Bruce's first moment of triumph soon returned. He thought that he might never reach home. He thought of his Peggy. He was overwhelmingly homesick.

Was the sight of an African marsh and three springs – there were two others close to the one from which he had drunk – worth all his efforts, he asked himself?

'I remembered that magnificent scene in my own native country, where the Tweed, Clyde and Annan rise in one hill; three rivers, as I now thought, not inferior to the Nile in beauty, preferable to it in the cultivation of those countries through which they flow; superior, vastly superior to it in the virtues and qualities of the inhabitants, and in the beauty of flocks crowding the pastures in peace, without fear of violence from man or beast. . . . Grief, or despondency now rolling upon me like a torrent; released, not refreshed, by unquiet and imperfect sleep, I started from my bed in the utmost agony; I went to the door . . . everything was still; the Nile, at whose head I stood, was not capable either to promote or interrupt my slumbers, but the coolness and serenity of the night braced my nerves, and chased away those phantoms that, while in bed, had oppressed and tormented me.'

He spent five days in examining the sources again and measuring them, in exploring the neighbourhood and questioning Kefla Abai on his worship of the Nile. He was told that the Agaus prayed to the spirit of the river as 'the Everlasting God, Light of the World, Eye of the World, God of Peace, their Saviour, and Father of the Universe'.

Once a year, he was told, when the Dog Star appeared in the sky, the Agau chiefs gathered at the altar in the marsh. The priest sacrificed a black heifer, whose head was wrapped in its hide, sprinkled with Nile water. On the hill where the church of St Michael Gish had been built by the Ethiopians to supersede the old Agau worship the carcass was divided among the tribes and eaten raw.

In the hillside behind the village of Gish, as at other Agau settlements, a great cave had been excavated, screened by a thick hedge of thorn bushes, where the people and their cattle could take refuge in times of danger. 'After they have finished their bloody banquet,' Bruce writes, 'they carry the head, close wrapt in the hide, into the cavern, which, they say, reaches below the fountains . . . and there they perform their worship, the particulars of which I never could learn; it is a piece of free-masonry, which everybody knows, and nobody ventures to reveal.'

On November 10th he saw the last of his little dominion of Gish, convinced that he had made contact not only with the source of the Nile but with a system of river-worship as old as ancient Egypt. He made his subjects happy with gifts, and Irepone, at least, wept to see him go. A century and a half later a British consul[1] found that the Gish church, in use again, was known as 'St Michael Zarabruk' and wondered whether the second of these names meant that the explorer had been transformed into an Ethiopian saint.

Bruce was now travelling towards Gondar again, but went first to the house of another of Fasil's officers, Shalaka Welled Amlac, whom he had cured of fever at Kusquam. He was startled when the Shalaka's pretty sister claimed that, in the name of traditional hospitality, the stranger must share her bed. At this point in his story he takes refuge in a not very gallant quotation from Swift:

[1] R. E. Cheesman, *Lake Tana and the Blue Nile*.

But what success Vanessa met
Is to the world a secret yet;
Can never to the world be told,
Nor shall the conscious muse unfold.

In fact, he seems to have been inclined to settle down in this retreat, botanizing and hunting, when the words of another guest of the household shocked him into action. This was a wife of Fasil's, young and handsome, but melancholy.

He told her he was surprised that Fasil had not taken her to Gondar. The Governor had twenty wives besides herself, she said, but none of them went with him to the Emperor's town. Gondar was a place of war, where it was the custom for conquerors to marry the wives of their enemies whom they had forced to retreat; she expected that Fasil would marry Michael's wife, Esther.

This was a sharp reminder of his promise to return from the Nile source as quickly as possible. Under Welled Amlac's protection he passed quickly through the disturbed Galla country of Maitsha and on November 19th reached the gates of Kusquam.

A Hyena

13

Vengeance in Gondar

Gondar lived in a fever of doubts. The usurper Susenyos still sat drinking in his palace, but such power as he had had was collapsing round him as the news of Michael's return from the north grew more certain. Fasil had at last arrived in the city, and as a final device to protect himself, Susenyos had appointed him Ras and Bitwadet, in place of his own chief supporter, Sanuda. But Fasil was using his new authority to prepare for the restoration of Bruce's master, Takla Haymanot, and Sanuda himself was intriguing with Michael.

Bruce found that Esther was recovering from the illness caused by her anxiety: she had met Fasil, who had assured her of his loyalty to the Emperor. But the Empress Mentwab was not to be seen. She had shut herself up in a corner of her own palace to pray that she might escape from Michael's vengeance. Esther's son, Confu, and his friends, were gathering troops to join Michael and the Emperor.

Susenyos could still play the part of a brigand in his capital. In a drunken midnight foray, he plundered a number of houses in Gondar, Bruce's among them. The Scot was not harmed, for he was living at Kusquam, but some of his instruments, documents, and drawings were damaged. The next day he was summoned to the palace for his first and last interview with Susenyos.

The pretender 'was sitting, his eyes half closed, red as scarlet with last night's debauch; he was apparently at that moment much in liquor; his mouth full of tobacco, squirting his spittle out of his mouth to a very great distance; with this he had so covered the floor that it was with great difficulty I could chooose a clean place to kneel and make my obeisance'.

This made a sickening contrast with Bruce's memories of Takla Haymanot. The squalid spectre of royalty complained that the traveller, who considered himself a great man, had paid him no attention and had not shown him his foreign tricks of horsemanship. He demanded Fasil's grey horse of which he had heard, and gold from the revenue of the governorship of Ras el Fil. He threatened the Scot with blinding or death.

'I am no great man even in my own country,' Bruce replied, 'one proof of which is that I am in yours.' Takla Haymanot had shown him great kindness, and such gold as he had received had been spent on the Emperor's service. The profession of arms was his birthright, derived from his ancestors, and it had been his duty to teach his young master what he knew of it.

At this 'an old man of noble appearance', who was the usurper's only companion, came forward. He was Sanuda. 'What have you to do with Yagoube?' he asked. 'He has been a friend not only to the Emperor but to all of us. All the people love him. If you had seen as much of him as Takla Haymanot did, we should not have been disgraced as we are.'

He turned to Bruce and said in a whisper, 'Don't be afraid of him. I am here. Go home.'

Susenyos rolled tipsily on his imperial seat. 'You are very angry with me today, daddy,' he said.

Soon the news came that Michael had crossed the Takazze. At this Susenyos and the Empress both fled towards Quara, Mentwab's native province. Not even his last supporters cared anything for the fallen pretender. His presence had become a danger to them and to the Empress herself. He was stripped of his robes, set on a fresh horse and told to find what refuge he could for himself.

Fasil, too, withdrew from Gondar. The city was masterless as its people waited for Michael and the Emperor to take command again.

Bruce himself was half afraid that his care for the body of the murdered Emperor Joas would be remembered against him by the Ras, who had ordered the murder. His friends combined to reassure him. Easther urged him to meet Takla Haymanot, as he had promised to do, at a mountain pass just east of Gondar.

When he set out, armed supporters of the Emperor flocked round to go with him. Yasin, his deputy in Ras el Fil, appeared with twenty horsemen, 'having on their coats of mail, their helmets upon their heads, and their vizors down; their pikes perpendicular with their points in the air', ready to be lowered for a charge. Confu, Esther's son, arranged that this party should be formally challenged as they came to the mountains, and Yasin gave the answer, 'It is Yagoube, the Emperor's Governor of Ras el Fil, with the slave Yasin, coming to do the Emperor homage and to die for him if he commands.' A drum was beaten and Confu's officer proclaimed, 'Yagoube is Governor of Ras el Fil, commander of the Emperor's Black Horse, Lord of Gish and *Baalomal*'.

This was very satisfying. It seemed to ensure that the traveller's position at court was fully restored. He was, in fact, well received by both Michael and the Emperor. The hillside above the great men's tents was white with the clothes of tens of thousands of men and women from Gondar who had come to welcome their rulers. 'The priests from the convents for many miles round came, with their crosses and drums, in procession, and greatly added to the variety of the scene.' The sun shone. The army had food to give away or sell. The whole gathering had the air of a colossal picnic.

But it was a day of fear, not of pleasure. The citizens were there to show their loyalty to a man they dreaded, to beg forgiveness for their submission to Susenyos and Fasil. The chief supplicants were the two leading figures of the Ethiopian Church, the *Abuna*, the country's only bishop, and the *Etchege*, abbot of its senior monastery. When Michael left Gondar and Susenyos had been enthroned these two men had been persuaded by Abba Salama, their much more forceful colleague, to excommunicate the Ras and the Emperor. They were now seeking pardon and had been told to come humbly to meet the army, clothed as penitents. They were sternly received. Michael rebuked them publicly and the Emperor would not speak to them at all. They had not even a tent to cover them from the afternoon sun till Bruce asked the Abuna to take shelter in his own.

Like many of the Coptic monks sent from Egypt to head the Church of a country which had very few other links with their own, the Abuna was a weak and lonely being. He could have very little contact with the Ethiopians, 'these black people', as this brown man called them. He knew nothing of any Ethiopian language: even his Arabic was not that of an educated Egyptian. Bruce claimed to have seen him ordain a whole provincial army of 10,000 men deacons by ritual gestures from a distance. He cursed the absent Abba Salama for having misled him into the excommunication and stole off to Gondar again.

Michael's army of Tigreans was 20,000 strong, 6,000 of its men musketeers. It was the most formidable force in Ethiopia, and no one knew what he meant to do with it. He had stated – or at least hinted – in his dealings with Fasil that his only aim was to bring Takla Haymanot back to his throne and palace; that when this was done he himself would resign his office as Ras in Gondar, returning to his own province (or, rather, group of northern provinces) as a simple governor. But he had also threatened vengeance against all who had acknowledged Susenyos. The rival chiefs and the Empress were, in fact, ready to see the Emperor restored, but none of them trusted Michael. His air was now more severe and brutal than ever.

Bruce found Takla Haymanot anxious and without a spark of his old gaiety. He was stern to most of those who spoke to him, though friendly enough towards the Scot himself. An incident on the march to Gondar showed how his spirit had changed.

Bruce had brought with him Fasil's horse as a present for his royal master, and the Emperor asked him to ride ahead and display its paces as they went. They had to pass through a stream where a bush, *kantuffa*, hung over the water. This plant was one of the chief obstacles to travel in Ethiopia. Its thorns tore the clothes of travellers: before an emperor set out on any journey a proclamation was traditionally made – 'Cut down the kantuffa in the four corners of the world, for I do not know where I may go.'

Bruce passed the ford without trouble. He was wearing a goat-skin cape on which the thorns could not catch. But the Emperor, whose eyes were on Fasil's horse, did not notice the branch till it struck him. He 'was dressed in the habit of peace, his long hair floating all around his face, wrapt up in his mantle or thin cotton cloak, so that nothing but his eyes could be seen', according to the Ethiopian custom by which it was disgraceful for a ruler to expose his features in public. The thorns tangled themselves so tightly in his hair and cloak that it was impossible to free him without pulling off his upper garment and leaving his face bare.

The royal boy showed no signs of distress. 'With great composure, and in rather a low voice he called twice "Who is the shum of this district?" ' The local Governor, a man of sixty, and his son were close by. They had not seen what had happened and came up smiling.

Beside the Emperor there always rode the executioner of the camp, who carried on his saddle 'a quantity of thongs made of bull hide, rolled up very artifically: this is called the tarade'. Without speaking Takla Haymanot made a sign with his head and hand.

'Two loops of the tarade were instantly thrown round the shum and his son's necks, and they were both hoisted upon the same tree, the tarade cut, and the end made fast to a branch. They were both left hanging, but I thought so awkwardly that they would not die for some minutes, and might surely have been cut down; but fear had fallen upon every person who had not attended the Emperor to Tigre.'

Takla Haymanot rode on, talking as if nothing had happened. To Bruce this seemed an omen of violence to come. The young Emperor had always been willing enough for bloodshed in war, where he was dangerously ready to risk his own safety, but before his retreat from Gondar he had never ordered an execution and had

often shown horror and disgust when Ras Michael sent offenders or
enemies to the hangman. In misfortune, his feelings of humanity
seemed to have shrivelled.

It was on Christmas Eve that the army reached Gondar. The
thousands who had come out to meet the Emperor had gone home
full of terror or fled from the city. It was rumoured that the Emperor
and Michael would burn the place to the ground; and this fear was
not lightened when, instead of going up to the palace, they encamped outside the city on the Kaha, one of the two rivers which
almost encircled the town. An attempt had to be made to welcome
them, however. Gondar had a company of singers, dancers and
buffoons, who appeared in the streets when there was some great
occasion to be celebrated and gathered in the courtyards of houses
for private festivities. They made songs for each occasion. 'Many a
time, on his return from the field with victory, they had met Ras
Michael, and received his bounty for singing his praises and wel-
coming him upon his return home.'

About thirty of these men and women came out into the parade
ground below the city with new songs in honour of the Emperor
and the Ras. But Michael had heard that on the day of his public
excommunication these same people had ridiculed him in rhymes
that called him crooked, lame, old and impotent. The Ras made a
signal to some of his cavalry.

In less than two minutes, says Bruce, all the company were
slaughtered, 'excepting one young man, who, mortally wounded,
had just strength enough to arrive within twenty yards of the
Emperor's horse, and there fell dead without speaking a word.

'All the people present, most of them veteran soldiers, and consequently inured to blood, appeared shocked and disgusted at this
wanton piece of cruelty. For my part, a kind of faintishness or
feebleness had taken possession of my heart . . . such a horror,
joined with an absence of mind, that I found myself unable to give
an immediate answer, though the Emperor had spoken twice to
me.'

On Christmas Day a more formal vengeance began. Gondar was

not to be destroyed: the citizens were warned not to leave it on pain of being treated as rebels. But prisoners were being brought in from the country. The first and most important was Abba Salama.

When he was brought to the camp tied to a mule the Guardian of the Hour had been violently abusive. He had claimed that, as a priest, he had the right to put kings in chains and nobles in irons and had again declared the Emperor excommunicate. Now he was before a formal court in the palace. The Emperor sat, as usual, screened behind a lattice. Ras Michael was with the judges and Bruce stood behind him. Abba Salama was charged with a long list of crimes – 'Various kinds of murder, especially by poison; incest with every degree collateral and descendant', and finally high treason by cursing the Emperor and absolving his subjects from their allegiance.

The priest took up his own defence, Bruce says, 'with great dignity, and an air of superiority very different from his behaviour the day before'. He laughed at the accusations of misbehaviour with women. These might be crimes among Franks or other Christians, he said, looking at Bruce, but the Ethiopians lived under the law of Moses, which apparently gave them complete sexual freedom, to judge by the acts of Old Testament patriarchs, who, as he explained, at length, had done as he did.

He then began to accuse the chief of his accusers, Ras Michael himself of murdering two Emperors, Joas and John, the father of Takla Haymanot, besides other princes. Michael seemed to pay no attention to this, reading a paper or speaking to men who were standing beside him. In a low voice, but in a way which was evidently meant to be overheard, he asked Bruce what was the punishment for treason in Britain.

In spite of the Scot's misgivings over the spirit of vengeance that seemed to brood over Gondar, he could not resist an opportunity to take his own revenge on a man who had plotted his death more than once and was again implying that he was a Roman Catholic 'Frank' whose presence in Ethiopia should not be tolerated. 'High treason is punished with death in all the countries I have ever known', was his audible reply to Ras Michael.

The accused priests's accusations mounted. The Empress, Aylo, and other members of her family, with Gusho, Governor of Amhara, had all became 'Franks', he said. In order to make Ethiopia Roman Catholic they had sent for priests who lived with them as the Frank Bruce did, a man who ought to be stoned to death as an enemy of the Virgin Mary. This was an appeal to the sort of Ethiopian nationalism which had been the main source of his own power as a church leader. Michael answered at last that the Guardian of the Hour must defend himself first. It would be time to accuse others when he had shown that he was innocent.

At this the man's bold spirit began to break down at last. He pleaded that he had cleared the way to power in Gondar for both Michael and the Emperor and begged that for old friendship's sake he should not be blinded or have his tongue cut out. He denounced the Abuna, whom he had persuaded to excommunicate the Emperor and Ras, as a Mohammedan, pagan, Frank and infidel. The judges refused to hear more. A written report of the defence was carried to the unseen and apparently silent Takla Haymanot, and the official who was the Emperor's Voice proclaimed that Abba Salama was guilty and must die that day. He was hurried out, cursing Emperor, Ras and Abuna, and hanged on a tree at the palace gate.

An avalanche of vengeance followed. Michael's enemies were blinded, hanged or beheaded.

'Blood continued to be spilt day after day till the Epiphany: priests, laymen, young men and old, noble and vile, found their end by the knife or the cord. Fifty-seven people died publicly by the hands of the executioner . . . many disappeared and were either murdered privately or sent to prison, no one knew where.

'The bodies of those killed by the sword were hewn in pieces and scattered about the streets, being denied burial. I was miserable, and almost driven to despair, at seeing my hunting dogs . . . bringing into the courtyard the heads and arms of slaughtered men . . the quantity of carrion, and the stench of it, brought down the hyenas in hundreds from the neighbouring mountains; and, as few people in Gondar go out after it is dark, they enjoyed the streets by themselves, and seemed ready to dispute the possession of the city with the inhabitants. Often when I went home late from the palace, and it was this time the Emperor chose chiefly for conversation, though I had but to pass the corner of the market-place before the palace, had lanthorns with me, and was surrounded with armed men, I heard them grunting by twos and threes so near me as to be afraid they would take some opportunity of seizing me by the leg. A pistol would have frightened them and made them speedily run, and I constantly carried two loaded at my girdle; but the discharging of a pistol in the night would have alarmed every one that heard it in the town, and it was not now the time to add any thing to the people's fears. I at last scarcely ever went out.'

Takla Haymanot was soon inquiring for Yagoube. His palace was half deserted, for the great men of the country were not coming to Gondar – fear rather than disloyalty held them back. As Bruce set out to obey the Emperor's summons he passed one of the Ras's officers who had three prisoners with him and was 'just beginning to cut one of them to pieces. As if he had been engaged about ordinary business', the man called to him to wait for a few minutes while the other two were killed – he wanted to speak to the traveller.

The Emperor was concerned to see that Bruce looked ill and worried. He could not believe that the mere sight and smell of death had upset him.

'Tell me, Yagoube,' he said, 'is it really possible that you can take such things as these so much to heart? You are a brave man: we have all seen it. We have blamed you, stranger as you are in the country, for taking so little care of yourself, and yet you are as much disturbed by these things as the most cowardly woman or child could be.'

Bruce answered that he did not know whether he was brave or not, but that he did not want to have courage if this meant watching torture or living among corpses without protest. A civilized

man of the eighteenth century, he made a distinction between war
and massacre or deliberate cruelty which may seem old-fashioned
in our day.

'War,' he said, 'is the profession of noble minds; it is a glorious
one; it is the science and occupation of kings; it softens men's
minds, by obliging them to society, to assist, befriend, and even
save one another though at their own risk and danger.' His friend
Engedan had just come into the room. 'There,' he added, 'is a young
man who has the humanity and gentleness as well as the bravery
of my countrymen who are soldiers.'

'You want war, do you, Yagoube?' said the young Emperor
seriously. 'You will have it soon. Engedan has come to tell us how
near it is.'

In fact, Ras Michael's enemies were massing again. The food
supplies of Gondar had been cut for a while, and though the roads
to the city were open again, Gusho and Powussen were gathering
their forces to the east, and Fasil, too, had got an army together to
the south, though, as usual, no one knew what he meant to do
with it.

This was bad news for Bruce, who, in his depression and disgust
over the bloodshed at Gondar, had been making plans to leave
Ethiopia for his return to Egypt by way of the kingdom of Sennar.
He meant to set out from his own province of Ras el Fil, which
he had never visited, and to prepare his way by sending letters
and messages to Sudanese chiefs through his deputy, Yasin, who
was in contact with them.

The Emperor was hurt and angry when he heard of these plans.
He was very uncertain of his own future. Michael, who had expected to be able to raise money and supplies at Gondar, as well as
to gather support from its neighbourhood, had, in fact, received
very little and could scarcely give his sovereign food enough for his
household. The Empress sent Takla Haymanot a little gold, but she
would not return to Kusquam and her supporters held aloof. It was
proposed to send Bruce to Ras el Fil with Yasin to buy horses and
coats of mail for the cavalry there from Sudanese merchants who

came to the border town of Gallabat to trade, but the Emperor feared that if his stranger did leave Gondar he would never come back.

It was with great difficulty that Bruce persuaded him to allow a messenger to carry his letters to the Sudan. The Scot took an oath not to attempt to leave until this crisis of the coming war was over. He also swore that if the Emperor was victorious or made a settlement with the rebels and if his own health recovered when he reached Scotland again, he would return with all the men of his family he could gather, fully armed and equipped, to serve Takla Haymanot.

'I cannot but hope the impossibility of performing this oath extinguished the sin of breaking it,' writes Bruce. He comforted himself later with the thought that it was a personal contract between himself and Takla Haymanot which ceased to be binding when the Emperor died: he believed (wrongly) that Takla Haymanot was killed shortly after he himself left Ethiopia. The agreement freed him from a fear which had dogged him since he first reached Gondar, the fear that – according to 'that ancient and general rule of the country, never to allow a stranger to return to his home' – he would be kept in Ethiopia for the rest of his life, as many other Europeans had been since the first Portuguese came to a fifteenth-century Emperor's court.

He must have needed such reassurance, for it was at this time that his only companion from western Europe, Luigi Balugani, died at Gondar. Bruce's attitude to the artist who had shared his adventures remains puzzling. When he returned to Europe he insisted that the death of the young Italian had happened a year earlier, before he reached the Blue Nile. This was not mere forgetfulness. Apart from the Italian records of their travel to the sources at Gish which Bruce brought home with him, there are unmistakable references to the artist in Bruce's own account of this journey, though the name of Balugani is never used. The evidence of a witness to the truth of his story would have been very valuable to Bruce. That evidence existed in Balugani's own handwriting, but the explorer could not use it against London sceptics and critics because of his apparently deliberate misdating.

It is certainly true that no one who knew him could have doubted that Bruce was the true leader in all his expeditions, that no companion planned his journey for him or pushed him forward if he was slow to face an adventure. In the planning of his journeys James Bruce was intensely practical. Whenever he could he accumulated facts and observations, topographic, astronomical, zoological, botanical, with tireless and entirely rational assiduity. But there was one point on which he could not give way to facts and reason. He must be the sole discoverer of the Nile source or admit (in his own mind, at least) that his efforts had ended in total failure. Nothing but his fear, a wildly irrational one, that his unique achievement might be questioned if any other educated man of the Western culture was known to have reached the Nile's source with him, can explain his concealment of Balugani's part in the journey, just as his unwillingness to admit that any Westerner had been at Gish or the Tissisat falls before him explains his attempt to disprove the claims of Paez and Lobo.

To Bruce, Balugani may never have been more than a servant, though a faithful one, liked by almost all who had to deal with him. But the Italian's death surely does help to explain the gloom which hung over those months at Gondar when the traveller waited for the battles that were to decide his fate as well as Ras Michael's and Takla Haymanot's. He was still busy enough, and the days had their brighter moments. No doubt it was then that he did most to train the young negroes of the Emperor's Black Horse. These had usually been captured in annual man hunts organized by the Ethiopian court. There were 300 of them 'all clothed in coats of mail and mounted on black horses', and Bruce had a high opinion of their ability.

'By strict attention to their morals, removing all bad examples from among them, giving premiums to those that read and wrote most and best (for they had all time enough upon their hands; especially in winter), and, above all, by the great delight and pleasure the Emperor used to take in conversing with them alone, countenancing and rewarding them in the line he knew I followed, this body became, as to firmness and coolness in action, equal perhaps to any of the same number in the world.'

Bruce's difficulty was to hold the little corps together. Almost every noble wanted to have one of them as a door-keeper.

In Bruce's day feeling against the slave trade was already strong, though hundreds of thousands of negroes were still being shipped to the Americas. He did not condemn slavery, but he demanded that the British Government should protect the slaves from the 'enormous cruelties' they suffered – 'the abuses and neglect of manners so frequent in our plantations are what the legislature should direct their attention against'. This was not, perhaps, a very practical proposal when it was written, at a time when the British legislature had just lost all control of its chief slave-owning colonies. But no American abolitionist could have put the case for humane treatment of the negroes more strongly.

'After having been torn from their own country and connections, reduced to the condition of brutes to labour for a being they never before knew, after lying, stealing and the long list of European crimes have been made, as it were, necessary to them . . . then, after we have made them monsters we describe them as such, forgetful that they are not now as their Maker created them but such as, by teaching them our own vices we have transformed them into, for ends which, I fear, one day will not be found a sufficient excuse for the enormities they have occasioned.'

Meanwhile Bruce was gathering not only arms and horses for his troop, the cost of which ran him into debt, but also scientific and historical information and Ethiopian manuscripts to take home with him. Here the arrival at Gondar of an unusual visitor gave him help. This was the son of the ruler of Shoa, who brought gold, a thousand horsemen and a promise of general support to Takla Haymanot.

It was a great occasion for the Emperor, in his capital already half threatened with siege. Shoa, which is now the central province of Ethiopia, was then a southern outpost. For generations it had been almost an independent kingdom. Its princely family, the ancestors of today's Imperial House, were of the blood of the Solomonic line. Settlements of Galla tribesmen had almost separated them from the neighbouring provinces, but they had held their own prosperously enough without taking a part in the political crises of Gondar or its civil wars.

Prince Amha Yasus was treated with great ceremony. The Emperor received him sitting on his throne, 'very richly dressed in brocade, a very fine muslin web wrapt loosely about him, so as to hang in plaits, and in some parts show, and in some conceal, the flowers of cloth of gold of which his waistcoat was composed. His hair was loose, combed out at its full length, and falling about his head in every direction; and a fork, like a skewer made of a rhinoceros horn, with a gold button or head upon it, stuck through his hair near the temples; he was all perfumed with rose-water; and two people stood on opposite sides of the tent, each of them with a silver bottle full of it'.

The guest was not allowed to prostrate himself as other visitors did. Instead of standing or kneeling when he spoke to the Emperor, he was gently forced to sit on a stool, where he was 'deluged so with rose-water that I do believe he never in his life was so wet with rain'. There was no proclamation of his father's offices and titles, as there would have been in the case of any lesser governor – as there had been for Bruce when he was going to meet the Emperor again outside Gondar. This would have been a confirmation of an imperial grant and the whole purpose of the ceremony was to emphasize the independence of Shoa and the almost-equality of its reigning family with the Emperor's own. 'The etiquette could not have been more punctually and uniformly observed in any court of Europe, and it would have just signified there what it did here.'

Amha Yasus was tall and well made: 'he had a very beautiful face, small features, and the most affable manners'. All the princesses and noblewomen at court, except Esther, fell in love with him, says Bruce. 'I have thought, when I have seen them together, that the Emperor, Engedan and himself were three of the handsomest men I had ever beheld in any country.' All three were intelligent, brave and humane, except for 'that accursed indifference, or rather propensity to shed human blood' which Takla Haymanot had learned from Ras Michael. 'For natural talents', Bruce adds loyally, the Emperor was the first of the three.

The Shoan's visit was not made without a purpose. It seems likely that his father was anxious to find out whether the young Emperor was a friend worth having, and whether he was likely to be able to hold Ethiopia together if Michael lost his power. In fact, Takla Haymanot and the prince became very friendly. Amha Yasus's mother was a sister of Gusho of Amhara, and Bruce believed that he had used his influence with this rebel uncle to persuade him to accept the Emperor again, though not the Ras.

Amha Yasus also had an interest in Bruce himself. He had heard from monks of the great monastery of Debra Libanos, in Shoa, that there was a white man in Gondar 'who could do everything but raise the dead'. The Emperor told Bruce to visit the prince each morning, and they were soon going everywhere together. In their long conversations the explorer was able to gather information about Ethiopian history and customs and about African countries south and west of the lands he visited himself. Amha Yasus told him of an imperial chronicle kept at Debra Libanos, which Bruce had looked for in vain. The Prince offered to send for a copy. This was duly brought across three hundred miles of troubled country and became the foundation of Bruce's account of Ethiopia's medieval history.

Another visitor was less important but to Bruce even more extraordinary. He was Guangoul, chief of the Angot Galla, in the north-east, who arrived riding on a small, saddle-less cow with enormous horns. He had with him five hundred foot soldiers and forty horsemen, 'armed, like himself with shields of no resistance, and hedge-stakes burnt and sharpened at the end instead of lances'. This warrior had come, it seems, to offer support to the Emperor and Ras Michael.

'He was a little, thin, cross-made man . . . of a yellow, un-wholesome colour, not black nor brown. He had long hair plaited and interwoven with the bowels of oxen, and so knotted together as to render it impossible to distinguish the hair from the bowels, which hung down in long strings, part before his breast and part behind his shoulder, the most extraordinary ringlets I had ever seen. He had likewise a wreath of guts hung about his neck, and several rounds of the same about his middle, which served as a girdle, below which was a short cotton cloth dipt in butter, and all his body was wet and running down with the same.'

The chieftain wore a pair of short drawers reaching half-way to his knees and nothing more above or below them. 'He was then in full dress and ceremony. He had a shield of a single hide, warped by the heat. He carried a short lance in his right hand, with an ill-made iron head. . . . Whether it was necessary for the poizing himself upon the sharp ridge of the beast's back, or whether it was meant for skilful riding, I do not know, being quite unskilled in cowmanship, but he leaned exceedingly backwards, pushing his belly forwards and holding his left arm and shield stretched out on one side of him; and his right arm and lance in the same way on the other, like wings.'

The Emperor waited to receive Guangoul in a tent below the city, but when he saw this strange figure he burst into laughter and had to hide himself behind his throne. The ivory chair stood empty. The Galla thought it was meant for himself and sat down on it, 'with the butter running from every part of him' on to the crimson silk cushion.

It was high treason to sit on the throne. The shout of amazement that went up probably saved Guangoul's life, for he leapt up and was hustled out of the tent, staring wildly round without under-standing what had happened to him. The Emperor was speechless with laughter, however, and Guangoul was allowed to visit Ras Michael.

This strange farce was welcome in a time of anxiety. Princess Esther, who was pleased with anything which could make the Galla seem contemptible, insisted on seeing it re-enacted. Michael had a dwarf among his servants, 'very ugly, with a monstrous big head, but very sharp and clever,' whom he used as a sort of herald to carry messages to his enemies in times of trouble. Doho seemed suited to play the part of Guangoul, but he was a learned, religious and essentially self-respecting man, and he refused to let himself be decorated with ox-guts. Bruce suggested that hanks of cotton steeped in butter could take their place.

'All hands were immediately set to work: the cotton was provided: Esther's servants and slaves decked Doho to the life. I spotted his face with stibium, and others anointed him with butter: an old milk cow was found that suffered a rider without much impatience and in came Guangoul.

'Never was anything better personated, or better received, the whole hall resounded with one cry of laughter. Doho, encouraged by this, and the perfect steadiness of his cow, began to act his part with great humour and confidence; he was born in the neighbourhood of these very Galla, knew their manners and spoke their language perfectly.'

Nobles and courtiers – Amha Yasus, Esther's son Confu, and Bruce himself – stood round the stool that represented the throne.

'The cow was brought into the middle of the room and [the pretended] Guangoul descended with his lance and shield in great state. A cushion was not spared, and Doho did not spare the cushion: the butter showed very distinctly where he had been sitting. We all fell upon him and belaboured him heartily and chased him to the door. His speedy retreat was not counterfeited.'

This charade was immensely successful, particularly with the ladies of the court. But Michael, in an unusually expansive moment, let slip the news that the real Guangoul, like many more important leaders, had gone over to the rebels, who used him to ravage the Ras's lands in Tigre. Young Confu was sent after him with a force of cavalry which put an end to the Galla chief and his men. The civil war was coming to a head again.

14

~~~oOo~~~

Days of Battle

From the top of the great tower of his palace – the only one in the
half-ruined building that still had a usable staircase – Takla Haymanot II could look out on the smoke of rebel campfires and burning villages. Ras Michael's musketeers, most of them commanded
by Gebra Maskal, could be the decisive force in a country where
firearms were still comparatively rare, but Michael had been un-
characteristically slow to move, perhaps partly because he was at
last beginning to feel himself an old man, partly because he had
been waiting for the reinforcements from the neighbourhood which
never came. It rained and the half-naked troops were dispirited.

But the impatience of the young Emperor and the cries of
refugees streaming into Gondar at last forced him to march out.
He took with him 40,000 men, half of these from his own lands of
Tigre. According to Bruce's estimate, this was 10,000 more than
the forces of Gusho and Powussen. He also took all the great ladies
of the court who held lands which owed military service to the
Emperor. Since so few of the nobles had joined him, the presence of
these women would help to ensure that warriors from their estates
at least would indeed fight for the Ras.

For James Bruce this was a memorable campaign. It was the only
one in which he actually fought at the head of his black troopers,
the flower of the Emperor's Guard, all 'armed with coats of mail,
the horses with plates of brass on their cheeks and faces, with a
sharp iron spike of about five inches in length which stuck out in
the middle of their forehead, a very troublesome, useless piece of

9. An emperor riding in state, early eighteenth-century manuscript, BM
Oriental 713

10. One of the ancient Axum Steles as it stands today

their armour; their bridles were iron chains; the body of the horse covered with a kind of thin quilt stuffed with cotton, with two openings made above the flap of the saddle, into which the horseman put his thighs and legs, and which covered him from his hip (where the shirt of mail ended) down to a little above his ancle'.

Each of them carried a fourteen-foot lance, which was his chief weapon, and had a small battle-axe on his saddle. They wore copper helmets with great crests of black horsehair, and before the face, down to the top of the nose, a flap of chainmail served as a vizor. 'This was the most troublesome part of the whole, it was hot and heavy, and constantly fretted the cheek and nose when either the man or the horse was in motion; and therefore I always substituted a black silk net, which concealed my colour better, and for the rest of my face I committed it to the care of Providence.' Using Arab-style saddles and short stirrups which allowed them to throw their whole weight into a charge, this troop, like the medieval knights, could break through any force which tried to stand up to them, but they were too heavy with iron to move very fast. On a Sudanese steed seventeen hands high their Scottish captain must have been a truly colossal figure.

Even in war Bruce was a doctor as well as a fighting man, sometimes giving medical advice even to the enemy. He could also be an envoy whom both sides would trust. But he would not make use of what should have been his most formidable military skill – his famous marksmanship with the rifle which would have allowed him to shoot down rebel leaders when they exposed themselves. The rebels, indeed, were inclined to believe that every lucky shot must be his, but as he explained to their chief, Gusho, sharpshooting was no work for a gentleman. 'It is not a custom known in my country,' he said 'for officers to be employed to pick out distinguished men at such an advantage, nor would it be considered there as much better than murder . . . there are common soldiers chosen for that purpose, for which they are not the more esteemed.' He used his rifle only once in the fighting, and this was to drive off men who were trying to capture his horses when they were taken out to a stream to drink.

There was something curiously formal, almost dreamlike, about the shape of this short campaign. Two days' march from Gondar were the church and hill of Sarbakusa, which Bruce called Serbraxos. They stood at the opening of a long valley through which ran the road to the uplands of Begemder and the mountain of Wechne, where the royal princes were confined.

A prophecy said that a Governor of Begemder would defeat and kill an Emperor there. After this a new Emperor, Theodore by name, would come to the throne. All the enemies of the Ethiopians – the Moslems, the Galla, and the negro Shankalla – would be destroyed. The Empire would reach to Jerusalem, and there would be a thousand years of peace. This millennial vision was widely known and long remembered. More than eighty years later the able tyrant Kassa, who began the reunification of Ethiopia after generations of anarchy, was to take the name of Theodore as an indication that he would fulfil it.

The rebels of 1771 decided that Sarbakusa should be their battle-field. This would convince their army that an historic decision could be reached in the fighting. On the other side, the Ras believed that at Sarbakusa the Archangel Michael would appear and advise him again. He had heard nothing from this angelic (or, as Bruce hints, devilish) spirit since he had failed to take its advice to burn down Gondar before his retreat to Tigre. For him Sarbakusa was a fatal, a decisive battlefield, much more genuinely, perhaps, than it was for Powussen and Gusho. The rebels do not seem to have had with them any new pretender who could have called himself Theodore, though, no doubt, it would have been easy enough for them to bring a prince from Wechne. Their real aim, in fact, was to separate the reigning Emperor from Michael, either by capturing him or by forcing him to dismiss the Ras; and at every interval in the fighting messages were passing between the two camps assuring Takla Haymanot of the rebels' loyalty to himself.

Bruce rode out from Gondar with the Emperor and his guards, hoping (audibly) that the enemy's march discipline was as bad as that of Michael's army. In fact, the bulk of the rebels let them pass towards Sarbakusa almost as if there had been an actual agreement that this was the only possible battlefield. Long before it was reached, however, there was a skirmish where a daring Galla chief, Asahel, raided the rear which Yasin and the cavalry of Ras el Fil were covering. Esther's son Confu had been left at Gondar with a small body of soldiers to protect the city, but the boy left the post at the rumour of fighting and led a charge against the raiders. He soon seemed to be in danger, but in spite of Esther's anxiety Ras Michael would not send help to his stepson, who had disobeyed his orders. Bruce begged that some musketeers should be allowed to advance and give cover to the Ethiopian horsemen. A grudging permission was given him, and he ran out, waving his cloak and crying, 'Come on', stumbling and falling among the rocks and slippery grass of a hillside.

Confu's men rallied and drove the Galla towards the musketeers who had followed the tall Scot. The bullets dispersed the enemy. This was Bruce's baptism of fire. His friend Confu was forgiven for his lack of discipline, but he had been wounded. No one, his worried mother believed, could attend to him so well as Yagoube, who was sent back with him to the city, assured by Michael that he would not miss a battle, since there would be none till Sarbakusa was reached.

When he returned Bruce found the army there. Michael had occupied the hilltop. His first aim was to draw the rebels under the fire of his musketeers, whom he had posted on slopes between which their horsemen would pass. For this purpose he ordered his own men to retreat as if they were fleeing. But the Emperor was very unwilling to seem to withdraw. He ordered Bruce and his Black Guards to charge a band of Galla before him. 'The Galla were all borne down, with little or no resistance, by the length of our pikes and the superior weight of our horses, and those that were not slain were scattered over the plain. But a greater misfortune befell us from our friends than from our enemies, as a volley of shot was poured upon us from Serbraxos hill . . . which killed seven men, notwithstanding their coats of mail.' The Emperor himself was in great danger. His brother was wounded. But night was coming on, and the army encamped on the hill.

What Bruce called 'the first Battle of Serbraxos' was over. It had been indecisive, though Michael claimed to have lost fewer men than his enemies. The next day was spent in desultory peace talks. It rained, the armies shivered and lost confidence.

When the two sides were ready for battle again a great red flag was seen among the men of Begemder. It was said to be the standard of King Theodore. But the rain soon fell more heavily than ever. The courtiers spent their evening in feasting on the hill, and Bruce taught his companions how to drink toasts in the European fashion. He raised a great cow horn full of wine and proposed 'Long life to the Emperor, health, happiness and victory to Ras Michael, and a speedy sight of Theodore'. Even Ras Michael drank and laughed. Among the rest the horn went quickly round, and Bruce prophesied that the Emperor Theodore would never be so cheerfully toasted 'in the thousand years he is to reign'.

Next morning the armies were again ready for battle. Looking out from the hill-top, the Emperor's men saw 'a thick cloud of dust like the smoke of a large city on fire' rising when the cavalry of Begemder mounted and began to advance.

'The ground where they encamped being trodden into powder . . . and now raised by the motion of the horses' feet, was whirled round by a very moderate breeze that blew steadily; it every minute increased in darkness and assumed various shapes and forms, of towers, castles and battlements as fancy suggested. In the middle of this great cloud we began to perceive indistinctly part of the horsemen, then a much greater number, and the figures of the horses more accurately defined, which came moving majestically upon us, sometimes partially seen, at other times concealed by being wrapt up in clouds and darkness.'

Bruce was excited by the spectacle. 'Is not that a glorious sight?'

he asked his Lieutenant, Ammonios. 'What king would not be fond of war?'

'King David the psalmist curses those who delight in war,' answered the Ethiopian, a practical-minded soldier and a student of Scripture. 'Wait and see what a glorious sight we shall all make before sunset.'

The enemy came on with the great red flag of Theodore among them. Michael had placed his musketeers in positions to receive them. A volley disordered their line. The Emperor's heavy Horse broke through, Bruce among them, and Takla Haymanot himself pushed forward in pursuit till he was in danger of being surrounded and captured or killed. He was led back in safety, however, in spite of his own resistance to any sort of retreat. But soon he was exposing himself again. Bruce and his Black horsemen and Yasin with the troops of Ras el Fil rode forward to defend him against a second Begemder charge. As they advanced Gebra Maskal, the musketeer commander who had done most to check the enemy, suddenly appeared beside them.

'Where are you going, Yagoube?' he called. He stammered with excitement, and the Scot fancied that he was again trying to pick a quarrel, as in their first days together at Gondar.

'I am going to die. That is the business of the day,' Bruce answered dourly.

'Then follow me,' cried the musketeer. 'You shall not take one step today but I will go five before you.' He ran forward and ordered a volley which finally set the enemy flying.

Takla Haymanot's guards formed up around him to begin the fight again, but the rebels would not come forward. The 'Second Battle of Serbraxos' was over.

It was treated as a victory. The chiefs of the army, including the great ladies, sat at the doors of their tents while each of their followers who had killed a man appeared with the sexual parts of his victim and, brandishing his lance over his master's or mistress's head, repeated a formula which was never changed except for the names in it.

'I am John, son of George, son of David, son of Claudius. I am the rider on the brown horse. I saved your father's life at such-and-such a battle. Where would you have been if I had not fought for you today? You give me no encouragement, no clothes, no money. You do not deserve a follower like me.'

Bruce took no share in this scene. He was attending to wounded friends, including Engedan, while the Emperor gave rewards to those who had fought well. During the battle Bruce had spoken to a soldier who had found the flag of Theodore lying trampled on the ground and had bought it from him. When he reached the Emperor's tent he produced this banner.

There was great excitement. Had he killed Theodore himself? Who was the pretender? Bruce explained that he had not seen this still mysterious being.

'I am no king-killer,' said the royalist Scot. 'That is a sin from which, thank God, my ancestors were all free, though if I had come across this king I might have overcome my scruples.'

If anyone had killed Theodore, he declared, it must have been Gebra Maskal, the commander of the musketeers, whose bravery and activity had foiled all the enemy's attacks. Bruce had his reward, however. It was a massive gold chain with which Takla Haymanot invested him, while his secretary said: 'The Emperor does you this honour not as payment for your services but as a pledge of what he is willing to do for you if you put it into his power.'

But in spite of rewards and rejoicings, in spite of the failure of the rebel attacks, the war was not going well, particularly for Ras Michael. The Ras no longer fought at the head of his troops, though he directed the army's movements with great skill as he sat on the hill-top of Sarbakusa, sometimes playing draughts with his servants before his tent as he surveyed the battlefield. But his tactics had become purely defensive, and he needed a decisive victory. In spite of the enemy's losses, their army was growing. The loyal army could watch bodies of horsemen and infantry moving into the rebel camps and knew that these were the forces of chieftains who had

feared to move against Michael when he came south expecting
victory. They also knew that no reinforcements were reaching their
own side. Michael's men began to lose heart and desert him. Food
and water were growing scarce and the enemy lay between them
and Gondar, their source of supply.

The 'Third Battle of Serbraxos' was, in fact, a mere defence of the
hill, which Michael had fortified with a series of small stone walls.
One party of Galla actually reached the hill-top, but 'the ancient
spirit of the troops seemed to revive upon seeing the enemy were
the aggressors' and the rebel attacks were beaten off again.

At every pause in the fighting messages came to Takla Haymanot asking for peace, but peace without the Ras. The rebels, too,
had their troubles. An epidemic of fever had broken out in their
camp. Gusho of Amhara had already sent to ask Bruce for the return
of a favourite horse of his which had been captured in a skirmish.
Now he proposed to the Emperor that Yagoube should be allowed
to come and give him advice on the treatment of fever patients,
among them his wife and daughter. On the day after the battle
Bruce crossed the lines of the two armies by agreement.

There was no doubt on either side about the real purpose of
this visit. The Scot was to discover what he could about the rebels'
plans. When he came into the Governor's camp he ceremoniously
bared his head and shoulders as a sign that he carried the Emperor's
orders. Equally ceremoniously four men were sent to meet him,
two of whom supported each of his arms as he was presented to
Gusho.

'Hear what the Emperor says to you,' he began as he entered the
tent where the rebel chief sat 'on a kind of bed covered with scarlet
cloth and edged with a deep gold fringe. . . . In a moment he
rose; and, stripping himself bare to the waist, he bowed with his
forehead on the scarlet cloth, but did not, as was his duty, stand
on the ground and touch it with his forehead' – though, as Bruce
noted, there was a Persian carpet on the floor which would have
made the prostration as comfortable as it could be. 'Pride and
newly acquired independence had released him from those former

observances of which he had been brought up from his childhood.'

The message was then delivered. The fever, said Bruce, would grow worse as the rains grew heavier. Gusho would die of it; 'consequently, being out of your allegiance, God alone knows what will happen to you hereafter'. The Emperor's only wish was that, to escape death and damnation, the rebels should go home, as he wanted to be rid of them at once.

As he announced this very unrealistic prescription for political and physical health the envoy could scarcely prevent himself from smiling. Gusho broke into loud laughter.

'Aye, aye, Yagoube,' he said, 'I see you are still yourself. Tell the Emperor from me that if I were to do as you say, I should indeed be disloyal and afraid to die. Let him know that I will do him better service. If I were to go home and leave Michael with him, I can say – though I am not a doctor – that the Ras would prove in the end more dangerous to him than all the fevers of this country-side.'

Bruce did what he could as a physician, giving medicine for fever patients and warning Gusho that one of his nephews had smallpox and should be sent out of the camp if a much more serious epidemic was to be avoided.

All that had been said up to this point had been heard by Gusho's officers and servants. Now there was a long and very friendly private talk from which Bruce gathered that the rebel chief expected the Imperial army to retreat to Gondar almost at once. Bruce was warned, for his own safety, to keep close to the Emperor, who would not be attacked. Esther, he was told, would be unable to protect him in the withdrawal, though her sister, Princess Altash, might, since she was mother-in-law of Powussen.

At the end of the interview Gusho was ready to slip gold into his visitor's hand, 'with the same manner we do the fee of a physician in Europe'. But, as usual, Bruce was determined to preserve his independence, prudently.

'You forget,' he said, 'that I am no castaway, no Greek servant, but perhaps of equal rank to yourselves.' If he needed money, an agent of Metical Aga who was in the rebel camp would provide it in the ordinary way of business.

If anyone owed him a reward for his doctoring, it was Gusho's wife and daughters, whom he had done his best to cure. He might need help when Gusho's position 'was great and governing everything in Gondar'. If this happened, he would speak to the women; Gusho could promise now to do anything for his visitor that they asked him.

'You are a good prophet, Yagoube,' said Gusho. 'And so I shall.'

The pattern of the future was already becoming plain. Gusho expected to take Michael's place as Ras, and, in effect, Bruce agreed that this was likely to happen. But he could not tell just how it would happen. As he left the camp, with an Amharan officer to safeguard him and several servants carrying gifts of fruit and fish, a muffled figure met him. This was a servant of Engedan, who, with Confu, had been recovering from his wounds at Gondar when a raiding party carried them off to Gusho as perhaps not altogether unwilling prisoners. In a whisper this man gave him very much the same advice that he had got from Gusho – 'Your army will disband. Keep beside the Emperor.'

Bruce learned from the officer who was with him that the Empress was now supporting the rebels. 'She could not see Ras Michael fall without giving him a shove,' he said, 'though she has waited till the very last day before she took the risk, for fear of accident.'

The Scot reached the royal tent 'musing what power was to carry us to Gondar, disband the army, depose Michael, and not hurt the Emperor'.

He found Takla Haymanot lying sick and exhausted in his tent: the boy evidently realized that the campaign in which he had been looking for glory was ending in failure. It was Ras Michael who first questioned Bruce. He was given a general account of what had been seen and done in the rebel camp, but nothing was said about Gusho's forecast of a retreat and a meeting with the Emperor in

Gondar. When Takla Haymanot was well enough to talk, however, Bruce told him all that he had heard. The Emperor was full of fears. He ordered the Scot to go to his tent and say nothing to anyone.

Next day, when Ras Michael proposed to begin a final battle, his chief officers told him that this was impossible. It was known, they said, that Gusho had sent a message to the Emperor saying that there would be no attack on his forces if they withdrew to Gondar. The rebel chief had even agreed with the Abuna that his own army should be excommunicated if they interfered with the retreat. Michael's own Tigrean musketeers had made up their minds not to fight again at Sarbakusa. If the Ras would not withdraw he might be left to defend the hill by himself – his troops would simply melt away.

This was decisive. Orders were issued that the army should be ready to move off at eight in the evening. Not a tent was to be lowered in daylight however. 'The old general was ashamed to be seen, for the first time, fleeing before his enemies.'

While they waited for the dark Bruce ordered Yasin to take his Ras el Fil horsemen, not to Gondar, but directly to their own province, where he was to complete arrangements for the Scot's journey to Sennar. Yasin was disconsolate. He begged his master to go with his Moslems to Ras el Fil at once: 'there was not a man of the troops under him who would not rather die with me than abandon me to be murdered by the hands of these faithless Christian dogs, who never were to be bound by oath or promise'. Bruce was tempted to agree, but his double duty as a courtier and an explorer forbade him. He remembered his own promise to the Emperor not to go without his permission – and also that if he left his instruments behind him in Gondar he would not be able to make proper observations on his journey through the desert.

With the dark the whole army was free to move. Orders could not be enforced. 'A confusion, never to be forgotten or described presently followed, everybody making the best of their way to get safe down the hill.' At first Bruce himself kept close to the Emperor, but he was riding for the first time a great black horse from the

Sudan which Takla Haymanot had given him. It was excited by the crowd on the slippery hillside, 'men, horses and mules rolling promiscuously over one another', and was soon almost out of control. He tried to make his way by a watercourse which was being followed by women of the camp, carrying the large, round bowls in which bread was baked, but the path ended in a small precipice. As he halted one of the baking bowls came rolling down the hill like a wheel and bounded past the horse.

'Whether it touched him or not, I cannot tell; but it determined him, without farther deliberation, to spurn all control by his rider. On the first leap he made, it was with the utmost difficulty I avoided going over his head: I will not pretend to say what followed. I was deprived of all sense of direction till, stumbling often, and sliding down upon his haunches oftener, I found myself at the bottom of the hill, perfectly stupefied with fear but safe and sound in body though my saddle was lying upon the horse's neck.'

The road below was crowded and full of alarms, but Bruce forced his way forward till he caught up with Ras Michael, whose mule threw him twice as he struggled to reach Gondar before daylight. The palace was almost deserted: even the Emperor's slaves had taken refuge in the town's monasteries. But Bruce fell asleep stretched on a bull's hide. The unlucky campaign was over.

15

Farewell to Ethiopia

The Emperor sat in his palace, waiting for what was to come. He was almost unvisited – for some days almost unfed. Michael, too, sat in the house that belonged to him as Ras, waiting. The rebels had surrounded the city on every side. They had even cut it off from the two rivers, Kaha and Angareb, from which its water was drawn, and they at once rationed the citizens' supply. Most of the wealthier townspeople were willing enough to obey Gusho: Gondar was his birthplace, his father had been Ras in Gondar, and he owned a good deal of property there. The town was full of Michael's troops, but, disorganized and dependent on the rebels for food and drink, they were helpless.

When Gusho demanded that all firearms should be surrendered Gebra Maskal himself organized the handing over of his 6,000 muskets and rebel sympathizers in the city made sure that few others were concealed in private houses. The disarmed Tigreans were herded together and then marched out towards their homes, guarded by rebel troops, but still insulted and often attacked by townsmen and country folk. When Michael heard of this his spirit at last seemed to break and he wept.

The rebels had not been allowed by their leaders to enter the town, but while the men of Tigre were passing out, pelted with stones and mud, a handful of wild Galla stole in. They plundered some houses and then came to the palace where Takla Haymanot sat in the alcove of his presence chamber, with Bruce and two remaining courtiers near him.

The room was the pride of Gondar. Jesus II, who loved foreign luxuries, had had it lined by Greek craftsmen with Venetian mirrors set in gilded frames. Much of the glass was already cracked – there had been no one to replace it for many years past – but the savages had never seen such a sight. There was no guard to oppose or control them. They looked with astonishment at their own reflection. Then one of them struck a mirror with its lance and it shivered. With glee they set about destroying the rest.

There were three glasses in the alcove beside the Emperor, and when only one other remained unbroken Bruce began to fear that if the Galla came near Takla Haymanot he would strike one of them. Neither the Emperor nor his companions had any arms except the knives in their belts. The intruders could murder them all. Bruce and the two Ethiopians rose and stood before the throne to hold the Galla back. The silent Emperor, 'with a gentle movement of his hand', signed to them to have patience. As he did so a prominent citizen who was Gusho's agent in Gondar appeared with a body of young men whom he had armed as a sort of police. The Galla tried to resist, but were overpowered. The Emperor allowed his preserver to kiss his hands and then without another word gave him permission to withdraw.

This was the worst moment of peril. It remained to make peace. The victorious chiefs were not revengeful. The surviving murderers of Joas, all adherents of Michael, were handed over to the dead Emperor's Galla followers, who cut them to pieces and threw the fragments of their bodies into the streets; but this was, at least an excusable atrocity, and there were no others. Michael himself was deposed as Ras and Bitwaded. Then each of the chiefs came to Takla Haymanot to do homage and ask for what he wanted for himself.

The air was full of intrigue, for they were not agreed among themselves. Gusho was accepted as Ras, but Powussen, in discontent, marched off to Begemder, taking Michael with him as a prisoner. In exchange, perhaps, he sent the usurper Susenyos in chains to the Emperor, who made him a slave in his kitchen: after a little time the despised being was hanged for theft there.

The Empress, too, returned to Kusquam, jubilantly welcomed by the people. Fasil made his appearance, as usual after a delay which set the court guessing about his intentions and fearful of them. Bruce met him in the palace and found him in a humorously friendly mood. He pretended that the Scot had promised him a horse in exchange for the famous steed which had been his passport to the source of the Blue Nile. The horse was out of town, said Bruce.

'Well, well,' said Fasil, 'that shall not save you. Tell me where he is and I will send for him and give you the best mule I have.'

'With all my heart,' Bruce answered. 'You will find him, perhaps in the valley of Serbraxos, on the battlefield near the south ford of the river there.'

'You shall have your mule for all that,' said the Galla chief, laughing as they shook hands at parting.

This exchange pleased the Emperor.

'I wish you could tell me, Yagoube,' he said, 'how you reconcile all these people to you. It is a secret which will be far more important to me than to you. There is Gusho, for instance, so proud of his new position that he will scarcely say a civil word to me, yet he talks to you readily enough. And now Fasil has brought me a list of his own servants whom he wants to make officers of mine without giving me a chance to discuss the matter, but as soon as you come into the room he begins joking and pleasant conversation.'

This was a happy note for the ending of Bruce's experience as an Ethiopian courtier. Takla Haymanot was on his throne, safely enough for the moment, though he could not rule as the greater emperors had done. All the leading figures of the country were friendly to the stranger, though they were quarrelling again among themselves. Bruce could feel that he had fulfilled his own promises, so far as this was possible. His main work as an explorer was done. The country was at peace, though uneasily, and there should be few obstacles to a traveller leaving it.

But it was clear enough that there were new crises ahead which might hold him up indefinitely if he stayed longer. Ras Gusho was making trouble between the Emperor and the Empress: he was soon to be arrested and imprisoned. The chief provincial governors were preparing to take his place or to snatch one another's lands. No one felt sure what was going to happen in the northern domains that Michael had lost, or whether the old Ras might not try to assert himself again. Nothing was heard of him, but in the general uncertainty Bruce felt that 'his familiar spirit seemed to preside in the air and pour down mischief' on his country.

As usually happened when he was anxious and depressed, the Scot grew physically ill. He retired to Kusquam, where Princess Esther was living with her mother – the old Empress relied on his medical advice, for she, too, was ill and anxious. There had been plotting against the Emperor in her palace and he had threatened to attack it. The place was soon full of armed men preparing for its defence. Bruce, who was still carrying on some of his duties at court, was almost the only link between Emperor and Empress, and he secured an assurance from Takla Haymanot that Kusquam would not be disturbed.

This seemed to him the best moment for his own departure. The Emperor and Mentwab consented to let him go, though they did their best to delay him. He even parted on good terms with the Ethiopian priests, whose influence he had dreaded so long. His last recorded talk with one of them gives us an idea of Bruce's own views of religion and society.

One of the most respected of the Gondar clergy, Tensa Christos, was with the Empress when he was saying good-bye. This man put to him a question which, he said, he dared to ask only because Bruce was leaving next day. 'You are not a Frank. You think your religion is better than theirs. You say we are nearer the Catholics than you are. Now, what objection have you to our religion, and what is your opinion of it?'

This was precisely the sort of subject which Bruce had tried to avoid since he reached Ethiopia. His answer now had a tactful beginning, but was finally frank enough.

'As far as I am informed, I think well of your faith. It is that of the ancient Greek Church under St Athanasius, the successor of St Mark. If this is so, you cannot have a better, since it is the religion nearest to the Apostles'. No religion teaches a man evil. Certainly yours cannot if you have not corrupted it: if you have, it is no longer the religion of St Athanasius or the Apostles and is therefore liable to error.

'And now let me ask you two questions, Tensa Christos. Does your religion permit a man to marry one sister, to divorce her and marry the other, and then, while keeping the aunt, to marry the niece likewise? Does St Athanasius teach you to marry one, two or three wives, and divorce them as often as you please; to marry others and then go back to the first wives again?'

'No,' said the possibly embarrassed priest.

'Then as Ethiopians do this daily,' continued Bruce, 'you certainly are not living according to the religion of St Athanasius. Now I ask you, if any Christian from our part of the world – not a Frank but one who agreed with you in other things – was to preach against this and such-like practices often seen in Ethiopia, could he live among you, or how would you treat him?'

'He would be stoned to death, like a Frank or a Jesuit,' exclaimed the pro-Catholic Aylo, who was sitting beside the Empress. 'He would not live a week.'

'Yagoube is hard on me,' said Tensa Christos, turning to Mentwab. 'I am sorry to say that our people never will abandon their indulgences for the teachings of any strange priest, however perfect his religion or pure his life might be, or however corrupt their own manners were.'

'In that case, Tensa Christos,' said the Scot, 'do not be too sure that shedding the blood of those Franks, as you call them, may not be criminal in the sight of God. Their religion has at least prevented some from sins that are common here. Yours has not. If the Ethiopians do not need teaching, at least they need a good example. At least these Franks would give them this.'

This was a skilful turn in the argument, since the Empress as

11. The Tissisat Falls

12. At the source of the Blue Nile. *The Priest of the Nile*, Bruce (in Ethiopian costume) and (seated) Shalaka Waldo, with the church of St Michael Gish in the background. (Drawing by Bruce, probably after Balugani, at Parramba.)

well as Aylo would be glad to hear anything favourable to the Roman Catholics, though even she dared not say so. To end the talk before still more awkward questions could be introduced, Bruce crossed the crowded room and stood before the priest.

'Holy father,' he said, 'I have a favour to ask you. Your forgiveness if I have offended you, your blessing now that I am going; and your prayers on my long and dangerous journey through countries of infidels and pagans.'

There was a hum of approval from the courtiers. Tensa Christos himself was surprised.

'Is it possible, Yagoube,' he asked, with tears in his eyes, 'that you believe my prayers can do you good?'

'I should not be a Christian if I had any doubt of the effect of a good man's prayers,' said Bruce, stooping to kiss the priest's hand. As he did so Tensa Christos laid a small iron cross on his bowed head and repeated the Lord's Prayer, with an added 'God bless you'. The Scot made his last obeisance to the Empress and turned to go.

But this atmosphere of ecumenical goodwill was not very well maintained by Bruce himself. 'Twenty greasy monks,' he writes, 'had placed themselves in my way, that they might have the credit of giving me the blessing likewise after Tensa Christos. As I had very little faith in the prayers of these drones, so I had some reluctance to kiss their greasy hands and sleeves; however, in running this disagreeable gauntlet, I gave them my blessing in English. "Lord send you all a halter, as he did to Abba Salama." ' He meant the dead Guardian of the Hour. 'But they, thinking I was recommending them to their patriarch Abba Salama, pronounced at random, with great seeming devotion their "Amen – so be it".'

It was on December 26th, 1771, that he left Kusquam. With him were three Greeks, an old Turkish janissary from Cairo, a Copt who was going to Sennar, and a few Ethiopian servants in charge of the mules which carried their baggage. The old Turk, Hadji Ismael, was the most remarkable character among them. He was a sherif, a descendant of the Prophet Mohammed. Besides having made the

pilgrimage to Mecca, he had convoyed the Abuna from Cairo to
Gondar, and was on his way back to Egypt. Though he had seen
most of the Arab lands, this proud Osmanli had never learned to
speak Arabic well, but he was always ready to say what he thought,
to Bruce, Moslem chieftains or anyone else he felt moved to correct
or advise. He took the place as the explorer's chief assistant on the
way, that Yasin had held on the journey from Arabia to Gondar and
Strates on the expeditions to the Blue Nile.

All the same, this was a feeble party for the beginning of what
was to be the most dangerous and exhausting part of all his travels.
He was to go westwards to reach Ras el Fil, where Yasin was
preparing the way for him, then through the burning Sudanese
lowlands to Sennar on the Blue Nile. From there he would make his
way to the White Nile near modern Khartoum and then partly by
the river bank but largely through desert to Aswan in Egypt, some
1,200 miles in all, the worst parts of the way quite unknown to
European travellers. He refused the Emperor's last-minute offer of
an escort of fifty horsemen at least as far as Ras el Fil, for he believed
that he must move as inconspicuously as possible if he was to escape
the attacks of plundering raiders in the Sudanese borderlands.

From Kusquam they skirted the great green cone of the Hill of
the Sun, which rose behind the palace. At the summit of their path
they looked down on a vast stretch of dark country which seemed
to be a continuous forest, reaching as far as they could see. This was
the steep western wall of the Ethiopian fortress, rocky and broken
by watercourses beneath its screen of trees. It was a formidable
obstacle to travellers or invaders: even in the descent Bruce's party
often could not make more than a mile an hour.

The people of the country seemed unfriendly. A messenger from
the Emperor had passed the party, though they did not see him,
and Bruce thought that he might be encouraging their inhospitality
in the hope of turning them back to Gondar. As a precaution against
attack, however, he put on his coat of mail and rode alone, some
way ahead of the rest. It was already a borderland of mixed races.
There were a sect of dark Jews who claimed to be descendants of the

prophet Jonah – and would not eat fish because of their ancestor's obligation to a whale. There were Moslems and Christians and the pagan negro Shankalla. Passing strangers reported that a thousand Christians, Moslems and pagans were waiting for the caravan at a hill pass, and that the Shankalla would burn down the house of Confu, Esther's son, for which Bruce was making.

Confu's house at Cherkin stood on a hill-top above a forest market-place, 'which seemed a beautiful lawn laid out for pleasure, shaded with fine old trees, of an enormous height and size, and watered by a small, but very limpid, brook, running over beds of pebbles as white as snow'. The large house, looking far over the forest, stood on the edge of a precipice. It was built of canes, so bound together that neither wind nor rain could break through. The walls and floors of its state rooms were covered with carpets.

In this romantic setting Bruce was to take a second farewell which he would remember as an idyll of friendship, and enjoyment. For he found not Confu, his friend, but Princess Esther herself, with Takla Maryam, the beautiful daughter of the Emperor's secretary, to whom she had proposed to marry her Yagoube. Esther explained, perhaps half seriously, that since her husband had been carried off, a prisoner, to Begemder she had decided to go with the explorer to Jerusalem, to pray for Michael at the Holy Sepulchre, to die and be buried there.

This elegiac note was soon forgotten when Confu arrived with Engedan and a company of courtiers. 'There was nothing but re-joicing on all sides. Seven ladies, relations and companions of Esther, came with Confu; and I confess this to have been one of the happiest moments of my life.'

Confu had come to hunt. The countryside was full of big game, not only elephants, which were the chief quarry, but also rhino-ceroses, fierce buffaloes and lions. Men who wished to join in the chase had gathered to meet Confu at Cherkin. 'He and Engedan, from the moment they arrived, had been overlooking, from the precipice, their servants training and managing their horses in the market-place below.' Bruce would have been happy enough to stay in this enchanted mountain with Esther, but he could not resist the opportunity to join in a sport which he describes with enthusiasm.

'On the 6th (of January 1772), an hour before day, after a hearty breakfast, we mounted on horseback, to the number of about thirty, belonging to Confu. But there was another body, both of horse and foot, which made hunting the elephant their particular business. These men dwell constantly in the woods, and know very little of the use of bread, living entirely upon the flesh of the beasts they kill, chiefly that of the elephant or rhinoceros. They are exceedingly thin, light and agile, both on horseback and foot; are very swarthy, though few of them black; none of them woolly headed, and all of them have European features.'

Two men, 'absolutely naked, without any rag or covering at all about them', rode on each horse, one to guide the animal, over rough ground and among trees and bushes whose branches might have caught a clothed horseman and dragged him down, the other carrying a Slav broadsword brought from Trieste, sharp as a razor, but with part of the naked blade wrapped in cord so that it could safely be supported in the right hand while the left held the hilt.

When one of these pairs of hunters found an elephant feeding, the horse was brought as close to its head as was safely possible while the rider cried out, 'I am so-and-so. This is my horse whose name is so-and-so. I killed your father in one district and your grandfather in another. Now I have come to kill you – compared with them you are nothing but an ass.' This was to enrage the elephant, who, irritated by the noise if not by the threat, would try to seize the riders with its trunk.

The horse would be made to circle the great beast, which would move round till the swordsman could drop to the ground just behind it. While the elephant's attention was still on the horse the razor-sharp sword would slash into its heel. If the hunters' movements were not quick and agile enough they and their horse might, indeed, be torn to pieces or trampled into the ground. But usually the elephant's Achilles tendon was cut, or at least so weakened that it snapped under the strain of movement. The swordsman remounted and the pair galloped off. Though still strong and trumpeting, the animal was fixed to the spot where it stood till the huntsmen could bring it down with their spears.

This was the truly skilled and daring work in elephant hunting. The part of Bruce and his friends in this sport was not so glorious. It was to finish off animals already made almost helpless. It seemed less glorious still when a female elephant who had a calf with her was attacked. The mother was maimed; the young one, 'about the size of an ass, but round, big-bellied, and heavily made', had been allowed to escape. But when the hunters gathered for the kill the calf 'came out of the thicket apparently in great anger, running upon the horses and men with all the violence it was master of'. Bruce was astonished and touched to see the little beast's defence of its wounded mother and tried to spare it. 'The calf made several rude attacks upon me, which I avoided without difficulty, but I am happy to this day in the reflection that I did not strike it.' However, its attacks were so violent that it was finally thrust through.

The readiness of a young animal to come to its mother's rescue, not by instinct, he insists, but by deliberate choice, seemed to the explorer much more extraordinary than other African wonders of which he had to tell. Yet, as he noted, Englishmen who would not believe that Ethiopians could eat raw beef never questioned this story.

From their day with the elephants the hunting party turned to rhinoceroses – Bruce brought one down by stunning it with a bullet that chipped its horn, which was made into a cup[1] – and then to wild boars and buffaloes. One man showed an unexpected enthusiasm for the sport. He was Ammonios, who had served with Bruce at Sarbakusa. An elderly though courageous warrior, he spent most of his leisure in reading the Bible and would seldom speak of anything else. 'He was tall and awkwardly made: slow in speech and motion, so much as even to excite ridicule . . . in a word, as pedantic and grave in his manners as it is possible to

[1] Now at Broomhall.

express.' However, he had made up his mind to see something of hunting, as indeed he did.

'Whether the buffalo found Ammonios, or Ammonios the buffalo, is what we could never get him to explain to us.' The animal had been wounded: in turn it gored Ammonios's horse and brought him to the ground. It tore his cloak to pieces, and this gave him just time enough to get behind a large tree, and then behind another while the angry animal pursued him. Engedan and Confu watched, laughing, as the old soldier skipped hurriedly from tree to tree, 'peeping first one way and then another, to see which way the beast would turn. And well he might be on his guard; for the animal was absolutely mad, tossing up the ground with his feet both before and behind.'

Bruce was anxious as well as amused. 'This will be an ugly joke tonight,' he said to Confu, 'if we bring home that man's corpse, killed in the very midst of us, while we were looking on.'

The tree where Ammonios had taken refuge grew close to a river. Bruce called to him to throw himself into the water, while he himself attacked the buffalo with a spear. The old soldier, who could not swim, had to support himself on the roots of a tree that reached into the river till the buffalo was finally shot.

The hunt was over. Ammonios would say nothing beyond repeating a scriptural phrase, 'He that loveth danger shall perish in it'. But when Esther blamed her son for his laughter at the old soldier's suffering, Ammonios, who was fond of the boy, could not bear to hear him scolded, 'so that all resolved itself into mirth and joke'. But time was growing short, for messages from the Emperor and Empress urged Esther and her son to return to Gondar even if Bruce could not be persuaded to go back with them. He spent another week with his friends, whom he was never to see or hear from again, and then set off for Ras el Fil.

Yasin had sent his camels to carry his baggage into the hot lowlands which the Ethiopians called 'Hell'. It was only very slowly that they could make their way along difficult paths and through thick bush till they came to the hill village of Sancaho, which had once marked the Ethiopian frontier. Its people were negro Moslems who had a chief of their own, though they were subject to the Governor of Ras el Fil. This man, the Erbab Gimbaro, was a formidable being, taller even than the traveller himself and capable, it was said, of killing an elephant with one blow of his spear. He had been with the army at Sarbakusa, and Bruce, who had treated him well then, now sent the Erbab a message asking for food and also for two camels, since his own were too heavily laden. He was surprised to be answered by the chief's young son.

'My father salutes you,' said the boy. 'If you eat what he eats, you shall be welcome.'

'What does he eat?' asked Bruce.

'Elephant killed yesterday; and as for the camels you ask for, he has none. Elephants are his camels and rhinoceroses are his mules.'

This was an insult. In Ethiopia no Christian would eat meat killed by a Moslem, and there were certainly camels at Sancaho. It might be dangerous to the travellers to allow themselves to be treated with contempt, since this could encourage the negroes to attack them on their way. Gimbaro's village stood on the top of a precipitous hill, an *amba*, even steeper than Confu's at Cherkin, but Bruce decided that he must assert his authority.

He put a pair of pistols in his girdle and had a gun in his hand. With him were two servants, 'each carrying a large ship-blunderbuss' and armed with pistols as well. The path wound between great stones, placed to shelter archers or musketeers. There were no defenders, but the way was so steep that the three men had to pull one another over its most difficult stretches.

At the top they came into a room fifty feet long. 'It was all hung round with elephants' heads and trunks, with skeletons of the heads of some rhinoceroses and of monstrous hippopotami, and also several heads of the giraffa.' Lion skins were spread on the floor like carpets, and on one of these stood Gimbaro, naked except for a loincloth, 'the largest man I ever remembered to have seen, perfectly black, flat-nosed, thick-lipped and woolly-haired, a picture of those Cannibal giants we read of as inhabiting enchanted castles in the fairy tales'.

Perhaps the chief was as startled by the appearance of the Scots giant with his gun and attendant blunderbusses as Bruce was by this vision of legendary barbarity. He began to make excuses. He had not known whom the message came from, he said. His own reply about elephants and rhinoceroses had only been a joke. But Bruce would not be appeased so easily.

'Your message to me was the language of a rebel,' he declared. 'Are you willing to be declared in rebellion?' If he did not receive camels and bread at once in payment of tribute that Gimbaro owed him as the former Governor of Ras el Fil he would send a message to Confu – who had resumed the governorship on Bruce's departure – denouncing the Erbab as a traitor.

This threat was enough. The black giant provided everything that was asked of him. He said, too, that he would send out men to make sure that the travellers would not be attacked on their way to Yasin. Some of his advisers who were with him begged for a general reconciliation, and they all ate bread and drank beer together as a sign of peace-making. Next morning the Erbab brought breakfast to Bruce's tent and, after 'two or three glasses of strong spirits' won a promise that when the Scot returned that way he would spend a week at Sancaho hunting elephant and rhinoceros.

There were six days of hard and slow travel before the little party came to the miserable village that was the centre of the narrow frontier province of Ras el Fil, which took its name (meaning the Elephant's Head) from the shape of a neighbouring hill. Today the place is Gallabat, on the Sudanese side of the border, but Bruce knew it as Hor Cacamoot, which he translated 'the Valley of the Shadow of Death' – 'A bad omen for weak and wandering travellers as we were, and so far from home that there seemed to be but One that could bring us thither. We trusted in Him and He did deliver us.'[1]

[1] In fact, Bruce was exceedingly ill at Gallabat. Under the appalling heat (it reached 114°F in the shade) he developed a dangerous dysentery, cured

The travellers were now to set out for Sennar on the Blue Nile, the capital of the Fung Kingdom, which included most of the territory of the modern Sudanese Republic, but Bruce did not propose to make for this city directly. Yasin and he had planned a route which seemed to them the safest in a disturbed country. Beyond Ras el Fil lay the Fung province of Atbara whose Governor, Sheikh Fidele (or Fadl), lived at Teawa, known nowadays as Gedaref. Between them he and Yasin controlled most of the declining trade that still passed between the Sudan and Ethiopia. Fidele had insisted that Bruce must pass through his town, well to the north of the direct route to Sennar, if he was to avoid danger from raiding tribesmen, and messengers had been sent to Sennar asking that the rulers there should send guides to Teawa to meet him. His plan for this journey through a country quite unknown to any living European was as complete and prudent as it could be. But at Yasin's village he was given a disconcerting warning by an Arab sheikh with whom he had had friendly dealings at Gondar.

'I know Fidele well,' said this man, 'and I believe your chief danger will be from him. He has been a murderer and thief all his days – a man without fear of God, neither Moslem, Christian or Pagan.' So far as men were concerned, however, he believed Fidele to be a coward. The most important question for Bruce might be whether the Sheikh of Atbara was afraid of Yasin. If he was not, or if he believed that Yasin would take no further interest in the traveller after he left Ethiopia the long years' journey to the Nile might end for ever at Teawa.

This was alarming. Yasin admitted that, believing Fidele's promises, he had taken no special step to safeguard Bruce once he reached Teawa, where the King of Sennar's servants were to meet him. It happened that a group of donkey-drivers carrying salt into the Sudan had attached themselves to Bruce's little caravan for protection. It was arranged that an Arab messenger should travel

only by a negro medicine-man's herbs and Yasin's care of him. It was two months before he could go farther.

among them, going not directly to Fidele's town but to a camp of Arabs in the hills near it. This man would come into Teawa after Bruce had arrived there and if he found him in danger would ride off on a swift camel to Yasin. Soliman, a capable black Moslem who had carried messages to Sennar for Bruce and the Emperor, agreed to travel there again with the party and report to Gondar on the explorer's reception.

The last march out of Ethiopia could now begin. Yasin had provided food for the journey to Teawa, and something equally necessary in the half-desert country they were to pass through, two *girbas* for carrying water. These were ox-skins, 'squared when raw and the edges sewed together very artificially by a double seam, much resembling that upon the best English cricket-balls'. They were greased on the outside to prevent the water from oozing through or evaporating under the tropical sun. Each could contain about sixty gallons, and two of them made a camel's load.

At the frontier Bruce said farewell to Yasin, who had so often been his chief support since they crossed the Red Sea together. The girbas were filled in a river bed. The whole company repeated together the Moslem prayer for peace. Then on March 18th, 1772, the travellers passed from Ethiopia into the Kingdom of the Fung.

16

————◦•◉•◦————

Faithless Fidele

The Fung Kingdom of Sennar was a strange and mysterious land. Indeed, some things in its history are still uncertain; Bruce himself was the first traveller to give a reasonably clear account of it to the West. A few Europeans had, indeed, visited it before him, some of them on the way to Ethiopia, but these travellers had not been fortunate. If Sennar was remembered in Europe, it was for the murder of the French envoy to Gondar, Du Roule, in 1705.

Yes, this was a land with a very long history. It had been the 'Ethiopia' of the classical writers and the Bible. Early Pharaohs had conquered part of it: its kings, in return, had briefly conquered ancient Egypt and its people had preserved a shadow of the old Egyptian civilization and religion long after Egypt itself became a Roman province. Its rulers were converted to Christianity only within a century of the time when Egypt fell to the Mohammedan Arabs.

Isolated from the rest of the civilized world by deserts and the Nile cataracts which prevented the great river from becoming a regular means of communication, Christian states had maintained themselves in the Sudan throughout most of our Middle Ages. When, under pressure from their Moslem neighbours, their religion and their special civilization finally collapsed into a welter of tribal sheikhdoms and feudal baronies it was from black Africa that its new ruling race came.

Bruce believed that the first Fung were Shilluks, long-legged pagan fishermen and river pirates from the White Nile who moved in cane-built canoes so light that one man could carry three of them if he had to pass from stream to stream. Others have thought that their leaders were Hamites from the Red Sea coastlands north of Ethiopia. In any case the armies which overran the country were chiefly black men from the pagan south. The kingdom they made was a curious confederation of races and little states. In the south and in the capital, Sennar, its dominant people were black Nilotes. They were formally Moslems, but their habits and traditions showed traces of a pagan, even a remotely Pharaonic, past. In the north and east were Arabs and Hamites, some of whom were tribal nomads, others the more or less settled subjects of tiny kingdoms along the Nile. A hereditary chieftain (Wed Ageeb, as Bruce calls him) stood between these brown men and the black court at Sennar, raising taxes for the King and controlling the smaller chiefs.

It could be said that this kingdom lived by flies, which were at once the greatest curse of its nomad herdsmen and a main foundation of its rulers' authority and wealth. Bruce was the first Westerner to describe the insect, which the Ethiopians knew as *tsaltsalya* and the Arabs as *zimb* or *seriut*. This was not the tse-tse, whose characteristics and effects another of his name[1] was to examine a century later. It was, he says, a little larger than a bee, with a hair-like triple proboscis about a quarter of an inch long. As soon as the tropical rains began, great swarms of these flies appeared wherever the earth of the Sudanese plain and the Ethiopian borderland was fertile and loamy. When their buzzing was heard cattle and camels ran wildly to escape it. The flies attacked these animals to suck their blood and infected them with a disease, so that 'the body, head and legs swell out into huge bosses which break and putrefy, to the certain destruction of the creature'.

To avoid this the tribesmen were forced to leave their pasture-lands – largely forest or brush, for their beasts ate tree-leaves rather than grass – and move into the desert, where there was some growth in the wet season, but the flies could not breed. In these movements they had to pass through certain points where the Fung

[1] Sir David Bruce (1855–1931).

kings and the Wed Agib placed their armies and compelled the nomads to pay tribute in beasts or gold.

On the whole, this scheme of government seems to have worked fairly well for more than two centuries, but in Bruce's day it was beginning to break down. There was rebellion and civil war in the north, particularly in the Bayuda Desert, which fills the great loop of the Nile, where the northward-flowing river turns south-westward, then north again. Travellers and traders between Sennar and Egypt had normally crossed this loop, ferrying twice across the Nile, but because of the Bayuda unrest Bruce was to be the first European to attempt a far more difficult route through the Eastern Desert to Aswan.

Farther south the old balance of the Fung Kingdom had been upset by its own conquests. Its boundaries had scarcely stretched beyond the White Nile until, in a long war, the great western province of Kordofan had been conquered. But the victorious general, Mohammed Abu el Kaylak, was not properly one of the Fung. Through his success he had become the King's vizier, with an army of his own. When Bruce arrived in the Sudan, Abu el Kaylak was in Kordofan, acting quite independently of the King. He had left his brother, Sheikh Adelan, behind him as his deputy: he, too, paid very little attention to the King's wishes. Indeed, there was never again to be a strong sovereign in Sennar. Half a century after Bruce's visit the divided kingdom was to collapse before a small disorderly Turkish–Egyptian army.

On the first part of his Sudanese journey Bruce had to find his way through a half-desert country. Large parts of it, indeed, were covered with scrubby forest whose leaves, after the annual rain, would feed the camels and cattle of nomad tribesmen. But in March most of the streams and water-holes were almost dry. The tribesmen were moving north in their annual round of migration to find new pasture or to escape the flies that would destroy their beasts. Here the Fung Kingdom had lost control over these nomads, partly owing to the misgovernment of Sheikh Fidele, to whose town Bruce was travelling. Between Ras el Fil and Teawa there was scarcely a human settlement. Villages which had existed had been wrecked by nomad raiders who had cleared their crops and left their people to starve. The first watering-place his party reached, an artificial reservoir, was almost empty, but crowded with thousands of birds, weak with hunger and thirst and easily knocked down by the donkey-drivers, but useless for food, since they were 'reduced to skeletons'.

The woods were full of lions and hyenas, desperate enough in their hunger to attack men and asses, so that Bruce was forced to fire on them, though he was anxious to avoid the sound of gunshots which might draw the attention of plundering tribesmen. In the distance he had a magnificent view of Ethiopian mountainsides streaming with flame, where nomads had set light to dry tree-leaves and grass, partly to promote fresh growth after the rains, partly to destroy the breeding-places of the flies.

Soon the party had their first experience of the *simoom*, the hot wind of the desert. There was first a haze, 'a sort of blush upon the air', then a blast of heat which seemed to dry or poison the lungs, though the breeze was actually quite a light one. The only protection was to lie down pressing one's face into the earth. Even so it caused such headache and exhaustion that, after a march of only five miles, they had not strength enough to pitch a tent.

Next day they were horrified to find that their girbas were empty, though still distended. It seemed that the intense heat of the simoom might have evaporated their water. At the same time the weary party realized that they had lost their way in a wood. There was immense alarm: most of the travellers began to think that they might die of thirst, though, as Bruce notes rather scornfully, it was only four hours since they had drunk at the watering-place.

It was twelve hours more, however, before they reached the next well, having found their road again. The majority rushed to fill themselves with muddy, stinking water: Bruce washed and gargled to cool himself before drinking. But the sudden indulgence killed two of the party.

They had now reached a stretch of real desert without trees.

They halted in the remains of a village whose people had starved to death the year before, when their crops had failed or been destroyed by nomad raiders.

'We encamped among the bones of the dead; no space could be found free of them.' But at last they were close to a river bed that still held some water, within a day's march of Sheikh Fidele's little town. It had taken them a week to cover sixty-five miles between Yasin's village and Teawa, which itself was a poor place of some 1,200 men and their families, 'naked, miserable and despicable'. With only twenty-eight armed horsemen for its defence, it lay very much at the mercy of nomad Arabs, who, if they attacked its cornfields, might reduce this capital of a large province to starvation as disastrous as that of the village of dead bones.

Bruce found Sheikh Fidele himself sitting on the floor of a large mud-brick hall. An empty throne stood beside him – a symbol of the sovereignty of the King of Sennar. The black sheikh was demonstratively studying the Koran and pretended to be surprised by the travellers' arrival, though his deputy had, in fact, come out to meet them and lead them ceremoniously into the town.

Fidele seemed prepared to be friendly. He admired Bruce's size and strength, 'introduced some loose hints about Abyssinian women', and said that such a great man should not have had to suffer by travelling through a difficult, dangerous country. The explorer must go and rest, he said, in a house that was ready for him. This was close to the river, since Bruce had declared that he needed water for his religious ablutions – the Scot's real purpose was to be on the edge of the town so that messengers from Yasin or Sennar might reach him without being seen.

When Bruce rose to go there was a more surprising speech.

'You do not realize what dangers you have passed through on your journey here,' said Fidele. 'Your Yasin of Ras el Fil is the worst thief in Ethiopia. He had placed Arab tribesmen on your way to murder you. But you have a clean heart and clean hands. God saw their plots – and I may say that I, too, had a part in defeating them.'

Since it was Fidele himself who had insisted in his letters to

Yasin that the route to Sennar by Teawa was the only safe one, and
since in these messages he had called Yasin his brother and friend,
all this had an ominous sound. However, Bruce went off to his
riverside room, and dishes of meat were sent to him there. The
donkey-drivers joined in the feast. When it was over one young
man whispered to Bruce in Arabic.

'Fidele is a devil! The Sheikh of Atbara is the Devil himself.'

Bruce consulted his adviser, Soliman, who had taken his messages to Sennar and had been with him at his interview with Fidele.
The man declared that the Sheikh was a traitor who had deliberately deceived Yasin. In fact, it began to look as if they had fallen
into a trap at Teawa. There should have been messengers there to
meet them from Sennar and from the friendly Sheikh of Beyla,
half-way to the Fung capital, but none appeared except the Arab
who was to carry back news of their progress to Ras el Fil. Secretly
they sent him off with a message and made up their minds to wait
in their retreat, seeing as little of Fidele as possible.

However, the usual presents had to be made to the Sheikh.
Bruce, with Soliman and the old Turk, Hadji Ismael, carried them
to him – 'a large piece of blue Indian cotton cloth with gold flowers,
a silk and cotton sash, two pounds of nutmegs and ten pounds of
pepper'. These seemed to be well received and Bruce asked to be
sent off to Sennar as soon as possible and to have camels to carry
his baggage.

The camels were a fortnight's journey away, said Fidele. They
had been sent into the desert to be safe from the flies. However,
that, in itself, would not hold up the travellers: they could not
begin their journey till permission came from Sennar. He himself
was just going to write to the capital to ask for this, but business
went slowly at Sennar and there were disturbances on the road there.

This was surprising, Bruce declared, since in a letter to Yasin,
Fidele had asked that the party should come quickly to Teawa,
where everything they needed was ready for them. The Sheikh
lifted his hands in astonishment. Never (or at any rate not for
months back) had he written to Yasin on this subject, he protested.

If Bruce had indeed seen such a letter it must have been a forgery.
Knowing that the explorer had much gold with him, Yasin must
have produced it to get him into the desert, where he could be
robbed and murdered.

This was too much for Soliman. 'Have not your servants, Ibrahim
and Nasser, lived with us at Ras el Fil for weeks together as bearers
of these letters?' he asked furiously. 'Was I not speaking to them
this morning about the letters? Call them in and question them
here. What will Yasin think when he hears what you have said
about him?'

Fidele's voice grew suddenly soft and soothing. He was very
busy, he said, and might have forgotten one or two letters among
the many he had to deal with. 'But Yasin is my brother and I will
do everything for him or you that you could wish. Stay only this
week and if my camels do not come I shall send to the Arabs for
some, for this is the King's business.'

Bruce was not entirely reassured, but at least he could hope. A
day or two later he was called to the Sheikh as physician. Fidele
had been drinking and asked for the favourite digestive remedy of
the country, a vomit. Bruce's ipecacuanha did its work so quickly
and gently that the Sheikh was delighted. Soon he was looking for
the same treatment for two of his wives.

This was an important opportunity. The friendship of Fidele's
harem could be very useful to Bruce. One of the wives was a
daughter of Adelan, the powerful Vice-Vizier of Sennar. She had
been married to Fidele largely in order that she might report on his
doings to her father: if she was well disposed towards the traveller,
Sennar was likely to learn of anything that happened to him – and
her husband would know this.

The help of women had done much for Bruce in Ethiopia: it
could be equally valuable in the Sudan. 'Being in the prime of life,
of no ungracious figure, having an accidental knack, which is not a
trifle, of putting on the dress and speaking the language easily and
gracefully,' he was to write, 'I cultivated with the utmost assiduity
the friendship of the fair sex, by the most modest, respectful, distant

attendance and obsequiousness in public, abating just as much of
that in private as suited their humour and inclinations.'

The prospect of his meeting with the ladies of Teawa took, at
first, an unexpected turn. He found Fidele sitting and smoking –
'I suppose meditating mischief, for he had no other apparent employment.'

Things were in a difficult state in Sennar, the Sheikh explained,
since the Vizier Abu el Kaylak and his brother Adelan were both on
bad terms with the King. Bruce could not go on to the city at once.
He did not want to go back to Ethiopia. Why should he not settle
down in Teawa? If he would become a Mohammedan, 'which is
the only true religion', he could have Fidele's daughter for his wife
and become his deputy in Atbara. The Sheikh intended to make the
pilgrimage to Mecca next year. Then his son-in-law could become
Governor of the province while Fidele, on his return from Mecca,
would look for an appointment at Sennar suitable for an old
man.

This proposal may have been made seriously enough by a
puzzled barbarian uncertain of his own future. The gigantic traveller
with his collection of firearms and his followers who knew how to
use them could have been a useful deputy in a district where no
equal armament existed. But Bruce laughed at the offer. He could
have had any honour he liked in Ethiopia, he said, among people
who were Christian, 'yet I never would consent either to stay with
them or marry among them. What then could be my inducement to
marry here, to change my religion, and live in a country where there
is nothing but poverty, misery, famine, fear and dependence?'

Though still impossible, the Sheikh's plan may not have seemed
quite so fantastic a little later. Bruce was led into the harem, where
he found two wives both of whom were elderly and 'never had been
handsome'. Many slaves attended them. He explained to Fidele
that, according to the best medical practice, he must be free to ask
his patients a number of questions 'which if you choose to hear you
may, but no person else must'.

'What has he to do with us or our physician?' demanded the

elder wife. 'His only business is to pay you money when you have
made us well.'

'What would become of him?' asked Adelan's daughter, 'if we
were to be very ill? He would starve for lack of people to prepare
his meat for him.'

'Aye, and his drink, too, which he likes better than meat,' said
the first wife.

Fidele said that the traveller could ask what he liked – he did
not want to listen. 'I only wish to God you would cure them or
make them dumb altogether. Then they would not tease me with
their illnesses any longer: a sick woman is plague enough for the
devil.'

He took up a switch and drove the slaves out of the door, but
among them was 'a genteel female figure covered from head to
foot' whom he pulled in with his hand as the others left. 'Come in,
Aiscach,' he said and left the room.

The wives took their ipecacuanha as successfully as Fidele had
done. While he was giving the medicine Bruce noticed that the
veiled girl had uncovered her head and face. 'Soon after one of the
slaves, her attendant, as in play, pulled off the remaining part of
the veil that covered her. I was astonished at the sight of so much
beauty. . . . The rest of her dress was a blue shift which hung
loosely about her. She was the tallest of the middle size, and not yet
fifteen years of age; her whole features faultless, they might have
served alone for the study of a painter all his life if he was in search
of absolute beauty.' She was brown in colour, for her mother, the
elder wife, was an Arab.

This was Fidele's daughter. The mother noticed Bruce's
admiration.

'If Aiscach was ill,' she said, 'you would take better care of her
than of either of us.'

'If the lovely Aiscach was ill,' Bruce answered, 'I feel I should
myself be so much affected as not to be able to attend her at all.'

The women laughed. A voice spoke, surprisingly, in Amharic.
'Send for Yasin and your Ras el Fil horsemen. Carry her away with

you to Ethiopia. I'll go with you willingly and, I'll swear, so will she.'

It was an Ethiopian slave. When the medical visit was over she and Aiscach went to the door with Bruce. Swathed in her veil again, the beauty asked:

'Shall we not see you tomorrow?'

Bruce had won the support of Fidele's women: the Christian slave was a faithful messenger between them. But next day the Sheikh himself demanded treatment again, and before the traveller left him he showed the real reason for his failure to open the way to Sennar. He knew (he said) that when Bruce left Ras el Fil he had 2,000 ounces of gold in the boxes that were said to hold instruments, besides cloth of gold and other valuables. He asked for 50 ounces (or 500 piastres). If these were given him Bruce could leave in two days' time: if not, he would take them by force and get rid of his visitor in the easiest way.

'Well done! That is out; it is what I knew was in your heart,' said Bruce. 'But I have not three ounces of gold. Search all my cases and boxes – you can have all the gold you find there. The cloth of gold is a present from the Ethiopian Emperor to the King of Sennar. There is also a present for Sheikh Adelan and some trifles for other officials there. If you think these gifts are too great, you can take part of them and explain to the King and Adelan what you have done. But you will get nothing from me by force. I am not a girl or a child. I am well armed and have brave men with me. Try your force when you please. I dare say you will keep yourself out of danger so that you can boast of your brave doings to the King of Sennar.'

After this defiance the travellers could only remain in their riverside house with their weapons cleaned and loaded in case of an attack. They were still waiting for news of support from Sennar or Ras el Fil – as it happened, Bruce's own messengers had been slow in reaching Adelan and Yasin. A messenger did come from the Sheikh of Beyla. Bruce had given medicine to this chieftain, who was full of gratitude and had heard of his arrival at Teawa. It was arranged that a highly respected mullah – a Moslem theologian and lawyer – should come to the town. In such a man's presence Fidele could be expected to do nothing violent. The Sheikh of Beyla was also to call for help from Sennar.

Matters were coming to a crisis, however. When Soliman was sent to Fidele to complain about another threat of attack the Sheikh hinted that if Bruce's man would join in killing his master he would have a share in the spoils. Soliman pretended not to understand this suggestion, and Fidele sent him off with a demand that the Scot should bring him medicine again the next evening.

Bruce was suspicious. Friday was a festival day when Moslems avoided taking medicine and his patient had just proposed to murder him. He decided to go armed to the Sheikh's house and to take four companions with him. He had 'a small Brescian blunderbuss about 22 inches in the barrel which had a joint in the stock so that it folded double'.[1] This weapon could be hung from a belt under his left arm. It was completely concealed under the wide Arab burnous that he wore. Besides it he took a pair of pistols and a knife in his girdle. The Turk, Hadji Ismael, Soliman and two servants also carried firearms and swords. Thus prepared they set out as the night was falling.

Bruce left his companions in the courtyard of the house and was taken to Fidele alone. The Sheikh sat by himself on a broad sofa. He was, or pretended to be, drunk – either way this seemed dangerous.

'You are alone, are you?' he asked, as he puffed at his pipe. 'Have you brought what is needed?'

Bruce said that his servants were at the door with the vomit Fidele had asked for.

'Damn you and your vomit!' cried the Sheikh angrily. 'I want money, not poison.'

'I cannot give you either,' said Bruce. 'You should drink some warm water to clear your stomach, let your head cool, and then lie down and rest. I shall see you tomorrow morning.'

[1] It is preserved at Broomhall.

Fidele pointed to a stain on the floor. 'That is the blood of a king,' he said. 'Badi [the father of the reigning King of Sennar] was killed by my father in this room. You have twenty thousand piastres in gold, I hear. If you do not give me two thousand before you leave tonight, I shall put you to death with my own hand.'

A sword was lying beside him on the sofa. He drew it and threw the scabbard into the middle of the room. Tucking up the sleeve of his shirt above his elbow like a butcher, he exclaimed, 'I am waiting for your answer!'

At this point Bruce, too, made his threatening gesture. He threw off his burnous and held the little blunderbuss in his hand. 'This is my answer,' he said. 'I am not a man to die like a beast by the hand of a drunkard. Do not stir from your sofa or you shall die!'

Fidele heard the click of the joint in the stock of the blunderbuss as it was straightened. He thought Bruce had cocked his weapon and was going to fire at once. He dropped his sword and threw himself back on his sofa, crying that his threat had only been a jest, and then calling for his servants to come to him.

'If one of your men comes near me,' said Bruce, 'I shall blow you to pieces. None of them must enter this room till my servants are let in. They are at the gate, armed, and will break in at once if they hear me fire.'

It was Fidele's women who appeared first, and they opened the door for Bruce's companions, each with a blunderbuss in his hand and pistols in his girdle. Even when the Sheikh's servants appeared, this group were far too strong for them. Fidele, still huddled on his sofa, continued to declare that it was all a joke. Bruce and his men withdrew, making their way through dark passages into the dark street beyond.

At their house they found the Sheikh of Beyla's messenger, who told them that the mullah had arrived in the town and would be sitting with Fidele when he held a law-court next morning. Bruce and his men should come to this session and wait to hear what was said. Exhausted and a little reassured, the traveller fell asleep, but

he was wakened at midnight by Aiscach's Ethiopian slave with a
warning from the ladies of a new plot.

Fidele was determined to take his revenge for what had happened
that night, she said. He had just received news that one of the
Sennar generals, Ibrahim, had been defeated and wounded in a
fight with an Arab tribe. He had written at once to Ibrahim, saying
that he had in Teawa a white doctor (Bruce) who could even
bring a dead man to life and whose companions, skilled in the use
of firearms, could help to conquer the tribesmen. To obtain this
reinforcement, however, Ibrahim would have to send a body of
armed men strong enough to overpower the doctor and his followers as they slept, chain them with Fidele's help, and carry them
away. The ladies promised all the aid they could give, but said that
the traveller must be prepared for an attack by 'many wild men',
quite ready to kill him if he resisted.

The slave was sent off with thanks and presents for her mistresses. In spite of this latest proof of Fidele's malignant ingenuity,
Bruce fell soundly asleep again and woke refreshed. 'Though my
affairs had not the most prosperous appearance,' he writes, 'I felt a
calmness of mind to which I had been an utter stranger ever since
I left Ras el Fil.'

He set out with Soliman and Hadji Ismael for Fidele's court. The
mullah was there, a small, dark old man, worn and hollow-eyed. 'If
holy, we could not say he was the beauty of holiness.' He was said
to have worked miracles, 'and, more than once in his life to have
been honoured with the conversation of angels and spirits and, at
times, to have called the devil into his presence and reproved
him. . . . I understood afterwards he was much addicted to the
use of opium, to the effects of which he probably was indebted for
his conversation with spirits.' This is an unkind reflection to come
from Bruce, whom the mullah's wisdom served remarkably well –
in his scepticism of saints in general he had sent a message to the
holy man by the Sheikh of Beyla's servant promising a present if the
little caravan escaped from Teawa.

A second, younger holy man sat with Fidele. He was a sherif, wearing the green turban of a descendant of the Prophet, and was so highly respected that when the nomad Arabs burned buildings and crops in Atbara his house alone was spared. He had made the pilgrimage to Mecca and remembered the British ships at Jidda.

When this man saw Ismael's green turban, tattered though it and his other clothes were by months of travel, he rose and embraced the old Turk, his fellow sherif. The mullah did the same. The dignity of Bruce and his party was properly assured. The mullah asked if Bruce was the Frank he had heard of in Sennar, whom the King and Adelan expected there. Fidele tried to deny that this could be so, and the mullah turned to Bruce himself.

'Sheikh,' he said, 'did you come from Ethiopia? Have you letters for Sennar?'

This was the traveller's opportunity. He had come from Ethiopia, he said, with letters for the King from the Emperor, from the Sherif of Mecca and from Ali Bey of Egypt. 'Yet contrary to faith observed even in pagan nations, I am here detained by Sheikh Fidele, who last night attempted to murder me in his own house because I would not pay him two thousand piastres.'

'That is not true,' stammered the Sheikh.

'Every word of it is as true as that book is the word of God!' exclaimed Ismael, pointing to the Koran which lay in the sherif's lap. He turned to Fidele. 'Look at my turban,' said he. 'Do you call me a liar?'

'It was the Christian who lied,' said Fidele. The whole incident had been a joke, he explained to the mullah.

'The joke was surely over for you when you threw away your sword and called to your servants for help,' said Soliman.

'Should I have let myself be shot by an infidel?' asked Fidele. 'He pointed a pistol at me.'

The Sheikh had given his case away. 'I can see your inmost thoughts,' said Bruce weightily. 'Did you not send a message to Sheikh Ibrahim not twelve hours ago asking him to seize me in my sleep and carry me off to heal his wounded men? Was that a joke, too?'

It was the mullah's turn to speak. 'All this is very bad behaviour,' said he. 'If a man makes jokes with drawn swords, he may kill. You must send the hakim away. You can get camels for him from the Arabs. Men like him have no money. There are many of them wandering about the earth. They are dervishes, studying the herbs and curing diseases.'

'There is the truth, God bless it!' said Bruce triumphantly. 'I am a dervish – a poor man but innocent.'

'No one would hurt Yagoube that knew him,' said Hadji Ismael.

'Yagoube el Hakim, that is the name I heard in Sennar,' said the mullah. 'One of Mohammed Abu el Kaylak's officers is lying ill there and has been asking for him. You must send him forward.'

Fidele declared at last that the traveller could leave next week if camels could be found.

'Go in peace and get ready,' said the sherif. 'If the Sheikh cannot find camels, we shall help him.'

Even this might not have been decisive for Bruce, but news soon came to alarm Fidele. A caravan from Atbara had been held up by Ammonios (of the buffalo) in Ethiopia, its goods and camels seized and its men imprisoned. At first Fidele would not believe that this could be a reprisal for his treatment of Bruce: he denied that any message could possibly have been sent by the explorer to Yasin.

Bruce had, indeed, sent such messages, but he now declared that Yasin, and even Takla Haymanot, were not the only people who were concerned about him and were following his fortunes from a distance. The Sherif of Mecca himself could know what happened to him and would penalize traders and pilgrims from Atbara if he were harmed. If Fidele doubted this, he would see in four days' time a sign in the sky which would show that the traveller's fate was a matter of universal importance and might forecast disaster for Atbara.

In fact, the explorer knew from his astronomical tables that an eclipse of the moon was due.

Before this could happen, however, Bruce's freedom to go to

Sennar was already assured. First the guides sent by the Fung King and Adelan arrived in Teawa. This, in itself, was not quite decisive, for the King's messenger, Mohammed, was a friend of Fidele's and proposed a further delay. But then three mail-clad men of Yasin's appeared outside the town. They would not enter it or eat Fidele's bread as a sign of peace. The letters they carried said that if Bruce was not allowed to go in peace Yasin himself would come within a fortnight to attack Teawa and that he would force the Arabs who were his allies to burn every stalk of corn in Atbara.

Fidele could not stand out against a threat of this kind. At last the camels for the journey were suddenly found. Girbas for water were produced, though these were defective and had to be replaced with others. On April 16th, the very morning of the day of eclipse – which was to take place when darkness was falling – everything was ready for their departure. Even Bruce's horse, which Fidele had impounded, was standing ready for him.

He had heard that horses could not live at Sennar. He decided that he could make a last use of this one by staging a demonstration to impress his unfriendly host. He mounted with a double-barrelled gun in his hand, put the horse through its most impressive paces, and fired to left and right of him. His audience, who had never seen a weapon fired on horseback, were astonished and scared. 'This,' said he, 'is the way my countrymen ride and fight. Indeed, I do the thing awkwardly, for I am a man of peace, a dervish, and no soldier.'

'If many men of peace such as you were here, your countrymen could get all Atbara for themselves,' said Fidele. 'Even your horse seems to have the sense of a man.'

This was the moment for a lordly gesture. 'Such as he is,' Bruce said, dismounting, 'a prince [Confu] gave him to me, and such as he is I now give him to you as a proof that I am your friend and that I should not grudge you a few paltry piastres if I had not been under a vow of poverty.'

'Fidele, how could you be willing to torment such a man as this?' asked the mullah, who had been particularly alarmed by the exhibition of horsemanship. 'I told you what he was, our books speak of them. They are not infidels, but spend their lives wandering in search of wisdom and must always do so till Hagiuge Magiuge come, and then there will be an end of the world.'

'I suppose now you are all at peace we shall not see that sign in the sky you foretold,' said the sherif.

'I should be thought a liar if it did not appear,' said Bruce. 'Do you wish to see it?'

'If it will do no harm,' the sherif answered.

'Then you shall see it and it will do no harm now. I hope it will bring health and a good crop to this kingdom.' He went off to say good-bye to the women, including a mournful Aiscach, to whom he gave a parting present of Indian satin and handkerchiefs. They were full of fear when the moon was hidden and the men, too, were suitably impressed and relieved when it slowly cleared again.

It was late next day before they finally left Teawa, travelling on by night to escape the heat. There were deserted villages on the way, their crops burned and their wells filled up by Arab nomads – this was the price Atbara had had to pay for the tribes' mistrust of Fidele's misgovernment. They had a warm welcome at Beyla, where the Sheikh, grateful for the medical help Bruce had given him, most exceptionally refused to accept a present – it was given to the mullah instead. The man Adelan had sent to meet them was their reliable guide, but the King's servant who had come with him still tried to delay them. They came easily enough, however, out of waterless woodland to the fertile low country that lay round Sennar.

This plain was a strangely orderly sight after their long journey through troubled country. It held a great semicircle of villages, more or less equal in size and set at equal distances from one another, all built of neat, cone-shaped huts. These were the cantonments of the King of Sennar's infantry. The men were all negro slaves from the south, living with their families. 'Having settlements and provisions given them, as also arms put into their hands, they never wish to desert, but live a very domestic and sober life.' They were pagans adoring the moon when it shone and had priests with them maintained by the nominally Moslem Government in Sennar.

Here was the organization that had strengthened the Fung Kingdom in its days of prosperity and had given it control over the Arab tribesmen. In spite of its good order, it had one great military weakness – the soldiers had scarcely a firearm among them. Bruce soon had reason to be grateful to the Nuba soldiery. When his party were going towards the ferry over the Blue Nile which would take them into Sennar they were suddenly struck by a whirlwind 'or what is called at sea a waterspout'. One camel was lifted off its feet and thrown down, breaking its ribs. Bruce and two of his companions were thrown down and plastered with the red mud of the plain, 'almost as smoothly as could have been done with a trowel'. They took refuge in a village, where they were cleaned, fed and rested by people who could scarcely speak Arabic.

'I had seldom in my life, upon a journey, passed a more comfortable night. I had a very neat, clean hut, entirely to myself and a Greek servant that sat near me. Some of the Nuba watched for us all night and took care of our beasts and baggage. They sang and replied to one another alternately, in notes full of pleasant melody, till I fell asleep, involuntarily and with regret.' But this idyll was not to last long. They had to wait a few days till their arrival was reported to Adelan and he had made arrangements for their reception. Then they crossed the river and entered Sennar.

17

The City of the Fung

Sennar was a great city for its time. It had 'many good houses after the fashion of the country', all built of clay and with flat roofs, unlike the round, conical-roofed huts that were usual elsewhere. Some of them were two stories high, and Bruce was led to one of these, belonging to Adelan, where he and his party were to live under the Vice-Vizier's protection.

But in spite of its size and the comparative comfort it could give, Sennar was for Bruce a place of fear and foreboding which seemed to live under an evil spell. The land for some miles round it was rich and fertile, yielding heavy crops. But animals could scarcely live on this 'fat earth'. They could not breed there and life was short for human beings. In the dry season when Bruce arrived the water of the district, apart from the Blue Nile itself, putrefied and stank and sickness descended on the town, 'epilepsies, apoplexies, violent fevers, obstinate agues and lingering painful dysenteries still more obstinate and mortal'.

The population could be maintained only by bringing in slaves from the south, but in spite of this renewal they were viciously self-indulgent and unfriendly, hating all strangers, and particularly white men. 'War and treason', wrote Bruce, 'seem to be the only employment of this horrid people whom Heaven has separated by almost impassable deserts from the rest of mankind; confining them to an accursed spot, seemingly to give earnest in time for the only other worse, which he has reserved to them for an eternal hereafter.'

The morning after his arrival on April 30th, 1772, Bruce was summoned to visit the King. Taking Hadji Ismael and Soliman with him, he was led to a large palace, mud-built and only one story high, most of whose rooms were empty and bare; they seemed to have been barracks for soldiers, but few men were to be seen on guard.

Ismain[1] sat in a small room on a mattress covered with cloth-of-gold cushions, but he himself was not a magnificent figure. He wore only one garment, a wide, loose shirt of blue Indian cotton which was the usual dress of Sennar. His colour was brown, for his mother had been an Arab. 'He had a very plebeian countenance on which was stamped no decided character; I should rather have guessed him to be a soft, timid, irresolute man.'

This being was a divine king, to use an anthropological phrase not yet known in Bruce's day. According to the system of ideas which the Fung had probably inherited from their Shilluk ancestors, he incarnated the life of his people. He must ceremonially plough the earth to ensure good crops. If it seemed to a council of his leading officers that he was no longer fit to govern the kingdom well, he could be killed in a traditional way by an official who was a member of his family and was expected to pass part of each day with his possible victim.

With the King sat three men, wrapped in white garments to show that they were learned in the law. One was the Cadi or chief judge of Sennar, a Moroccan, who was one of Ismain's leading advisers, but had quarrelled with the powerful Vizier, Abu el Kaylak, and his brother Adelan. The second was Cadi of Kordofan, Abu el Kaylak's special domain; he was at the court as a spy on the King for the Vizier. The third controlled large stores of surplus grain which had been built up as a safeguard against the failure of the crops.

The King looked in a rather confused way at the letters Bruce brought from the Ethiopian Emperor and the Sherif of Mecca. He

[1] Or Ismail – the first is Bruce's spelling.

was surprised to find that the explorer could speak Arabic as well
as Amharic.

'You are a doctor and a soldier,' said Ismain, 'but the Sherif's
letter tells me that you are also a nobleman in the service of a great
king called Englise-man, who rules the Indies and has Moslem as
well as Christian subjects whom he allows to be governed by their
own laws.'

'I never said that to the Sherif,' Bruce answered, 'but it is true.
I am as noble as any man of my nation and am also a servant of the
greatest king now reigning on earth – India is only a small part of
his dominions.'

'The greatest King!' said one of the Cadis. 'You have forgotten
the Ottoman Sultan. There are four great kingdoms in the world.
Turkey, Persia, Bornu [the chief state of the Western Sudan] and
Ethiopia.'

'Those are all heathens and slaves, except the Turkish Sultan,'
exclaimed Hadji Ismail, using his favourite expression of contempt
for all men and countries he disliked, even if they were Mohammedan. 'There are the Turk, the King of England and the King of
France. What are Bornu and the rest? Heathen!'

After this short excursion into world politics as seen from the
Sudan came the question which puzzled almost all Bruce's African
hosts.

'How is it,' asked the King, 'that you, who are so noble and
learned that you know everything and speak all languages, and so
brave that you are not afraid to travel with a few old men through
countries like this one and Ethiopia, have not stayed at home to
enjoy yourself, eat, drink and take pleasure instead of wandering
like a poor man exposed to all sorts of dangers?'

'You must know of such men in your religion, learned or noble,'
said Bruce, 'who because of sins they have committed or vows they
have made, renounce the world and become humble and poor, so
that they are often insulted by the wicked, who have not the fear
of God before their eyes.'

'They are dervishes,' declared the Cadis.

'Then I am a dervish,' Bruce declared, 'bound to travel in hardships and danger, doing all the good I can to poor and rich and hurting nobody.' He declared that he had been travelling for almost twenty years.

'You must have been very young when you committed those sins,' said the King. He supposed they had all been with women.

Modestly Bruce admitted that some probably were, 'but I did not say that I was one of those who travel on account of their sins, but that there were some dervishes that did so on account of their vows, and some to learn wisdom'.

Apparently this was found satisfactory. The explorer, who had been standing in the royal presence, was told to sit down on a cushion.

'Do you know when Hagiuge Magiuge will come?' the Cadi of Sennar asked him. These mysterious beings, which had been mentioned by the mullah at Teawa, were equivalent to the Biblical Gog and Magog. Bruce answered that he knew nothing about them. What was said of them in the Cadi's books?

'Hagiuge Magiuge,' the man of learning explained, 'are little people, not so big as bees or like our fly, which will come in great swarms out of the earth. Two of their chiefs are to ride on an ass. Every hair of that ass is to be a pipe and every pipe is to play a different kind of music, and all who hear and follow them will be led to Hell.'

'If they were twice as little as you say and twice as numerous, I would not be afraid of them,' Bruce declared. 'I trust in God I shall never be so fond of music as to go to Hell after an ass, for all the tunes he or they can play.'

The interview was over. It had been friendly enough, but as Bruce passed out into the square before the palace the passers-by taunted him as a foreigner and he remembered that this was the place where the French envoy, Du Roule, and his suite had been murdered, though as diplomats they were 'under a protection which should have secured them from all danger, every part of which I was then unprovided with'. The thought of Du Roule's death seems never to have been far from his mind during his months in Sennar.

That evening he was recalled to the palace to give the King the presents he had brought. Ismain was sitting in a larger room, naked except for some cloths spread on his knees, while a servant rubbed him with stinking grease, some of which dropped from his hair like water. It was elephant's fat, the King explained, which strengthened virility and kept the skin smooth. Bruce ought to use it, he suggested: it would prevent his hair from being so red. When the greasing was finished the King went into the next room, where cold water was poured over him. Then he was rubbed over again with sweet-smelling ointment, 'after which he sat down, as completely dressed, being just going to his women's apartment.'

Bruce produced the Ethiopian Emperor's gift of cloth of gold which, he explained, had been sent in the hope that Ismain would protect him and quickly send him on to Egypt. There was a time when he could have done this, the King said, but things were changed in Sennar, which was going to ruin. Bruce was given a glass of sherbet to drink in his presence as a pledge of personal safety, but he got no other satisfaction before Ismain went off to his harem.

He had to wait a week before seeing Sheikh Adelan, who, he hoped, would be able to do more for him than the nominal sovereign. This visit made an impression very different from that of his audience in the half-deserted palace. The Vice-Vizier's house, on the edge of the desert at Aira, three and a half miles from Sennar, stood in the centre of a fenced square, each side of which was half a mile long. Inside the fence were rows of horses tethered facing the sheds which were their riders' quarters.

'It was one of the finest sights that ever I saw of the kind,' wrote Bruce, an enthusiastic admirer both of horseflesh and of military order and discipline. The steeds 'were all above sixteen hands high, of the breed of the old Saracen horses, all finely made and as strong as our coach horses, but exceedingly nimble in their motion; rather thick and short in the forehead, but with the most beautiful eyes, ears and heads in the world. . . .

'A shirt of mail hung upon each man's quarters opposite to his horse, and by it an antelope's skin with which it was covered from the dew of night. A head piece of copper, without crest or plumage, was suspended by a lace above the shirt of mail. To them was added an enormous broad-sword in a red-leather scabbard, and upon the pummel hung two thick gloves. . . .' There were said to be four hundred horses and their riders in the enclosure, all the personal property of Sheikh Adelan; the men were slaves bought with his money. Five or six similar squares sheltered the royal cavalry. 'Whether they were all in as good order as Adelan's I cannot say, for I did not go further, but no body of horse could ever be more magnificently disposed under the direction of any Christian power.'

Adelan himself was an imposing figure, wearing a cloak of silk and camel's hair lined with yellow satin and a cap with two points – an emblem of authority inherited from ancient Egypt.[1] He was perhaps sixty years old, more than six feet tall, and 'of the colour and features of an Arab'.

In war, Bruce says, Adelan 'was a fair-player and gave everybody his chance'. He was the first to attack and the last to leave a fight.

His business at Aira was the important, and also dangerous, one of raising taxes from the nomad tribes as they moved northwards into the desert to escape the flies which attacked their beasts or south again to their pastures when the rains were over. The tribute was paid either in gold or in beasts – camel's flesh was one of the chief foods of Sennar city. Bruce was told that one tribe paid 100,000 ounces of gold. Adelan taxed ten such tribes. Farther north the Arab chief, Wed Agib, had to deal with six others. This tribute was the chief support of the Fung Government. It was only with the backing of an army of cavalry that the tribes could be made to pay.

'You suppose you have come through great dangers,' said

[1] O. G. S. Crawford, *The Fung Kingdom of Sennar*.

Adelan to Bruce, 'and so you have. But what do you think of me? I am day and night here in the open, surrounded by hundreds and thousands of Arabs, all of whom would eat me if they dared. Look at the door' – they were in his house, in a room hung gorgeously with mirrors and scarlet silk – 'those men you see are their chiefs whom I am now taxing, and I have brought them here so that they may judge whether I am ready for them or not.'

'You could not do better,' said the explorer, thinking of the orderly rows of horses and their riders. For himself, he explained, what he wanted was a safe conduct through the country to Egypt. He gave Adelan the letter from Takla Haymanot asking for this protection.

'My brother, Mohammed Abu el Kaylak, can do more for strangers than I can,' Adelan answered. 'You will be lucky if you meet him at Sennar, but if not I shall help you when I have dealt with all these Arabs.' He advised that while Bruce was in Sennar he should never go into the streets without a black companion. He might also go to the palace, so that he could say when he reached home that he had seen a king 'that neither knows how to govern nor will allow others to teach him, who does not know how to make war and yet will not sit in peace.' He also gave the rather disturbing news that Ali Bey of Cairo, Bruce's protector in Egypt, had been driven from power by his son-in-law, Mohammed Abu Dahab.

In spite of this the traveller felt cheered by his interview. Since he left Ethiopia he had not met a man in authority who spoke so frankly as Adelan, and apparently meant what he said. But on the short way back to Sennar he met 'ignorant brutish people' who with threats demanded gold, cloth or tobacco. He could not forget that weeks might pass before the Vice-Vizier was free to give him more help.

In the city the King seemed to be growing hostile and suspicious. His servant Mohammed, who had been sent to Teawa to meet Bruce, appeared to have passed on Fidele's story about the traveller's boxes full of gold. Bruce felt encouraged, however, when he was asked to treat several of the Ismain's wives, who were sick, since 'all my acquaintance with the fair sex had hitherto been to my advantage'.

'I must confess, however,' he writes, 'that calling these the fair sex is not preserving a precision in terms.' He was introduced to three women who sat together on a sofa, clad in voluminous blue cotton shirts.

The most conspicuous, the King's favourite, seemed to Bruce 'next to the elephant and rhinoceros the largest living creature I had met with'. She was about six feet tall and far more than proportionately fat.

'A ring of gold passed through her underlip and weighed it down till, like a flap, it covered her chin, and left her teeth bare, which were very small and fine. Her ears reached down to her shoulders and had the appearance of wings: she had in each of these a large ring of gold, somewhat smaller than a man's little finger and about five inches diameter. . . . She had on her ankles two manacles of gold, larger than any I had seen upon the feet of felons, with which I could not conceive it was possible for her to walk, but afterwards found they were hollow.' One of the other queens had gold chains hanging from her ears to her nostrils and a ring through the end of her nose. 'I think she must have breathed with great difficulty. It had something of the appearance of a horse's bridle.'

The three complained of innumerable ailments. As soon as the consultation began each of them stripped off her shirt and sat naked with the garment on her lap. 'I could not but observe that the breasts of each of them reached the length of their knees.'

Bleeding was the favourite medical treatment, and when Bruce had produced an instrument for cupping which did not require the use of a lancet this was done – 'the room was overflowed with an effusion of royal blood'. Bruce was called back for a second visit when the queens and some other court ladies demanded vomits. 'The ipecacuanha had great effect, and warm water was drunk copiously. . . . It was most prodigiously hot, and the horrid black figures, moaning and groaning with sickness, gave me, I think, some slight idea of punishment in the world below.'

His worst moment came when the senior queen demanded that he, too, should throw off the long blue shirt which, in the Sennar fashion, he was wearing as his only garment. 'The whole court of female attendants flocked to the spectacle. Refusal or resistance was in vain. I was surrounded with fifty or sixty women, all equal in statue and strength to myself. The only terms I could possibly, and that with great difficulty, make for myself were that they should be contented to strip me no farther than the shoulders and breast.

'Upon seeing the whiteness of my skin they gave all a long cry in token of dislike, and shuddered, seeming to consider it rather the effect of disease than natural. I think in my life I never felt so disagreeably. I have been in more than one battle, but surely I would joyfully have taken my chance again to escape from that examination.' He could not help thinking that if the King had come in at this point his travels might have had a painful end; 'though I can solemnly declare there never was an idea in my breast since ever I had the honour of seeing these royal beauties that could have given His Majesty of Sennar the smallest reason for jealousy: and I believe the same may be said of the sentiments of the ladies. Ours was a mutual passion, but dangerous to no one concerned.'

Bruce's medical attention to the harem brought him no gratitude in this case. On the contrary he had reason to feel more anxious. In the palace the King's servant Mohammed threatened him with a drawn sword and went unpunished. He could only sit waiting in Adelan's town house, where, using the Vice-Vizier's name, he could refuse to admit any stranger. Even so, he was never idle. He worked on notes of his travels. And he had found a friend in Sennar who was very ready to give him information about the Kingdom of the Fung.

This was Ahmed, the Sid el Kum or Master of the Royal Household, the man whose duty it was to kill deposed kings, or princes who might be a king's rivals. Ahmed had been tortured by calculus and was thankful for the relief Bruce's pills had given him. He also suffered from epilepsy, which he believed to be due to the enchantments of an enemy.

In spite of his office, the Sid el Kum was one of the gentlest beings that Bruce met in an ungentle city. He had been born in the pagan south and seemed to the explorer to be a pagan still. Nuba priests who claimed to be powerful sorcerers were often with him. When Bruce asked some of these men why they did not cure Ahmed of his illnesses they answered ingeniously that these were caused by a Christian devil not subject to their spells.

The Sid el Kum believed that the Scot was no more a Christian than he himself was a Moslem, and Bruce did not undeceive him. 'I was no missionary, nor had I . . . any desire to enter into conversation about religion with a man whose only office was to be the deliberate murderer of his sovereign.' Bruce's royalist principles were shocked by the idea of king-killing, in Sennar as they had been in Ethiopia, but he did not hesitate to discover what he could about this custom, and Ahmed was willing to tell all.

A king, he said, must be killed decently and privately, his throat being cut with a sword. The Sid el Kum himself had no part in deciding when this was to be done – he merely carried out a decision of other people. In this way he, Ahmed, had killed the last king, Nasser, Ismain's brother, having previously killed his son in the father's presence, so that Nasser could be sure the boy's death was swift and according to precedent. He had no doubt that if Ismain's turn came – as it might at any moment, since his most powerful subjects disliked and despised him – this king, too, would prefer a quick and (so far as possible) kindly end by the properly appointed hand of his own relations to murder by someone else or a public execution. On the other hand, Badi IV, the father of both these kings, had been stabbed in the back with a spear at Teawa by Sheikh Fidele's father. Though Badi had been duly deposed and Adelan had ordered his death – though, indeed, he was actually invading the country with a force from Ethiopia at the time – this procedure was incorrect, and the killer himself was put to death for a breach of the law.

However little choice Ahmed may have had in his business of killing kings, his authority and influence in Sennar were great. But for this Bruce might scarcely have escaped the dangers of the city. These were growing still more pressing. Fidele came to Sennar, repeating his story of the traveller's riches and urging the King to plunder him. Adelan left his station at Aira for another: though this was not much farther away, it was less easy to be sure of his protection in a sudden crisis. The man on whose financial help the traveller had counted when he planned his Sudanese journey, a merchant, Hadji Belal, in touch with the suppliers of the British captains at Jidda, refused to give him the money for which he had credit – money needed to buy camels and provisions for the next stage of his long march. This was the first and only time when the banking arrangements Bruce had made for regions no European financier had seen broke down.

He had hoped and expected to be able to travel with an important visitor to the city. This was a West African, one of a group of negro eunuchs who were attendants at the Moslem shrines in Mecca and Medina. From time to time these men were allowed to revisit their native countries and collect offerings of gold for the Holy Places. The eunuch, whom Bruce calls Mahomet Towash, was returning from the towns on the Niger some two thousand miles west of Sennar, when he fell ill with malaria. Bruce's quinine ('the bark') cured him, and he was anxious that his white doctor should go with him to Egypt. Quite unexpectedly it was learned that the eunuch had gone from Sennar secretly, persuaded by King Ismain to leave Bruce and his party behind him. This was a crushing disappointment, since the 'holy man' should be able to count on all the camels, provisions, guidance and protection he needed on his desert journey; though later Bruce was to think that it had been a providential escape from disaster.

The Sid el Kum was the traveller's only helper. He argued with Hadji Belal. He promised to bring out the King's own servants to protect Bruce if he was in danger. He advised him to have everything ready for a quick departure and meanwhile to remain in Adelan's house, prepared to defend himself there.

On the night of August 25th, the very date when they had hoped to leave with the Towash, the little party were sitting sadly in Bruce's room while their one lamp was burning low when a battering was heard at the outer door of the house. They snatched up their weapons and Bruce arranged that Hadji Ismael should fire first, if necessary, since his right of self-defence as a sherif would be respected when a white man's bullet might be regarded as aggression against Moslems. The Scot went forward himself and found that a dozen men had broken through the outer gate and were trying to force an inner one.

'Are you mad?' called Bruce. 'You are attacking Adelan's house and there are men here with firearms that can kill you all if we shoot once through the door.'

'How sound you sleep!' said a soothing voice. 'We have been trying to waken you for an hour. The King is ill. Tell Yagoube to come to him at once and open your door to us.'

It was Mohammed, the King's servant, who was speaking. He was told that Bruce would go to the palace in the morning, that a message had been sent to the Sid el Kum for his help, and that they would defend themselves till he came. One of Bruce's men fired a pistol into the air from an upper window, and the assailants ran away.

Next morning Bruce heard from Ahmed that they had been arrested and that the attack had been reported to Adelan. The Sheikh would certainly insist on executing men who had tried to break into his house. This looked like bringing things in Sennar to a crisis. The King was determined to protect his servant. There might be civil war in the city.

In desperation Bruce made up his mind to leave his possessions with the Sid el Kum and go to see Adelan himself. But he must have money. His companions reminded him that, after all, there was gold in his baggage. It was the great chain which the Ethiopian Emperor had given him at Sarbakusa. He had been anxious to take this trophy home with him, but now it had to be brought out. By persuasion and threats the Sid el Kum forced Belal to give enough for the gold to provide what was needed for the journey to Egypt.

When this was done only six of the chain's heavy links were left to the explorer.

By September 5th he was ready to leave Sennar. In the evening the King sent for him.

'You are not so gay as when you first came here,' Ismain said, as he smoked his hubble-bubble.

Bruce answered, laconically, that he had no reason to be.

The King made a new proposal. Bruce, he knew, was going to Adelan. He himself (he said) had told the Vice-Vizier to send for him. A tribe of Arabs had rebelled. Bruce, he believed, had firearms that would kill twenty or thirty men with one volley. ('Say fifty or sixty,' interjected the Scot 'if it hits them'.) Adelan would use him to punish the tribesmen and Bruce could have some of their camels for his journey.

As usual, the explorer refused to take part in an African quarrel. The irrepressible Hadji Ismael, who had come with him to the palace, called from the door in his broken Arabic: 'Why did you not tell those black heathens you sent to murder us the other night to stay a little longer. You would have known then what our firearms can do.'

This brought the King to his real purpose. 'Adelan has been told that my servant Mohammed, who brought you from Teawa, has taken part in a drunken frolic at the door of his house and he has sent soldiers to take him and some of his companions out of Sennar,' Ismain said. When Bruce saw Adelan he was to ask him to spare Mohammed's life and free him. If he succeeded, the reprieved man would be ordered to guide the traveller to Egypt.

Here at last was the opportunity for an unopposed escape from Sennar. No guide through the deserts could have been less welcome than the devious and unfriendly Mohammed. But so long as the King believed that Bruce was going to Adelan to ask for the man's life there would be no attempt to interfere with him when he left the city. Sending his baggage before him, he passed through the gates at nightfall. Next morning he set out not for Adelan's camp but on the road to the White Nile and the north.

18

━━━◇∘◉∘◇━━━

Sand and Simoom

Bruce's men were as pleased with the escape as he was. 'They promised to bear fatigue and hunger cheerfully and to live and die with me, provided I would proceed homeward and free them from the horrors of Sennar and its King'. There were only four of them now, three Greeks and Hadji Ismael, since black Soliman, his most useful adviser, was to return to Gondar with letters from Adelan to the Emperor. It was a minute party for a scarcely known route fully eight hundred miles long. One of them, Georgis the Greek, was half-blind, and the Turk was elderly. Four of their five camels were fully loaded. Bruce explained to them that they might take turns of riding on the other for a time, but when they came to the desert all of them would have to make their way on foot across the sands.

Their first march was pleasant, however. After the rain which had almost flooded Sennar city in their darkest days there 'the corn now sprung up and covering the ground made the whole of this immense plain appear a level, green land, interspersed with great lakes of water and ornamented at certain intervals with groups of villages, the conical tops of the houses presenting, at a distance, the appearance of small encampments. Through this winds the Nile, a delightful river there, above a mile broad, full to the very brim, but never overflowing. Everywhere on these banks are seen numerous herds of the most beautiful cattle of various kinds, the tribute recently extorted from the Arabs. . . . The banks resemble the pleasantest parts of Holland in the summer season.'

It was the Blue Nile, of course, actually called the Bahr el Azrak (Blue River) at Sennar. When he came to the White Nile three weeks later he realized that it was very deep and kept its flow much more constantly great than that of the Blue Nile. 'Rising in latitudes where there are continual rains,' he thought, 'it suffers not the decrease the Nile does by the six months' dry weather', but he still assumed that his river, which brought the floods from Ethiopia, must be considered the main stream.

Before he reached the White Nile, where Khartoum is today, he had passed through country which is now partly watered by the great Sennar Dam, but then dwindled towards mere desert, on the edge of which half-starved people ground seeds of wild grass to make their bread. He had visited Wed Agib, the Arab chief responsible to Sennar for the northern Sheikhs and kinglets, who received him kindly, though with curiosity, since he had never seen a Western European before.

There was news that Adelan was punishing the King's Mohammed and Bruce's assailants – news, too, that Yasin's men from Ras el Fil had burned Teawa and chased Fidele to Beyla. Evidently the traveller was not sorry to know of this revenge. Wed Agib told him of the dangers of the two possible routes to Egypt; across the Bayuda Desert in the great loop of the Nile and then following the river itself or through the Eastern Desert directly to Aswan. He gave Bruce a letter to his sister, the Sittina 'or Lady' of Shendi, where there could be a last choice between these two lines of travel.

Soon after he passed the meeting-place of the Blue and White Niles Bruce reached the point that is the limit of the regular rains which gave pasture and crops to the south of the Fung Kingdom. There was a ribbon of green growth – sometimes perhaps a mile broad, sometimes very narrow indeed – only along the Nile banks or at rare oases. Bare red hills or stretches of sand or coloured rocks stretched endlessly to the east and the sun was so torrid that the travellers could scarcely move by day. It was a country of splendid horses Bruce found, bred on the edge of the desert and fed on roots dug out of the dry soil. Its people were Arabs of an ancient race, speaking the language of the Koran more purely than the men of central Arabia itself. Here, on October 4th, they came to Shendi, the capital of a tiny riverside kingdom and the home of Wed Agib's sister.

Shendi had been a meeting-place of great trade routes, and consequently a famous market. Merchants travelling from Egypt along the Nile and across the Bayuda loop of the river, from Suakin on the Red Sea, from Ethiopia and Sennar, from the far south-western countries near the Niger, from Darfur and Kordofan, could meet there. But in times of violence and civil war all these movements had grown fewer. There was still some trade: Bruce found that most goods were cheaper and more plentiful at Shendi than at Sennar, but the town itself was small and shrunken, with only 'two or three tolerable houses' among two hundred and fifty lesser huts.

It was full of alarm because the planet Venus was seen shining all day, 'in defiance of the brightest sun, from which she was but little distant' in the sky. Bruce reckoned that the phenomenon must be visible every four years. If this was so, the sight had been forgotten. 'The bulk of the people in all countries are the same; they never foretell anything but evil.' In this case the men of Shendi expected all sorts of disasters, war or famine, and when the explorer unpacked his quadrant and telescopes they blamed him for bringing the doleful omen with him. He succeeded in suggesting tactfully to their leaders that Venus was a sign of good luck, and in the end this made him popular in the town.

In a few days he took his letter to the Lady. She sat behind a screen through which she could see him, but could not be seen, while they talked about Adelan's dealings with King Ismain, and she asked, as so many others had done, why a white man like Bruce had come to troubled African countries. After a time he surprised her.

'Allow me to complain, madam,' he said, 'of a breach of hospitality by you which I have experienced from no other Arab.'

'How can that be?' she asked.

'You called me a white man,' said Bruce. 'From this I know that you can see while I am not allowed to see you. The queens of Sennar were not so hard on me: I had a full sight of them without asking for it.'

This was a line of thought which can seldom have been heard of in Moslem lands, but the Lady took it well. She must have known of Bruce's sufferings in King Ismain's harem and she laughed heartily. She asked Yagoube's medical opinion on the best means of preventing her hair from falling. Then she proposed that her visitor should come back next day, when, she hoped, her son, King Idris, would have returned from an oasis where he was inspecting his cattle.

On this second visit Bruce was led into a passage with doors on either side of it. One of them opened 'and Sittina appeared magnificently dressed with a kind of round cap of solid gold upon the crown of her head. . . . She was a woman scarcely forty, taller than the middle size, had a very round, plump face, her mouth rather large, very red lips, the finest teeth and eyes I have ever seen.'

She stopped for a moment, saying seriously, 'How are you?' Bruce went forward and kissed her hand. He was told to go through another door, 'and there was the screen I had seen before, and the Lady sitting behind it.'

'Are the women in your country handsome?' asked the Lady.

Bruce spoke as a patriot. 'The handsomest in the world,' he said, 'but they are so good that nobody thinks at all of their beauty, nor do they value themselves on it.'

Perhaps this was no more tactful than truthful, but the Lady had a question to put for which she really felt the need of an answer.

'And do they allow you to kiss their hands?' she asked.

Bruce told her that in Britain this was a form of greeting only for kings and queens. It was the highest reward for dangerous and difficult services when a queen gave her hand to be kissed.

'Do you know that no man has ever kissed my hand but you?' asked this Queen.

'It was meant respectfully, cannot hurt you and ought not to offend you,' said Bruce.

'It has done neither, but I wish my son Idris could come and see you.' The Lady explained that it was because her son was expected that she had dressed so finely.

Bruce hoped that the young King would find a way of sending him safely to Egypt.

'Safely! You are throwing yourself away. Idris himself,' the Lady declared, 'dare not attempt such a journey.' Why had the traveller not gone with Mahomet Towash, who had left Shendi only a short time before? It now appeared that the eunuch had not only gone forward a second time without waiting for Bruce: he had also taken all the desert guides with him.

A journey could scarcely be made without at least one of these men and Bruce had made up his mind to take the route from the westward bend of the Nile near Berber directly across the desert to Aswan. It was the shortest way, but there were fully five hundred miles of it. Only an experienced guide could lead travellers from well to well, could help them to survive sandstorms and the scorching blast of the simoom, could keep them out of the way of nomads who would plunder and kill them. Most of the guides were nomads themselves. They had earned a high reputation for honesty and reliability. On this, indeed, their profitable work had depended in the days when there were many desert caravans. But since trade had fallen off the numbers of professional guides had grown fewer and they were less trustworthy.

'You must not go without a good man. I will not allow it,' said the Lady. However, a guide would turn up if Bruce waited. 'While you stay, let me see you every day and if you need anything send to me for it.'

A guide did appear. He looked poor enough. His name was Idris, like the still absent King's. He was not a nomad but an Arab from Egypt who had made many desert journeys, and was going home for good. He had fallen ill at Shendi and had got into debt. Bruce had to make the payment that would clear him and get his camel and clothes out of pawn. The Lady herself cross-examined the guide very thoroughly. In the end she approved of him. They were ready to go. At their last interview Bruce asked to be allowed to kiss her hand again, 'which she condescended to in the most gracious manner, laughing all the time, and saying, "Well, you are an odd man! If Idris, my son, saw me now he would think me mad." '

This was almost the kindliest moment, the most pleasantly sentimental, of Bruce's travels. It fortified him for the most dangerous and painful of his journeys. The little caravan went easily enough along the Nile till they reached the villages of Berber, passing the ruins of Meroe, the ancient Nubian capital, which Bruce was, apparently, the first Westerner to recognize. They were ferried across the Nile's last great tributary, the Atbara river, which Bruce had known in Ethiopia as the Takazze. Then, where the Nile itself was beginning to make its turn north-westwards, they were to strike out into the desert.

There were now nine of the travellers – Bruce, Hadji Ismael, the three Greeks, Idris, a young relation of his who joined him at Berber and two Nubians who were to take care of the camels. They filled four girbas with Nile water. For food they had twenty-four goatskins crammed with durra bread, dried and then rubbed to a powder. A handful of this put into a half gourd, 'about twice the size of a common tea-basin', and soaked till it had swelled to six times its volume was to be each man's food morning and evening, with a gourdful of water for drink during the day. As they prepared to go they were joined by half a dozen poor negro pilgrims from the Western Sudan, 'much against my will', says Bruce, 'for I knew that we should probably be reduced to the disagreeable necessity of seeing them die with thirst before our eyes, or by assisting them, should any accident happen to our water, we ran a very great risk of perishing with them'.

It was on November 11th, 1772, that they moved away. While the camels were loaded Bruce bathed in the Nile, 'and thus took leave of my old acquaintance, very doubtful if we should ever meet again'. They marched over hard ground with occasional patches of thin grass where the camels could eat a little.

When they halted in the evening Bruce asked Idris the guide to show him the direction in which Aswan lay, so far before them. He fixed the line with his compass and afterwards found it almost precisely correct, though, as Idris warned him, they had to move aside at times to reach wells or for other reasons.

A day later they faced their first misfortune. Their shoes were wearing out. They had been walking over great stretches of rough stone, and their feet, though hardened by so many weeks of travel, were inflamed by the sun-baked ground.

They were far into the desert when they were 'at once surprised and terrified by a sight, surely one of the most magnificent in the world. . . . We saw a number of prodigious pillars of sand at different distances, at times moving with great celerity, at others stalking on with a majestic slowness; at intervals we thought they were coming in a very few minutes to overwhelm us. . . . Again they would retreat so as to be almost out of sight, their tops reaching to the very clouds.' At midday they seemed to be sweeping down on the travellers. Then 'eleven of them ranged alongside us about the distance of three miles.'

They disappeared only when the wind dropped. 'It was in vain to think of flying; the swiftest horse, or fastest sailing ship, could be of no use to carry us out of the danger, and the full persuasion of this riveted me to the spot where I stood, and let the camels gain on me so much, in my state of lameness, that it was with some difficulty I could overtake them.'

Most of Bruce's companions were horrified and depressed, especially when they found next morning that they had been half-buried in wind-blown sand while they slept. They were in terror of thirst, for one of the West Africans had opened a girba during the night, and the skin had almost emptied itself. There were more sand-pillars that day. At dawn the sun's rays striking through the moving sand 'gave them an appearance of pillars of fire. . . . The Greeks shrieked out and said it was the day of judgement. Ismael proclaimed it to be hell.' The West Africans moaned that the world was on fire. Idris told Bruce privately that his own fear was not of the sand-pillars but of a redness in the air which forecast the simoom.

After a night's rest the caravan was comparatively cheerful again. There were no more sand-pillars, and before long they could see the top of the hill of Shrikrib, where they would find the next wells.

As they looked towards it Idris called, 'Fall down on your faces. Here is the simoom'. A haze appeared from the south-east, 'in colour like the purple part of the rainbow, but not so compressed or thick'. The heat struck them even before they could lie down and hide their faces. It was almost suffocating, even when the strange haze in the air had passed. 'For my part,' writes Bruce, 'I found distinctly in my breast that I had imbibed part of it, nor was I free from an asthmatic sensation till I had been some time in Italy, at the baths of Poretta, near two years afterwards.'

Bruce's companions could only whisper their despair to one another. He decided that he must rally them. He pointed to his own face, so swelled that he could scarcely see, his neck covered with blisters, and his feet inflamed and bleeding. In a voice almost stifled by the simoom he ordered that each man should be given an extra gourdful of water and he pointed to the Shikrib height where their girbas would be refilled.

'I believe I never was at any time more eloquent, and never had eloquence a more sudden effect.'

His men declared that it was Bruce's own condition that shocked them most. They would not be afraid for themselves if as their leader he would agree to take better care of himself. One of the camels should be unloaded and he should ride it to spare his feet. But Bruce insisted that the camels must be a last resource in case any of them became too ill to walk farther.

Late in the evening and moving very slowly, they came to the narrow rocky gorge where the ten wells of Shikrib lay. The place attracted all the desert creatures, though there was no herbage, and the water was full of dead animals. It had to be filtered through a cloth before it could be drunk; but there was plenty of it. The camels were fed and given a chance to drink enough to carry them to Egypt. Idris declared that at this point they were just half-way across the desert from Berber to Aswan. Bruce wanted to check this by fixing the latitude of the rocky gorge, and the Greeks were so anxious to find that their guide was underestimating the length of the journey they had already made that, in spite of their exhaustion, they eagerly helped to set up the quadrant. By their leader's reckoning, however, Idris was right.

As he made his observations a large antelope walked round him, even biting the cloth he had spread to kneel on. 'It would have appeared to by-standers (had there been any)', he thought, 'that we had been a long time acquainted. The first idea was the common one, to kill it. I easily could have done this with a lance; but it seemed so interested in what I was doing that I began to think it might perhaps be my good genius, which had come to visit, protect and encourage me, in the desperate situation in which I then was.'

At Shikrib two of the West Africans died after drinking, though Bruce's own party were refreshed and more cheerful when they left the wells and a deep pool in a cave where they had been able to bathe in really cold water. They were soon reminded of their danger again when they passed some sand-hills which, their guide told them, covered the remains of a caravan of some thousands of camels and their drivers that had been overwhelmed by such moving pillars as they still saw, at intervals, not far from themselves. Now, however, they were coming to a region where there was some thorny scrub whose leaves gave a sort of pasture. Here, two days from Shikrib, they found another well, Tarfawi, and Bruce, whose feet had 'swelled to a monstrous size', sat by the camels in the early dark, while the others went to draw water.

He was worrying over an estimate of distance – based typically enough in his century on a calculation of the ancient Alexandrian geographer Eratosthenes – which suggested to him that Aswan might lie much farther to the west than he had thought, when he heard the chain that tethered the camels clink. In the light of the camp fire he saw the figure of a stooping man glide past. There was another clink as if the chain had been heavily struck and the camels began to stir.

Of all the dangers of the desert men could be the worst. It was impossible to forsee the movements of nomad tribesmen, and crimes could be committed among the sands which would never be fully explained, or even known. The little party had looked anxiously for signs of human movement near their route and had been glad to find none. Now it seemed as if unknown plunderers might be preparing to attack.

Bruce had his gun beside him. He rose and shouted in the direction of the figure he had seen, telling the man to come forward if he wanted anything, but to keep away from the camels and the baggage or expect to be shot. There was another glimpse of movement, but no answer till Idris's young nephew, who had heard the call, ran up to help him. They found that two links in the camels' chains had been broken, apparently by blows with a sharp stone, and there were footprints on the sand.

A second fire was lit to give the camp light on both sides. Bruce ordered the girbas to be brought up from the well, though there had not been time to fill them completely, and the party formed a defensive position partly screened by thorn bushes. The men understood their danger well, but their spirits, which sank almost to a despairing resignation before winds, sands and thirst, revived against a human menace. Hadji Ismael, in particular, was full of fight. They were well enough armed to face anything short of a large body of raiders, but arms alone might not be enough. If they lost their camels, or their shrinking store of food, if their waterskins were damaged, they would die in the desert as surely as from lance-thrusts or shots, though more slowly.

But in the morning no attack came. They dared not wait long near the well for fear that the men who had tried to break the camels' chains might have gone, or sent, to bring up other plunderers, but Bruce, Ismael and the two Nubian camel-drivers followed the footprints in the sand, which led them to two ragged tents concealed under the shelter of a rock.

In one there was a single woman; in the other two 'perfectly naked, frightful emaciated figures, not like the inhabitants of this world' – a man and a woman who had a very young child with them. Bruce seized the man by his hair and threw him on his back, threatening him with a knife. The nomad was too terrified to resist, and though his wife, more boldly, reached for a lance, she was knocked down by the Hadji.

Bruce ordered that the captives should be separated, so that each of them might be questioned and out of the hearing of the others. As the child's mother was led away she said to her husband mournfully, 'Did I not say you would suffer for the murder of that good man.' She asked to have her child with her, and this was allowed. Bruce was touched when the baby, instead of seeming frightened, crowed and held out its little hands to him as it was carried past.

But his companions were not in a merciful mood. The man had tried to steal their camels, without which the whole party would die. If he and his wives were left alive, they might, somehow, be able to call up people of their tribe, the Bisharin, to pursue the little caravan or waylay it. For safety's sake they should be killed at once. Hadji Ismael was already looking for the sharpest knife he could find.

Bruce, however, had a plan that was more rational as well as kindlier. 'Hold your hand,' he said to the Turk, 'till we see if this thief is a liar also. If he proves to be, you shall then cut off his head and we shall send him, with the lie in his mouth, soul and body to Hell.'

Ismael agreed that this was reasonable. He stood by, with Bruce's own sword in his hand, while the prisoner was warned that he and his wives would die if they did not answer truly and fully what was asked of them.

The Bisharin was asked who the good man was for whose murder his wife had blamed him. It was a negro from Shendi, he said – in fact, Mahomet Towash. He explained that, tempted by the gold the eunuch was carrying to Mecca, one of his Bisharin guides had gone to his own sheikh and arranged that forty men should meet the caravan at a spot towards which the other guides would lead it. The nomads had knelt, as if to kiss the holy man's hand, and when he came forward to greet them had stabbed him in the back. They had pretended to make peace with his armed servants and had then murdered them, too.

The prisoner and his wives had been left behind at the well because their two camels were lame, though their milk was all the family had to keep them alive. He had meant to steal Bruce's camels and use them to rejoin his chief, who was on the Nile two days' journey away.

'What would have become of me if you had taken my camels?' said Bruce. 'Should we not have died?'

The man hesitated and then admitted that this was so.

'If another party of your people had found us here, would they have killed us?'

He hesitated again, and then answered, 'Yes, surely, they murdered the holy man and would murder anyone not protected by a Bisharin.'

'Now, there are two last questions,' said Bruce, 'and your life depends on them. Do you know of any party of Bisharin who are soon to pass here or at any of the wells farther north? Have you sent any message to your people since you saw us last night?'

There had been no message, the man said, and could have been none, because his camels were lame. It was not likely that the Bisharin would come to Tarfawi for some time. They would not visit the wells beyond it, because these belonged to another tribe, the Ababdeh – the people whose chief had sworn friendship with Bruce when he was on his way to the Red Sea.

Bruce called for Ismael, and the prisoner, expecting death, swore again that all he had said was true. The Turk and his sword were wanted not for an execution but for the questioning, of the mother, who was told that her child would be killed, and then herself, if she did not answer freely. She told precisely the same story.

When Bruce rose to go, 'she burst into a flood of tears, and tore her hair in the most violent excess of passion; shrieking out, to have mercy upon her, and pressing the little child to her breast, as if to take leave of it; then laying it down before me, in great agony and bitterness of heart, she again shrieked out, "If you are a Turk, make it a slave, but do not kill my child, and spare my husband." '

Bruce felt that he had never heard Arabic used so eloquently, with 'expressions at once so forcible and so simple'. His own tears fell and he could not keep up the farce of threats which he did not mean to carry out. But his companions still had to be persuaded that it was safe to let the man live. They were ready to spare the women and child, but Bruce pointed out to them that if they killed the Bisharin's camels the wives would die of starvation, while if the animals were left alive and recovered from their lameness the rest of the tribe might hear about the caravan.

'It has appeared to me,' he said, 'that often since we began this journey we have been preserved by visible intervention of God's protection, when we should have lost our lives if we had gone by the rules of our own judgement only.' They all worshipped the same God; perhaps this was a trial of the reality of their faith. They should leave the women and child at the well, making sure that their camels were really too lame to move, and instead of killing the man should take him with them, keeping him constantly chained to one of themselves. He could be a useful guide whose knowledge, particularly of the movements of his own tribe, and how to avoid them, would supplement Idris's. He would be warned that if they did meet a party of Bisharin he would be cut down before fighting began. On the other hand, Bruce would promise that if the man proved helpful new clothes for himself and his women would be given him when they reached Aswan, with a load of grain for the family and a good camel to take him back to them.

This humane plan was adopted by all: it turned out to be a valuable one in practice. Twelve handfuls from the meagre supply of powdered bread were left with the women to supplement their milk, and the party set off again, the right hand of the Bisharin chained to the left of one of the Nubian camel-men.

That day the simoom struck again, and one of the camels died, 'partly famished, partly overcome by extreme fatigue'. They cut slices from its flesh and dried them in the sun to add to their food supply. Near the next well they found the bodies of a man and two camels, shrunken by the heat, 'yet no vermin had touched them, as in this whole desert there is neither worm, fly, nor anything that has the breath of life'.

Only the Bisharin, reared in violent heat and semi-starvation, kept up his strength and spirits. He was very friendly to Bruce. Out of rags torn from his own loincloth he made wrappings for the Scot's feet which eased his walking. But it was at night, when the temperature fell sharply enough to make all of them shiver, that his sores became excruciatingly painful.

Two mornings later one of the West Africans seemed to be struck with madness. Though not physically incapable, he would not rise from the ground and had to be left to his fate. That afternoon a second camel died.

'I had begun to prepare for the worst,' writes Bruce. 'I saw the fate of our camels approaching, and that our men grew weak in proportion; our bread, too, began to fail us, although we had plenty of camel's flesh in its stead; our water, though in all appearance we were to find it more frequently than in the beginning of our journey, was nevertheless brackish, and scarcely served the purpose to quench our thirst; and, above all, the dreadful simoom had perfectly exhausted our strength and brought upon us a degree of cowardice and languor that we struggled with in vain. I therefore, as the last effort, began to throw away every thing weighty I could spare, or that was not absolutely necessary, such as all shells, fossiles, minerals and petrifactions that I could get at, the countercases of my quadrant, telescopes, clock and other such things.'

In the afternoon they came on a naked body lying face downwards. It was that of the murdered eunuch. Behind some rocks were the bodies of his three chief servants. Along the way to the next well they found scattered the corpses of the West African pilgrims who had been with the eunuch. The Bisharin had allowed them to escape, knowing that, without food or water, they would soon collapse among the rocks and sand. Bruce, who would have travelled (and perhaps suffered) with Mahomet Towash if he had had his way, felt that this was a case where Providence had protected him and his men.

There was a wild duck at the next water pool, the first bird of the kind they had seen in the desert. Bruce ordered that it should not be killed, but should be frightened into flight, believing that it would make for the Nile and give some indication of the direction of the river and its distance from them. It flew straight to the west, rising so high before they lost sight of it that he concluded, rightly, that they still had far to go.

That night Hadji Ismael and the blind Greek, Georgis, were so ill and depressed as to say that they would go no farther, but must be left behind to die. Bruce insisted that they should ride by turns on one of the camels. He had again refused to do this himself: 'I well knew', he says, 'that if I had set them that example, besides destroying the camels, it would have had the very worst effect upon their dastardly spirits; and, indeed, we very soon saw the bad effects of this humane consideration for the two invalids.'

Next morning they found the last of the eunuch's party. It was his horse, which had made its way from well to well far beyond its human companions. But it, too, was dead.

The following day they saw men. Bruce's party were resting among some scrub near the top of a sandy slope when seventeen nomads with camels approached them from below. He formed his men up with their arms in their hands and called out that he would fire if the new-comers did not halt. They soon proved friendly enough. They were Ababdeh going to gather senna to be sent to Cairo as a drug – it was one of the few plants which could survive in the waterless desert. They could not spare two camels, which Bruce would have bought from them, but, by laying a lance on the ground with its point towards Aswan they gave an indication of the route to the town, which was two days' riding away.

The travellers could not ride, however: indeed, they could

scarcely totter. Their spirits rose for a little when they saw ground
before them covered with what seemed to be green grass and yellow
marigolds, but when they came closer they found the plants were
senna and colocynth, useless as food for man or beast.

This was an almost unbearable blow. Their water was almost
finished and their powdered bread, too. They had, indeed, dried
camel flesh, but, 'by living so long on bread and water an invincible
repugnance arose either to smell or taste it'. Hadji Ismael and
Georgis had become so stiff through riding on the camels that they
could not bear to touch the ground. Bruce's own feet made him
almost helpless. He made up his mind that they must throw away
his instruments to lighten the camels' loads so that they might all
take turns of riding over the last stage to Aswan.

But after a night of bitter cold the camels could not be brought
to their feet. There was nothing to be done, but to abandon all
their possessions except their firearms, from which they dared not
part. The camels were killed, and the Bisharin managed to drain
from their bodies the reserve of water that these animals could
carry in their stomachs for days through the desert. It was quite
fresh and tasteless, says Bruce, though rather blue in colour. This
supply, he reckoned, might just take them to Aswan.

He himself was in despair. All the fruits of his travels, his manuscripts and drawings, the records of his scientific observations, were
to be left in the desert. The pride in his achievement which had
buoyed him up for ten years was shattered. 'I felt for my country',
he writes, 'that chance alone, in this age of discovery, had robbed
her of the fairest garland of this kind she ever was to wear, which
all her fleets full of heroes and men of science, in all the oceans they
might be destined to explore, were incapable of replacing on her
brow.'

However, that afternoon they saw three kites, the scavenger
birds of Egypt, which are seldom far from inhabited country. At
night they saw trees. Next day they were among hills like those
Bruce remembered at Aswan. After taking his last bread and water,
he staggered up to a height, hoping to see the Nile, but nothing

was visible except a succession of granite ridges, some of which, he knew, must be beyond the river. When he sat silent, however, he could hear the noise of rushing water: it was surely, he thought, the sound of the famous First Cataract, just above Aswan town. Then, as night fell, a line drew itself across the landscape. It was a flock of water birds flying very low, and evidently seeking food along the banks of the river. Surely the travellers were very near the Nile. Idris, who had followed him, agreed that they must be close to Aswan.

'A cry of joy followed this annunciation . . . all burst into floods of tears, kissing and embracing one another, and thanking God for his mercy in this deliverance; and unanimously in token of their gratitude, and acknowledgement of my constant attention to them in the whole of this long journey, saluting me with the name of Abou Ferege, Father of Foresight, the only reward it was in their power to give.'

By half past ten the next morning they were on the outskirts of the town. Most of them pressed down to the wide river to drink, but Bruce, more cautious or more exhausted, sank down in the shade of palm trees and fell asleep. The impossible desert journey was over. From Berber to the Egyptian town it had lasted just twenty days.

19

<img — decorative divider>

Out of Africa

They were well received at Aswan. Hadji Ismael, starving, ragged and dirty, but wearing his green turban as a sherif, was the first to go into the town. In his broken Arabic he announced that he had come from hell, walking through a desert where the earth was on fire and the wind was flame. He was taken to the Turkish commander of the town, a janissary officer like himself, and he sent a soldier to find Bruce.

'Go to the palm trees,' said Ismael, 'and when you see the tallest man you have ever met, more ragged and dirty than I am, call him Yagoube and ask him to come with you to the Aga.'

Bruce was indeed an alarming figure. His outer clothes were torn and he had not had a whole shirt for months past. His beard was long and unkempt. He was so emaciated that his height seemed greater than ever and he could scarcely stand on his swollen feet. The Aga was at first shocked by the sight of such a being, but men who had known him on his first visit to Aswan recognized him again. He rested for some days in a hospitable house and then persuaded the Aga, not without difficulty, to lend him fast camels for a return journey into the desert to look for the baggage that had been abandoned there.

It was found untouched as they had left it. All the precious manuscripts and drawings were recovered. Bruce was able to produce the Sultan's firman, which was duly revered, and to draw money from an Aswan merchant. His next thought was to fulfil his promise to the Bisharin who had been both his captive and his guide and helper. The man was given a camel, clothes for himself and his wives and a load of millet. He went off full of gratitude – offering, indeed, to come back and serve Bruce for the rest of his life.

Now they could take ship again for the long, easy voyage to Cairo, carried by the current, or by oars when the wind was contrary. This was a chance to rest and sleep soundly, but Bruce was too worn out to make the most of it. The ending of effort and danger produced 'an universal relaxation of spirits . . . a kind of stupor or palsy of the mind . . . I seemed to be as if waked from a dream, when the senses are yet half asleep, and we only begin to doubt whether what has before passed in thoughts is real or not'.

Physically he was suffering from a common plague of African travel, the guinea-worm which had developed in one of his legs. He had an attack of malaria, and his feet were still torn and painful. It was an uneasy convalescent who sailed back towards the European civilization he had left ten years before.

Before Europe came Cairo. Bruce could not be quite sure of his welcome there now that Ali Bey, who had accepted him as his physician and had written so strongly in his favour to other Moslems in authority, had been displaced by his son-in-law, Mohammed Bey Abu Dahab. The two Mameluke chieftains were actually still at war. Ali's attempt to make himself completely independent of the Turkish Sultan with the help of Russia had collapsed, but he was at the head of a small army in Syria. When Bruce reached the Egyptian capital he took refuge in the Greek monastery of St George, very much against the will of the monks, who seemed to have forgotten his old friend and ally, the Archimandrite Christopher.

He had scarcely got to sleep that night when a dozen soldiers broke into the room. 'Get up; the Bey wants you,' their sergeant ordered, rudely. Bruce protested, especially when one of them tried to seize him by the arm.

'Keep your distance, you insolent blackguard!' he said. 'Remember I am an Englishman: do not lay your hands on me. If the Bey calls me, he is master in his own country and I will go to him. But, hands off! Though I have not seen him these three years he knows what is due to his own character better than to allow a slave like you to lay his filthy hands on a stranger like me.'

It did not take him long to prepare for the interview. He had been sleeping on a carpet in the only clothes he possessed – a waist-coat and trousers made from a coarse woollen blanket, with another blanket wrapped over his shoulder, and a thick, rough girdle in which he carried his pistols and an Ethiopian knife. He had neither shoes nor stockings. In this condition he was mounted on a donkey, the only kind of riding animal usually allowed to infidels in Cairo. It had no stirrups, and he had to balance himself painfully to keep his maimed feet off the ground. The soldiers carried long poles with which they hurried the donkey through the dark streets. 'I had every reason to sympathize with the beast for the severity of the blows, of which I was a perfect judge, as, whether through malice or heedlessness, every fourth stroke landed upon my back and haunches, so that my flesh was discoloured for more than two months afterwards.'

The palace, when he got there, was glowing with lights, and the Bey himself was in full dress, his girdle, turban and dagger-handle glittering with diamonds. This splendour was embarrassing to the traveller, who was bent with the pain of walking and scarcely dared to put his dirty, wounded feet on the rich Persian carpets. Abu Dahab, whom he had seen as an officer of Ali Bey when he was last in Cairo, did not recognize him at first, but when he did was full of apologies for having brought a stranger out so hurriedly. He had wanted, he said, to thank Bruce for the kindness to Hadji Ismael, who had been in the palace. The Bey was, in fact, an intelligent man, much interested in learning, who welcomed this chance of talking to a visitor able to tell him about distant countries.

'But this is not the time,' he said. 'Go home and sleep and I shall send for you. Eat and drink, and fear nothing. My father-in-law is gone, but by the grace of God I am here in his place; that is enough.'

Bruce left him, much reassured. As he went through the ante-room a slave appeared with a basket of oranges. This the traveller took as a gesture which would show the bystanders that he was high in the Bey's favour. But it was more than that. When he lifted a single orange the slave whispered, 'It is all for you. Put your hand to the bottom, the best fruit is there.'

It was a fat purse full of gold. Bruce kissed it and gave it back again.

'This is forbidden fruit for me,' he said, 'though it is the best. The Bey's protection and favour are more to me than a thousand purses.'

This was the declaration of financial independence that he liked to make in order to maintain his prestige; but the refusal of money by any one – above all by a man 'dressed like those slaves who carry water and wash stairs' – was so intensely surprising to the Bey's messenger that he insisted on taking Bruce back to his master.

The Bey, too, was surprised, though apparently not angry. 'Surely you must need money,' he said; 'those are not your usual clothes.'

Bruce was diplomatically grateful. 'You already have my prayers,' he declared. 'I must not deprive you of those of widows and orphans whom that money could help.' He explained that he could draw all he needed from his Cairo bankers, Julien and Rosa. 'Besides, I am in the service of the greatest King in Europe, who would not fail to supply me abundantly if my necessities required it.'

The Bey was impressed and asked what else he could do for him. Bruce was ready with a request which he must have been planning while he was travelling to Cairo. He had countrymen, he said, who traded to the Red Sea from India, but they were not allowed to sail to Egypt itself. Their ships had to stop at Jidda, where they paid heavy customs duties and also had to make presents to the Sherif of Mecca. The Sherif was exacting more and more money from them, so that the trade was in danger of being stifled altogether.

Bruce probably reckoned that the Bey was not likely to feel very friendly to the Sherif, master of the Moslem Holy Places, since it was Abu Dahab who had been sent to Arabia by Ali to conquer Mecca.

'Are there not guns in your ships?' the Bey asked. 'Why don't you blow Jidda to pieces?'

'Our ships are all armed for war and full of brave officers and skilful seamen,' Bruce answered. 'But,' he added virtuously, 'Jidda is not part of our King's dominions, and in foreign countries we never use force except in our own defence.' However, he said, his countrymen would like to be able to come to Suez and trade directly with Egypt.

'That would be to my advantage,' said the Bey. 'You have not told me yet what I am to do for you.'

'When it is known at home what you have done for my country at my request,' Bruce answered, 'it will be a greater honour to me than any ruler has ever done me.'

It was agreed that they should decide together the conditions and customs duties for British-Indian trade at Suez, and Bruce went off in triumph, clothed ceremoniously in a new robe. The same soldiers received him and mounted him, not on a donkey this time but on a mule with gilt stirrups.

'I went back with full as much speed as I came, but free from those salutations of the quarter-staff which I still felt on my haunches. The scale of politeness was now turned in my favour; and to shew their respect for me the soldiers knocked down every person they overtook in the streets, giving him first a blow upon the head, then asking him why he did not get out of the way.'

This was the last achievement of the long African journey, and one in which James Bruce took a good deal of pride. In a sense which he could not foresee it has had, perhaps, more influence on history than anything else in his career, for there was in it the germ of the idea of that 'overland route' to India which had a part in international crises and wars for nearly a century after his day, and finally, when the land barrier between Suez and the Mediterranean was cut by canal, led to the occupation and control of Egypt by the

British and all the events which have followed from that in our time.

In Bruce's day, however, there was scarcely a hint of such developments. He did, indeed, work out with the Bey a scheme of customs charges for British merchandise at Suez far more favourable than those at Jidda. This was embodied in a firman, binding on the Egyptian authorities, which was sent to Arabia along with a letter from Bruce dated February 1st, 1773, to his friends, Captain Thornhill of the *Bengal Merchant* and Captain Price of the *Lion*, 'or any other of the English vessels trading to Jidda'. This gave advice on the advantages and financing of trade with Egypt and the precise bearings of places on the Gulf of Suez previously unvisited by British ships.

The letter also contained a characteristic caution and warning:

'As I have no view in this but your advantage, so I will not take upon myself to answer for any consequences. You know what Turks are. I never saw one of them to be trusted in money affairs. You must keep your eyes open and deal for ready money. You will, however, be much safer, be better used, have better markets, and be much sooner dispatched;[1] and if any of your cargo remains unsold, you may leave it here in great security, with a certainty of its selling in winter.'

The Suez Adventure, as it was called, was duly begun from India, with the support of Warren Hastings, who was soon to be the first Governor-General of the East India Company's lands.

Hastings's interest in the Suez route, particularly as a new and shorter line of communication with London, was keen. In this, as in many other things, he was obstructed by a majority of his council, led by Sir Philip Francis, who seem to have done their best to prejudice the East India Company directors against the Red Sea route which was developing according to Bruce's plan. The Governor-General had scarcely succeeded in organizing a regular system of dispatches through Suez when the Ottoman Government in Istanbul took alarm. They demanded that ships from India should

[1] i.e. at Suez than at Jidda.

13. One of the strips of paper on which Bruce wrote his daily notes during his journey through the Sudan (now at Broomhall)

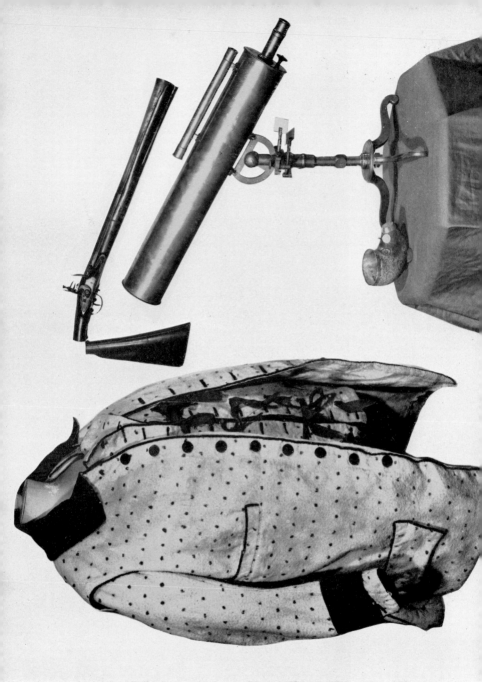

14. Some of Bruce's relics at Broomhall including his folding Blunderbuss and telescope and a cup made from rhinoceros horn which he used on his journey

again go no farther than Jidda. Finally, in April 1781, the Turkish Sultan issued a firman closing 'the Suez Sea' completely to Europeans. It was to be reserved for Moslem pilgrims travelling to Mecca. Franks, the firman declared, made a habit of building up trading privileges in Moslem ports till they grew strong enough to annex whole countries. This was what they had done in India. It must not happen in Egypt.[1]

The privilege Bruce had won for British-India merchants was quashed and with it the prestige he could claim as the opener of a new trade route. But he had sown a seed which became a formidable tree as soon as steamers made it possible to reach India swiftly from Suez.

When the Suez firman was drawn up Mohammed Abu Dahab was just about to set out for the last battle with his father-in-law. He was anxious that Bruce should go with him, but, as usual, the Scot wished to keep out of African quarrels; and it was time for him to go home and enjoy the fame and rewards that he counted on.

Then came a conversation which, as he reported it, carried an implied reproach to King George and his Ministers seventeen years later. What would he do at home? asked the Bey: he would not be a soldier, he was not a merchant.

'Have you any other trade or occupation but travelling?'

'No other,' answered Bruce.

'Ali Bey, my father-in-law, often observed there was never such a people as the English; no other nation on earth could be compared with them, and none had so many great men in all professions, by land and sea. I never understood this till now', said Abu Dahab. 'I see it must be so when your King cannot find other employment for such a man as you but sending him to perish by hunger and thirst in the sands, or to have his throat cut by lawless barbarians.'

Disturbances were to be expected in Cairo when its master left for war, and Bruce set off at once for Alexandria and a ship that would take him to Europe. He found a French captain ready to sail, and a friendly Turk warned him to leave as quickly as possible.

[1] 'The Overland Route', *Bengal Past and Present*, vol. IV.

There were rumours that Ali Bey had been captured; because of the defeated ruler's alliance with the Russians the town mobs were likely to attack any foreign Christian they could find. In fact, the sound of musket shots could be heard from Alexandria and the sky above it was lit by burning houses when his ship left the harbour.

As usual, the Mediterranean was unkind to him. The winds were high, and the old vessel sprang a leak off Derna, where he had been shipwrecked more than six years before. After the storm was over and the leak stopped Bruce lay groaning with the pain of the worm in his leg when the captain came to him with a question.

'Tell me how many of those things' – he winked – 'you have on board. . . . *Ces morts*. How many dead men have you in those trunks? Last night the crew were going to throw all your boxes overboard.'

Apparently the instrument cases which had been carried so painfully over deserts and mountains were now believed to hold mummies.

Bruce handed over his keys. 'In case another gale should come,' he said, 'open the trunk you think likeliest to have a dead man in it. There will be none, but try the other cases if you like. If you find a single corpse you can throw them overboard.'

There was, indeed, a second storm off Malta, but no mummy was found. On March 25th, 1773, the ship reached Marseilles after a three weeks' voyage.

It was almost exactly ten years since James Bruce had sailed from Italy to Algiers. He was desperately ill. His Greek servant Michael, the one man who had been with him through the whole of his Nile journey, had tried to extract the guinea-worm from his leg, but it had broken and he was in agony. The doctor at the Marseilles quarantine station advised amputation of the leg: this under the conditions of the day could mean death. Bruce decided on a drastic medical treatment which succeeded in the end, but left him weak and limping for many months. The long odyssey was over, or almost over, and he was preparing to claim the reward of all those efforts, but he was not yet ready to go back to London or Scotland.

It is clear[1] that he had already made his plans. He would present himself as the faithful servant of King George bringing both the glory of discovering the source of the Nile and countless gifts – his drawings of ancient architecture from North Africa, his Ethiopian manuscripts, his seeds of strange plants, his drawings of beasts, birds and fishes, his account of unknown lands and peoples, and for British traders the privilege of access to Suez. He had already begun to write down some of his experiences and the historical conclusions that he drew from them during the weary months when he was held back at Sennar. This would be completed. His friends had already assured him that all the learned world would be waiting for a book from him.

And then Ulysses must join his Penelope. To be sure, he had never found time to marry the faithful lady he expected to be waiting for him, but he seems to have felt no doubt at all that his Peggy would have resisted all other suitors. He had been a cautious and practical-minded as well as a daring traveller, very well aware of the oddities of human character; but, in some moods, his adventures seem to have had for him the quality of a long romance, reminding him of 'the fairy tales', full of mailed warriors, strange kingdoms and strange beasts, wicked enchanters – the Naib, Abba Salama, Fidele – and of places that lived under a malign spell like the deadly city of Sennar.

Now the prince of romance was coming home: it was in the proper nature of things that the princess should be ready to reward his courage. Ten years earlier he had persuaded himself that it was for her sake that he was setting out to win fame in Africa. He had, indeed, met other princesses on his travels, but these were mere memories. He felt as sure of finding Margaret Murray again as he was that 'the greatest King in the world' would indeed recognize and reward the man who had been dismissed from his consul-generalship eight years before.

[1] Particularly from a letter of Belville, his friend in Aleppo, April 25th, 1772.

The news that he was returning had reached France before him and he had all the welcome he could have wished for at Marseilles from the friends of his French friends in Syria and particularly from a local *savant*, Journu de Montagny. Buffon, who had helped to supply him with scientific instruments before he began his Nile journey and was eagerly waiting for information about the fauna of Ethiopia and its neighbourhood, came to meet him. They travelled to Paris together. The great biologist had just published the second volume of his *General History of Birds*, part of the vast *Histoire Naturelle* in which he described and classified all the animals and minerals of which he could hear. Bruce gave him a full account of his discoveries and discussed with him how his own book of travels should be written. Social life in Paris was overcast by the last illness of Louis XV, but the traveller met many of its learned men and social leaders. He gave seeds of Ethiopian plants to the royal botanic garden and a copy of the Apocryphal Book of Enoch to the King's Library.

In the third volume of his *Histoire des Oiseaux*, Buffon paid him a glowing tribute.

'A new aid which has just come to me and which I hasten to announce to the public is the communication, as frank as it is generous, of the thoughts and observations of an illustrious traveller Monsieur le Chevalier[1] James Bruce de Kinnaird, who on returning from Nubia and the heart of Abyssinia, stayed some days with me and told me of what he had learned on a journey which was no less painful than perilous. I was truly astonished as I looked through the immense collection of drawings he had made and coloured himself – animals, birds, fish, plants, buildings, clothing, arms, etc., of the different peoples, in a word, all the objects which we would wish to know of have been described and perfectly represented; nothing seems to have escaped his curiosity. It remains for me to wish to be able to enjoy this very valuable work fully. No doubt the Govern-

[1] Though not a knight, Bruce was usually addressed on the Continent as *Chevalier* or *cavaliere*, an indication of nobility which he probably thought very fitting.

ment of England will order its publication: that highly respected
nation, which takes the lead of all others in discoveries, cannot but
add to its glory by giving to the world promptly those of this
outstanding traveller who has not been content to describe nations
well but has also made very important observations on the cultivation of different kinds of grain, on the navigation of the Red Sea,
on the course of the Nile from its mouth to its source, which he was
the first to discover, and on several other points of geography and
means of communication which may be very useful to trade and
agriculture.'

This was a splendid recommendation of Bruce's achievements to
Europe, and particularly to Britain, for Buffon's work was read by
the learned everywhere. From Paris he was not yet ready to go
home, however. He was still ill and in need of rest. He was advised
to go to the warm baths of Poretta, in Italy, where his worm-
wounded leg might be properly cured. These healing springs were
near Bologna, the home of Luigi Balugani, and Bruce was a guest at
the house of the Marchese di Ranuzzi, who had been Luigi's
patron. This does not suggest that the Scot felt he had anything to
hide in his treatment of the young artist: indeed, he had already
corresponded with another member of the family, Filippo Balugani,
who looked out for him some drawings that had been mislaid and
asked to be allowed to meet him and 'give thanks for so many bene-
fits to my dear brother'.[1]

Bruce spent two months in Bologna working on his uncompleted
drawings in the intervals of medical treatment. The baths did their
work. He was well again, and if there were questions among the
Bolognese about Luigi's death they do not seem to have troubled
him. He set out for Rome, this time with a letter from the French
Foreign Minister, the Duc d'Aiguillon, to France's Ambassador at
the Vatican, Cardinal de Bernis, recommending this 'Englishman,
renowned for the extent of his knowledge, and his zeal for the growth
of the sciences and arts', who had brought back to Europe from
Abyssinia the fruit of his work and discoveries. Protestant Britain

[1] Letter of August 8th, 1773, Broomhall Papers.

had no regular diplomatic dealings with the Papacy, whose capital
was the home of King George's Jacobite rival. The ageing Prince
Charles was, indeed, no longer the 'bonnie' hero of the 1745 Rising
and his kingship was not fully recognized even by the Pope, his
host, but he still claimed to be Charles III. The British Minister to
the Grand Duke of Tuscany at Florence, Sir Horace Mann, had for
years kept a watchful eye both on Vatican politics and on the little
Stuart court and the Scots and English exiles who still clustered
round it in Rome. Mann is best remembered now as the friend to
whom Horace Walpole wrote the endlessly entertaining letters
which record the gossip and scandal of Georgian London, but
he was a great figure in Italy when Bruce came to visit him in
November 1773 and left again most abruptly and alarmingly.

It was at Florence – so it seems – that the traveller had learned,
dramatically enough, that Margaret Murray was no longer waiting
to marry him. A message had been sent to her at her home telling
of his return to Cairo, but she was no longer in Scotland to receive it.

According to what was apparently a family tradition,[1] she had
fallen ill and had been taken to Italy by her anxious brother, partly
in search of health, partly in the hope of finding Bruce there. The
Murrays were told, however, that he had died in Ethiopia. They met
a Roman nobleman, the Marchese Filippo Accoromboni, and
Margaret was persuaded to marry him.

At the theatre at Florence, so the story says, she and Bruce met
without warning. The Marchesa fainted, and her lover, in an
explosion of passion, declared that he had been betrayed by her
husband.

After a discussion of his disappointment with Horace Mann, he
vanished, leaving a letter behind him which convinced his host that
his intentions were very violent indeed. Mann wrote off at once,
hoping this message would catch the traveller on his road, begging

[1] Note on the Batoni portrait of James Bruce in *Illustrated Catalogue of
Portraits on loan in the New Galleries, Corporation Buildings,* Glasgow, 1868. The
information was probably supplied by his granddaughter, Mrs Cumming
Bruce.

him 'to desist from the carrying into execution what seemed to be the only motive for your going to Rome'. Bruce's purpose there, he said, 'cannot fail of being attended by the most serious and probably the most tragical consequences. I once more beseech you, Dear Sir, to reflect on this: if you still persist it will convince me that when an Error is unfortunately fixed in a reasoning mind it is almost impossible to remove it.'[1]

Bruce had evidently left breathing fire and vengeance against the Marquis. The result was not 'tragical', at least for Accoromboni, Bruce, or Mann; but in the eyes of the world it was ridiculous. In the eighteenth century there were many things which could be held to justify a duel, but marriage with a young woman who had not seen a former lover for eleven years was not one of them.

A Scots priest, the Abbé Peter Grant, who had a social talent which made him the friend of most English-speaking people in the city, Jacobites or visiting Hanoverians, Roman Catholics or Protestants, did his best to mediate in the quarrel. He persuaded the Marquis to say that if he had known of Margaret Murray's engagement to Bruce there would have been no marriage. But mere reported words were not enough for the disappointed lover, who demanded something in writing that could be regarded as an apology. He sent a letter to Accoromboni which called plainly for a duel.

It was not for merely verbal satisfaction, he wrote (in Italian), 'that sick and covered with wounds I have journeyed so far by land and sea to find you.

'Without any provocation or injury from me you have deprived me of my honour – me, an innocent man engaged in the service of my country – by violating all the rights that are most sacred before God and man. You now make difficulties about giving me in writing what you willingly confess in words. A man of honour and innocence, Marquis, knows no such subtleties as these, and it would be well for one of us today if you had been as scrupulous in doing an injury as you are in repairing it.

[1] Letter of November 16th, 1773 – Broomhall Papers.

'I am your equal, Marquis, in every way, and only God can give me justice for the wrong you have done me. Full of innocence, and with a clear conscience I commit my revenge to Him and draw my sword against you with confidence inspired by the reflection that I have done my duty and by a sense of the injustice and violence I have suffered from you without reason.

'At half past nine (French time) I am coming to your gate in my carriage; if it does not please you let your own be ready and let us go together to see which of two things is easier – to injure a man in his absence or to defend the affront in his presence.'

By half past nine (presumably) the Marquis gave his written reply. It was a prudent one.

'When the marriage with Miss Murray, today my wife, was arranged it was never said to me that there had been a previous promise to yourself, otherwise such a matter would not have been concluded.

'As for yourself, on my honour, I have never spoken of you in any way as you were entirely unknown to me. On this account, if I can serve you, command me.'[1]

For Margaret all this may have been tragedy enough. It is said that she never recovered from the shock of Bruce's reappearance, she certainly died soon after it. But though Rome laughed, no doubt, over this extravaganza, the laughter was friendly. The city was full of people from Britain, Jacobites and aristocratic tourists. Prince Charles had taken a pretty young wife, Princess Louise of Stolberg-Gedern, and in the first year of this finally disastrous marriage had roused himself from the drunkenness and depression of his decade of failure. They called Louise 'the Queen of Hearts'. She was the great-granddaughter of a Bruce and showed a proper family interest in the latest great man of the name.[2] Hostesses and guests were eager to hear of his African adventures. Pope Clement XIV received him and presented him with a number of gold medals struck during his reign.

[1] Letter of November 30th, 1773.
[2] Letter of the Abbé Grant, December 22nd, 1773, Broomhall Papers.

A whole series of learned societies in Italian cities made him one of their honorary members.

It was slowly that he turned homewards, again stopping at Paris for discussions with Buffon. The story of his ludicrous quarrel with the Marchese Accoromboni and some comic versions of his African stories went with him, or before him, to London. For some of those who would meet him there was already a hint of violence and exaggeration in the name of James Bruce.

A Bee Cuckoo

20

⤜∘◉∘⤛

The Road to Ardwhillery

'I hope my terrible voyage to Abyssinia will not be money thrown away', Bruce had written from Marseilles to the Edinburgh lawyer, John Mackenzie of Delvine, whom he had left in charge of his affairs.[1] 'I may venture to assure you not from my own opinion but that of all that are competent Judges, I have performed them all with Great Attention and do not doubt you will acquit me of any Imputation of Idleness or Dissipation!'

This businesslike attitude to his own achievement was genuine enough. He did expect to be paid, one way or another, for all that he had done, but fame and glory were his main concern when he reached London at last on June 21st, 1774. And London was not indisposed to listen to him. Strange regions of the earth and men who could describe them were in fashion.

For a dozen years King George's Government had been at peace with its European neighbours. The eyes of politicians and journalists could safely stray to the ends of the earth, particularly, of course to India, where they had become conscious of possessing not simply an immensely powerful and profitable trading company but also a vast empire for whose government they must take some responsibility. They wanted to know more about other southern and eastern lands. The great (and wealthy) amateur of science, Joseph Banks, had returned from his voyage round the world with Captain Cook and their discoveries in the Pacific to become the leading figure of the Royal Society and finally almost its dictator.

[1] Delvine MSS, National Library of Scotland, 1241.

A genuine Stone Age man brought from Tahiti, Omai, had become a favourite ornament of London drawing-rooms. A Scottish giant from unknown Africa could be at least equally interesting. Less than three weeks after the traveller's arrival Horace Walpole was writing to Sir Horace Mann in Florence:

'Africa is, indeed, coming into fashion. There is just returned a Mr Bruce, who has lived three years in the Court of Abyssinia, and breakfasted every morning with the Maids of Honour on live oxen. Otaheite and Mr Banks are quite forgotten, but Mr Blake [a man known for social extravagance] I suppose will order a live sheep for supper at Almack's, and ask whom he shall help to a piece of the shoulder. Oh yes, we shall have negro butchers, and French cooks will be laid aside!'

There is no hint of serious criticism, even of real scepticism, in all this. Walpole is merely amusing himself with the fantastic elaboration of what seems to him an already exaggerated story. Clearly Mann has not told him of his own dealings with 'a Mr Bruce' and Walpole himself has not met the traveller. There is no suggestion that 'imputations of idleness or dissipation' are being raised against Bruce. His journey is a social sensation, as he had expected it would be. But in the gossip of London society it is also a joke, and this is something that he did not expect.

London was prepared to hear what he could say. It was, perhaps, a little prejudiced against him by the knowledge that he had allowed himself to become a lion in France and Italy before coming back to Britain, that he had left plants and drawings and at least one manuscript about which the learned were particularly curious in Paris to mark his gratitude to the French Crown; for Paris was London's great rival in Europe. But the fact that French scientists took him so seriously was a reason why he must be seen and heard.

King George did receive him graciously enough. The drawings of classical architecture in North Africa, the making of which had, in Bruce's opinion, been the main object of his appointment as Consul-General at Algiers, were duly handed over to the royal collection. He reminded the King that all those who had arranged for this work – and suggested proper rewards for it – were now dead – Egremont, Halifax, Robert Wood.

'I am alive and will not forget,' said George, reassuringly.[1]

George III had, indeed, a retentive memory: it seems likely that his view of what had happened a dozen or ten years before was rather different from James Bruce's. He may not have forgotten that he had thought a man experienced in North African affairs would have made a more useful representative at Algiers than an amateur of Roman architecture and archaeology, however assiduous such a researcher might be. Almost certainly he did remember that Bruce had, in fact, been dismissed from his post.

The Scot had persuaded himself – and many other people – that it was as 'the servant of the greatest King on earth' that he had made his almost incredible journey. His supreme offering to his sovereign was the glory of a great discovery which had been sought in vain by a long series of rulers since the times of the Pharaohs – the discovery of the source of the Nile. Beside this all the geographical, biological, historical, linguistic, political knowledge he had gathered in Ethiopia and the Sudan was of secondary importance. But King George was not a Pharaoh or a Caesar: he had not sent James Bruce to the Nile, whatever some of his ministers may have hinted on the subject, and the problem of the great river's source was not a particularly exciting one for him, even if Bruce had been the first to solve it.

A dozen years earlier the King's ministers had been trying to build up an image of peaceful glory and progress for the new reign which would replace the picture of warlike success in all quarters of the world that William Pitt had created for Britain in the last years of George II; but by 1774 the King himself was absorbed in strictly practical politics. After long and painful struggles with party leaders much abler than himself he had at last found a Prime Minister, Lord North, who could manage Parliament for him in the way he wanted. Lord North, it seems, was not much

[1] Draft Memorial at Broomhall.

inclined to be interested in African opportunities or adventures. Peace in Europe and Asia was still his Government's aim, but he was being forced to look anxiously towards North America, where the colonists' revolt against taxation from London was pushing him towards what was to be, for Britain, the most dangerous of the century's wars. When Bruce claimed credit for the Egyptian firman that opened Suez to British traders from India the Prime Minister's comment was chilling: he doubted whether the East India Company would find this particularly useful.

Altogether, Bruce's first weeks in London were disappointing. The self-confidence which, in a young man, had impressed people in power such as Chatham and Halifax, and had quelled or persuaded African rulers, was not so impressive in a burly Scots laird of forty-four, too obviously convinced that he knew more of the subjects he wanted to talk about than anyone else in Europe. Indeed, it could seem comic or simply rude. Bruce had got into the habit of dealing with men in authority as something more than an equal, in rank as well as in knowledge, but fashionable London was not at all impressed by hints at his very distant descent from Scottish kings.

Educated Englishmen had no difficulty in accepting what Mr Banks or Captain Cook had to tell them about Pacific Islands which scarcely any white man had seen before them: after all, several scientists and whole crews of officers and seamen had come back from the South Seas to confirm one another's reports of what had been found there. But everyone had at least heard of the Nile and Abyssinia. Classical authors and Dr Johnson's *Rasselas*, had spread firm, though mainly false, ideas of the sort of life that could be looked for in the one ancient African empire. James Bruce himself was the only witness to his own travels. What he had to say about feasts of raw meat, chieftains draped in ox-guts, burning purple winds, the official king-killer of Sennar and at least a dozen other things which no one in the rational eighteenth century had thought of imagining seemed, from the first, too much to be swallowed.

When he was cross-questioned with even the politest hint of

polite scepticism, by people who, too obviously, knew nothing whatever about the realities of Africa, Bruce was apt to freeze into proud silence.

He still had to write the book of his travels which was expected from him, but he had decided to go home to Kinnaird before making a serious beginning on it. He wanted to take a businesslike view of his own affairs. His 'commissioner', John Mackenzie of Delvine, had sent him a lively letter on June 30th.

Dear Sir,

I have yours of the 25th Intimating your arrival at London on which Lucky Event I felicitate myself as well as you, for few things I wish more than to know you survive – I think you may now say with Truth and Justice, *per varios casus, per tot discrimina rerum tendemus in Latium* – or Londinium.

You tell me I may expect you here Immediately on the receipt of Copys of your papers with the Carron Company.

This (tho' you should run me through the Body) I can scarce credit, for were you to occupy the Tabernacles of Whitfield or Wesley for three months to come, you would have a thronger[1] audience from John Bull than either to have a detail of your travels wherein I suspect you will be oblig'd to Indulge Itching Ears of many of the Great. And I shall be perfectly satisfied if you reach this northerly climate in a month, altho' none here can wish your return more than I do in whom you was pleased to repose so much blind Confidence.

I sent you, some posts ago, the 2d articles you entered into with the Carron Comp'y and the obligation I exacted from them . . . They are a Loupy Sett (as most projectors are) violent in their Expectations, but tardy and superficial in their performance or Execution, yet I expect to convince you at meating that you have sufer'd as little by your distance and in your absence as others who have molested them with Lawsuits (whether Justly or unjustly I do not pretend to say) . . .

[1] More crowded.

I never laid claim to understand Coale myself tho' you may who have seen so many various occurrences in traversing so large a part of the Globe. It is now time you should be Coole and Enjoy *Otium Cum Dignitate* and Instruct Others – and among them

My Dr Sir

Your most Obedient Ser^t

Jo Mackenzie.[1]

Perhaps a faint nervousness can be read between these cheerful lines. Mackenzie and John Higgins of Neuk, Bruce's factor (in English, land steward) had indeed watched his interests jealously enough at times in their dealings with the Carron Company, but they had not carried out all the instructions he had left with them. Like other Scots lairds of the time, he was an 'improving' landlord who wished to increase the size of farms on his estate, and the rents he could draw from them. He had ordered in 1762 that the leases of some tenants should not be renewed. But to part a man from his farm was unpleasant work, though common enough at the time. As the years passed it had seemed more and more uncertain whether the Laird of Kinnaird would ever return and the tenants were still there in 1774.[2] Bruce's home-coming was to be clouded with the unpopularity which clearances on an estate always produced. And he was not at all unwilling to 'molest' the Carron Company with a lawsuit, though the sale of his coal to it supplied him with a large part of his income.

Perhaps he was surveying a future legal battlefield when James Boswell met him on August 9th in the Edinburgh Parliament House, the seat of the Court of Session – 'just returned from his most curious travels, a tall stout bluff man in green and gold.'[3] The explorer was talking to two eminent Scots lawyers – a judge, James Burnett, Lord Monboddo, and an advocate, John Maclaurin, who was to be a judge as Lord Dreghorn. Boswell himself was not

[1] Broomhall MSS.

[2] National Library of Scotland, Delvine MSS 1242–4.

[3] Boswell's Journal, *Boswell for the Defence*.

only an advocate, the son of a judge and the ardent disciple and future biographer of Dr Samuel Johnson but also an enthusiastic, though anonymous, journalist. He saw in the meeting the opportunity of a 'scoop' for the *London Magazine*, to which he contributed. Both Monboddo and Maclaurin were authors with wide interests and inquiring minds in that intensely literary Edinburgh of the Golden Age.

The judge was considered a philosophical eccentric in his day, largely because his theories forecast Darwinian evolution. 'Have they tails?' he had cried when Joseph Banks's companion in the South Seas, Dr Solander, described the primitive Australian aborigines. These were men whose curiosity about Africa Bruce was quite prepared to satisfy. 'Monboddo set him dead and Maclaurin snuffed him keen' Boswell noted with satisfaction. The reading world was waiting for a first authentic account of his travels. A good many strange stories had, indeed, appeared in newspapers and magazines, picked up at second or third hand from people who had talked to the explorer, and usually garbled in the process. It was this sort of publication which had made James Bruce unwilling to speak freely. But James Boswell felt that he could do better than the casual gatherers of gossip.

After the group in the Parliament House broke up he sought out the explorer in his lodgings. But conversation with two learned men was one thing and journalistic interviewing was another. James Bruce resisted and resented the questioning of a man who did not know a guinea-worm from a serpent and seemed to believe that Arabs wore wigs. For him Boswell was not a favoured name, even when it belonged to an exceedingly distant cousin who was proud that the blood of Bruce flowed in his veins. When he was at last provoked into talking he began by talking of his arrival at Jidda when 'a Scotsman, a Captain Boswell' had refused to help him and he had fallen back on the hospitality of Englishmen. He showed the scar on his leg left by the guinea-worm and Boswell dug some further information on Ethiopia out of him, 'as from a flinty rock with pick axes'.

How dare you approach me with your travells. There is not a single word of them true There you may be right, and altho I never dined upon the Lion or eat half a Cow and turned the rest to grafs, yet my works have been of more use to mankind than yours and there is more truth in one page of my Edin.ʳ directory than in all your five Volumes 4º. So when you talk to me dont imagine yourself at the Source of the Nile!

I. Kay Del. et Sculp.ᵗ Publifhed as the Act Directs 179¹

15. This cartoon by John Kay, shows Bruce in conversation with Peter Williamson, the adventurer who produced the first Edinburgh street directory; it expresses the sceptical reaction to Bruce's account of his journey

16. James Bruce, later in life. Engraved from a drawing by David Martin,
in the *Scottish National Portrait Gallery*

'All extraordinary travellers', Boswell afterwards reflected 'are a kind of shows; a kind of wild beasts. Banks [whom he had also met] and Bruce however were animals very different from one another. Banks was an elephant, quite placid and gentle, allowing you to get upon his back or play with his proboscis; Bruce a tiger that growled whenever you approached him.'

'I conjectured', he wrote in his journal,[1] 'that he had come to London with high expectations from Government and had been disappointed. This had soured his temper, not very sweet originally; and he had come to Scotland, at which he had conceived a strong aversion when young from the bad usage of a stepmother who had obtained unjust settlements from his father – and come in bad humour with it and its inhabitants just to try to see how much he could squeeze out of his estate to support him in England'.

This was a subjective judgement, though perhaps not intentionally an unkindly one. There is no reason to think that life in London had anything like the intense pull on James Bruce's ambitions that it had on James Boswell's. His love of Scotland was strong and he chose to pass most of the rest of his life there. But Boswell's opinion was not very different from that of a good many of his fellow countrymen, then and later. If Bruce was disappointed with London, Scotland, on the whole, was disappointed with him and never understood him.

The interview in Milne Square made two articles in the *London Magazine*. It was these which introduced Bruce to many English readers. It was not a very good introduction. Inevitably Boswell paid his tribute to Dr Johnson: everyone, he wrote, wanted to know more about Abyssinia because of *Rasselas*. His own report of what he had been told was rather confused, except on the one point of the Ethiopians' eating habits.

'The Light of the Gospel beams upon them very faintly, for they are a fierce and cruel people. Not satisfied with devouring raw flesh, their custom is to eat collops cut from live animals. . . . A company of Abyssinians at dinner is a horrible spectacle.'

[1] *Boswell for the Defence*, August 9th, 1774.

The explorer himself was *Nec visu facilis nec dictu affabilis ulli* – neither easy to look at nor kindly in conversation.

'Some people have complained of Mr Bruce as being close and reserved in his speech since his return to Britain. But it should be considered that a gentleman of fortune, and who has the *blood of Bruce* in his veins is entitled to maintain a dignity of character . . . When he meets with men of knowledge and of classical inquiry he is very ready to take the trouble to giving them the satisfaction of which they are worthy.'[1]

Bruce was not very pleased with this piece of publicity. He was used to being considered a handsome, tall man: the quotation from Virgil described a monster, the Cyclops Polyphemus. When the traveller dined with Monboddo, whose literary parties were famous, Boswell was annoyed to find that he himself had not been invited to meet him again. 'It was below me to mind whether I was agreeable to him or not', Boswell reflected. 'Bruce is a rough-minded man and has not such principles as that one would court him . . . I had seen him as a curiosity and extracted from him a good essay for the *London Mazagine*; and there was enough.'[2]

For James Bruce the interview and its fruits were perhaps more important than he imagined. Boswell was not yet a great figure in the world, but he was a close friend of the one man whose views on Abyssinia were likely to carry most weight among educated Englishmen. Bruce had not met Dr Johnson, but after these dealings with his disciple the author of *Rasselas* was not likely to be prejudiced in his favour.

A third article in the *London Magazine* for February 1775 cannot have been more welcome than the first two. It was headed *On the Advantages which GREAT BRITAIN may derive from the Discoveries of Travellers in the reign of his present Majesty: A Rhapsody.*

It was signed 'Nunius', but contains references which suggest that it, too, was written by James Boswell in one of his more spritely moods.

[1] *London Magazine*, August and September 1774.
[2] Journal, December 15th, 1774, in, *Boswell: The Ominous Years.*

'What a prodigious noise has been made about the wonderful acquisitions to our knowledge by travellers in the age in which we live', it begins. 'Let us therefore consider what advantages we have gained, or really may gain, from these extraordinary expeditions. If it should be admitted that *amusement* is the only object, the end might have been answered as well in a snug apartment in London, with pen, ink and paper, as by all the apparatus of navigation, and risking the danger of the deep, and the cruelty of savages. Surely the *Arabian Nights Entertainment* and the *Adventures of Jack the Giant Killer* are as entertaining as *Hawkesworth's Collection of Voyages* or the *Travels of Mr Bruce*.'

The author admits that 'the utility of Mr Bruce's travels cannot yet be fully illustrated, that gentleman not having yet deigned to favour the world with his own account of them, but from the specimen given in the *London Magazine* one most useful discovery may be adopted from the Abyssinians, which is that of eating meat raw. I would not go to the high degree of *refinement* "eating the flesh of animals while they are yet alive," as it is *utility* alone that I have at present in view.' In future, the writer suggests, it may be possible to do without butchers and save the expense of fires for cooking.

This is nonsense rather below the level of undergraduate wit – well below Horace Walpole's. But it suggests how very little of the explorer's real achievement was reaching the public which the first news of his journey had interested, and which he counted on to give him fame. He was rebuilding part of his house at Kinnaird, he was looking into his contract with the Carron Company, 'the curiosity and kindness' of his friends occupied him for weeks on end, but it was only too pointedly true that he had not even begun to make the book about his travels which was expected from him. There could, indeed, have been a whole series of books, not only the story of his adventures, but monographs on Ethiopian history, on African animals and plants, on Ethiopian languages, on geography, on buildings. He knew more about most of those subjects than any other man living and could have spent the rest of his lifetime in developing and systematizing his knowledge and passing it on to other scholars. But though he was a man of limitless curiosity and many more or less original ideas, he had not the mind of a scholar. Disappointment at the discovery that the mere fact of reaching the source of the Blue Nile did not make him a great man in the eyes of King George and his subjects, seemed to freeze his will to record his knowledge and memories.

He was still hoping, indeed, that the Government would publish a collection of his drawings – to do this in a really impressive way would be too costly a business for a commercial firm. No doubt it was to forward this project that he went to London in the spring of 1775 and showed them privately to a number of interested and influential people. He was most at home in the house of Mrs Strange, wife of the engraver and sister of his Jacobite friend in Rome, Andrew Lumisden. She herself was the staunchest of Jacobites and had brought up her three sons to fight for King James or King Charles: in fact, they served King George with distinction. It was with affection that she called the imposing giant 'His Abyssinian Majesty', and it was in her drawing-room that he first saw Fanny Burney, who described their meeting with the liveliness of a novelist-in-training.[1]

'He is more than six foot high, is extremely well proportioned in shape, and has a handsome and expressive face. If his vanity is as great as his pride he would certainly become more courteous, if he knew how much smiles become him, for when he is pleased to soften the severity of his countenance, and to suffer his features to relax into smiling, he is quite another creature.' But he had become so shy of questioning and so imperious that it was scarcely possible to ask him 'How do you do?' or 'What time is it?' Sometimes, we are told, he had real difficulty in speaking, perhaps as a lasting result of the effect of the simoom on his lungs. 'His whole stomach seemed to heave like an organ-bellows,' says one observer. This physical weakness cannot have made him a less alarming companion.

[1] *The Early Diary of Frances Burney*, vol. II, pp. 14–26.

'This is the most awful[1] man I ever saw,' said a guest who was introduced to him. 'I never felt myself so small before.'

Fanny's father, Dr Charles Burney, was then writing his once-famous *History of Music*, and Bruce gave him a letter for publication which described not only the music and instruments of Ethiopia but also the harp which he had copied from an ancient Egyptian tomb. He came to Dr Burney's house to hear him and his daughters play on the harpsichord, and stayed for supper.

'He made me feel so very short as I sat next to him', wrote Fanny, 'that had not Mr Burney [a cousin], who is still less than myself, been on my other side, I should have felt quite pitiful. But what very much diverted me was, that whenever I turned to Mr Burney, I found his head leaning behind my chair, to peer at Mr Bruce, as he would have done at any outlandish animal. Indeed, no eye was off him; though I believe he did not perceive it, as he hardly ever himself looks at any body. He seems quite satisfied with thinking of his own consequence.'

But he was already beginning to feel a special sympathy for other wanderers who might have to describe strange lands to their fellow countrymen. Omai, the Polynesian brought to London by Joseph Banks, was being sent back to Tahiti. 'This poor fellow,' said Bruce, 'has lost all his time . . . He will only pass for a consummate liar when he returns; for how can he make them believe half the things he will tell them?' At first Bruce's own stories had seemed amusing and fantastic, but not necessarily untrue. But now he was beginning to encounter real incredulity.

It was on April 1st (perhaps an appropriate date) that at last he met Samuel Johnson at the house of his cousin, 'Single Speech' Hamilton. The great Doctor's first comment on him to James Boswell was cautious.

'Is not Bruce a sensible man, sir?' Boswell asked.

'Why, sir, he is not a distinct relater,' said Johnson 'I should say that he is neither abounding nor deficient in sense. I did not perceive any superiority or understanding.'

[1] i.e. awe-inspiring.

'But has he not a nobleness of resolution?'

'That is not to the present purpose. We are talking of his sense. A fighting cock has a nobleness of resolution.'

Significantly enough, Johnson added that Richard Jackson, lawyer and M.P., who was known as 'Omniscient Jackson' or 'Sensible Jackson' because of his wide knowledge and judgement, did not believe Bruce's account of his travels at all.

Certainly Johnson himself knew little about Ethiopia, in spite of his *Rasselas*. But he was rightly convinced of one thing. Bruce's most insistent claim was untrue: he was not the first European to have reached the source of the Nile. Like almost everyone else, Johnson fully accepted the idea that the Blue Nile, which gave Egypt its annual inundation, was the true 'Father of Waters'. But in what is the earliest piece of resounding Johnsonian prose he had pinned his faith to the Jesuit Lobo.

'The Portuguese traveller', he had written in the preface to his translation of a summary of Lobo's book in 1735, '. . . appears, by his modest and unaffected narration, to have described things as he saw them, to have copied nature from the life, and to have consulted his senses, not his imagination. He meets with no basilisks that destroy with their eyes, his crocodiles devour their prey without tears, and his cataracts fall from the rocks without deafening the neighbouring inhabitants.'

Lobo had described the source of the Blue Nile: if he had not been there himself, Paez certainly had. If Bruce's greatest boast was false, what else in his story could be true? Johnson told Sir John Hawkins, Boswell's rival as his biographer, 'that when he first conversed with Mr Bruce, the Abyssinian traveller, he was very much inclined to believe that he had been there, but that he had afterwards altered his opinion'.

This was a literary sentence of death from the Grand Cham of writing in London, the one famous Englishman whose name had been associated with Abyssinia before Bruce's journey. Something like a social sentence of death had come rather sooner. This was the result not of Bruce's self-deception about the discovery of the Nile source but simply of fashionable Londoners' total ignorance of conditions in Africa. According to Horace Walpole's account,[1] Bruce had told at a dinner party the story of the thorny kantuffa plant which tore away Takla Haymanot's head-covering and of the instant execution of the shum, or local governor, who should have cleared the kantuffa from the Emperor's path. In Walpole's version the kantuffa became a bramble which had stripped the Emperor naked and the shum the chief general of his army. In any case, these were not the manners of good King George or King Louis and some of the company found them incredible. Bruce was asked whether there were musical instruments in Abyssinia. Since he had written a full account of six of these for Dr Burney he could have had no doubt about the answer to the question, but, according to Walpole, he hesitated for a moment (one guesses because of the lung weakness which sometimes made it difficult for him to speak) and then answered, 'Yes, I think I remember one – lyre.'

George Selwyn, wit and M.P. famous for his power of sleeping through debates and waking only in time to vote for the Government, whispered to his neighbour, 'I am sure there is one less since he came out of the country.'

This not very brilliant pun went the rounds of fashionable London and became linked with another incident of Bruce's travels, his discovery of the painting of an ancient Egyptian harp in a rock tomb at Medinet Habu.

'Would you believe', Walpole wrote, 'that the great Abyssinian Mr Bruce, whom Dr Burney made me laugh by seriously calling the *intrepid traveller*, has had the intrepidity to write a letter to the Doctor, which the latter has printed in his book; and in which he intrepidly tells lies of almost as large a magnitude as his story of the bramble . . .' Bruce had not only described Abyssinian musical instruments 'but contributed a Theban harp, as beautifully and gracefully designed as if Mr Adam had drawn it for LadyMansfield's dressing room'. Clearly, Walpole thought, it could not be true that the original of such a drawing had stood for thousands of years in

[1] Letter to Sir William Mason, February 20th, 1776.

an open cave. Not even the greatest painter of the day, Sir Joshua Reynolds, had the secret of making his colours last so long, he declared.

Because eighteenth-century Londoners could not imagine what the conditions of a dark cave-tomb in the rainless air of Upper Egypt actually were Bruce was decisively nicknamed 'the Theban liar'. Decisively, but not openly, 'Remember this letter is only for your own private eye', Walpole warned his correspondent, 'I do not desire to be engaged in a controversy or a duel.' The explorer was too formidable to be laughed at to his face, but an invisible wall of unbelief and secret derision rose around him. He was elected a Fellow of the Royal Society, but its President, a Scot, Sir John Pringle, told Boswell that he was 'a brute' and not fully believed in London.

It was time to go home. He had found a retreat not more than thirty miles from Kinnaird, where he could imagine himself to be among the Ethiopian mountains again. Just beyond the nearest Highland hills, to which he had looked in his childhood, was the narrow water of Loch Lubnaig, where one could see the current of a river flowing to join the Forth very much as the current of the Little Abai flowed through Lake Tana on its way to Sennar and Egypt. The bulk of Ben Ledi rose between it and the Lowlands. One could hear a strange language spoken – not Amharic but Gaelic. There were deer to be shot and fish to be caught. The house which he called Ardwhillery – it is Ardchullarie today when we are more concerned than the eighteenth century was for Gaelic spelling – looked across the curve of the loch towards the mountain. This was a place where ambitions could be forgotten for at least a part of each year, and where a family could grow. For he had found a wife as well as a refuge. On May 20th, 1776, he married Mary Dundas, daughter of one of his neighbours, Thomas Dundas of Fingask and Carron Hall. It was the happy ending, for a while, of James Bruce's long adventure.

21

---∘⊙∘---

Munchausen

James Bruce was a marrying man. He needed affection and had seldom had his proper share of it. The loss of his first wife had darkened the world for him, and however clumsy his treatment of Margaret Murray may seem there can be no doubt that he had looked forward, through all his wanderings, to the day when their reunion would crown his years of hardship and adventure. When, after her loss, he did come home at last he soon began to think of marriage again.

For him this was a part of life which should make real claims on any man. When his friend Mrs Strange spoke of an acquaintance of hers who spent scarcely a moment of his life on anything but his studies, 'Then what the devil did he marry for?' Bruce demanded. 'I think his wife is but little obliged to him. Now a man is certainly right to give his day to his studies; but the evening should be devoted to society; he should give it to his wife or his friends, to conversation or to making love.'

His ideal bride must respond whole-heartedly to her sense of the beautiful. 'There's a woman who could never make a man unhappy', he exclaimed when he heard of a girl who burst into tears of emotion at the first concert she listened to. 'Her soul must be all harmony.'[1]

Lady Anne Lindsay, the charming and very intelligent daughter of a poor Scots earl, was, apparently, his first choice. She was a poetess, remembered for her ballad 'Auld Robin Gray'. Bruce had a

[1] The Early Letters and Diary of Frances Burney, II, 20.

rival, the Earl of Rosebery – 'Lord Rosemary', as he called him in contempt – but Lady Anne would have neither of them. The rejected wooer turned, instead, to young Miss Dundas, who had been born in the year when his Adriana died.

This was a prudent match. The Dundas family were rich and influential. For two generations they had been establishing themselves more and more firmly in this corner of Stirlingshire; in local politics they had been persistent rivals of the Bruces and the Grahams of Airth. David Bruce, in particular, had conducted a sort of non-violent vendetta with Thomas Dundas, and when James succeeded him and found himself faced with a lawsuit over what he called 'an inch of ground' he had declared furiously that Dundas would never have ground enough till he had a mouthful of it. A marriage alliance could end the feud and allow the two lairds to unite in pushing their claims on the Carron Company, which both supplied with coal.

Calculations of that kind do not explain the marriage, however. This again was a romance, as for James Bruce it had to be. There is even a very faint hint of Montague and Capulet in the story of his first meeting at a dance with two Dundas daughters, when, it is said, he told his friends that one of the girls must be his bride.

Mary Bruce was an adoring wife, for whom her husband was a hero, almost a god, certainly the greatest of great men, as a prayer in verse, written at Ardwhillery in August 1780, shows.[1]

> All giving power! Great Source of Life!
> O hear the Parent! Hear the Wife!
> That life thou lendest from Above,
> Though little, make it large in Love . . .
> Let me my length of life employ
> To give my sole injoyment Joy.
> His love, let mutual love excite,
> Turn all my cares to his delight
> And every needless blessing spare

[1] Broomhall MSS.

Wherein my darling wants a Share . . .
Ah! deck me in his eyes alone
With charms attractive as his own,
And in my arching wings caressed
Give all the Lover to my Breast.
Then, in our Chaste, Connubial Bed
My Bosom pillow'd for his head,
His eyes with blissful slumbers close
And watch with me My Lord's repose;
Your peace around his temples twine,
And love him with a Love like mine.
And, for I know his gen'rous flame,
Beyond whate'er my Sex can claim,
Me too to your protection take
And spare me for my Husband's sake . . .
Ye tender objects of my care!
Peace, peace, ye little helpless pair!
Anon he comes, your gentle Sire
And brings you all you can require . . .
Should I survive to see the day
That tears me from myself away,
That cancels all that Heav'n could give,
The life by which alone I live,
Alas, how more than lost were I
Who in the thought already die. . . .

Here was the balm that a tired and disappointed man most
needed: unquestioning trust and belief, the sort of sensibility that
could weep with joy and a power of self-expression which must
have made his wife a satisfying companion for an intelligent man.
The years of his second marriage were probably the happiest of
James Bruce's life.

Perhaps they were even too happy. When he had described
Ardwhillery to his friend Journu de Montagny the Frenchman
replied (September 15th, 1775) that he was both pleased and

jealous to know that Bruce was leading the most contented life which could be imagined, by the lochside – 'the bridle in your hand, the gun by your side and your eye on your books'. But all this and his coming marriage should encourage him to work. In quiet he could prepare to tell the world what he had done and learned.

But, in fact, Bruce did not give his days to study and his evenings to his wife and his friends, like the ideal husband in his own saying. Certainly he did not forget Ethiopia or allow those who talked to him to forget it, but the ambition for fame and public recognition ceased to drive him. The notes and manuscripts he had brought back from Africa were locked away. His correspondence with scientists, geographers and orientalists was allowed to dwindle. Many of them were French and the outbreak of another great war when France supported the not yet fully United States of America may have made contacts more difficult, but the real obstacle to the writing of the book or books expected from him was his absorption in his home.

He was active enough in some ways, pursuing a long and complicated lawsuit against the Carron Company. Writers on the company's affairs have suggested that in this he was being no more than a cantankerous nuisance, but it is by no means clear that this was always so. To many people of that day the first visible signs of the new industrialism were simply horrifying. It was Robert Burns who wrote of Carron itself:

> We cam na here to view your warks
> In hopes tae be mair wise
> But only, lest we gang to Hell,
> It may be nae surprise.

But Bruce was not an anti-industrialist; he certainly could not afford to be so, since a large part of his income came from the coal that fed Carron, but apart from this he was as ready to take an interest in industrial techniques and deliver opinion on them as he was to discuss Moses' passage to Sinai. Like many a more fully engaged industrialist, however, he was not prepared to look out on smoke and machinery from his own front windows. He had given the Carron Company the right to develop the coal-mines on his estate, but before leaving for Africa he had so arranged matters, as he thought, that a proposed new pithead and steam engine (for pumping water from the mine) would be well out of sight. He came home to find that the agreement on this subject had been broken. He objected, too, with some expert support, to what he considered wasteful methods of working his coal.

He considered that he knew a good deal about coal-mining. On one occasion his opponents challenged him to put his opinion to the proof by going through the deep galleries of a mine with them. They thought that the enormous laird would scarcely be able to get his broad shoulders through the narrow workings. He did, indeed, become so wedged between walls of mineral at one point that he had to be pulled or pushed through a tight passage. When he emerged, covered and almost choked with coal-dust and sludge, he said merely, 'I really am surprised by the dirtiness of the wastes.'

His great lawsuit dragged its way through the Scottish courts, through bills of suspension, reclaiming, petitions, and appeals, till after ten years, it ended in the House of Lords, quite satisfactorily for him. There were others to follow it. One must admit that he had the traditional appetite of Scots lairds for 'a guid gangin' plea'.

Before his chief legal victory his wife had died on February 10th, 1785, after several years of illness. The happy private world that he had made for himself collapsed. He was alone again among acquaintances some of whom had heard too much too often about Abyssinia.

'Weel, traveller,' said one of them, Sir William Bruce of Stenhouse, cryptically, 'die when ye like, ye'll die wi' the guid will o' your neighbours.'

Echoes of 'the Theban liar' were still in the air. He began to think again about the need to leave a great name behind him, to kill the idea that the story of his journey was no more than a romance. 'My friends unanimously assailed me on the part most accessible when the spirits are weak, which is vanity', he wrote in the introduction to his *Travels*. The most insistent of these friends was Daines Barrington, an amiable legal antiquarian who had been his school-fellow, and but for whom, Bruce declared, his book would never have been written. Another was John Douglas, Bishop of Carlisle and afterwards of Salisbury, a Scotsman who made a great career for himself in the Church of England largely by his skill as an apologist for George III's government. Bruce engaged a secretary, William Logan, who was with him for the rest of his life, and set to work.

With this activity other ambitions revived. He still felt that he had claims on King George and his Government. There were those promises, made half a lifetime ago, of the reward which was to come to him if his plan for the taking of Ferrol was brought off success-fully. He was to have had a baronetcy and a pension of £500 for life, and he believed that this promise had been renewed when he undertook to go to North Africa and bring back drawings of Roman buildings for the King. He had, in fact, brought back a far richer treasure of manuscripts, drawings of birds, beasts, fishes and plants and quite new knowledge of a dozen different kinds from unknown Ethiopia, the Red Sea and the Sudan. He had opened Suez to British ships – it was not his fault if this achievement had later been blocked. Above all, he had brought back the glory of unveiling the source of the Nile.

King George had, indeed, made some payment for his drawings, but this was all. Surely that hoped-for baronetcy had been more than earned. He now had a son. If the boy could succeed him as the second Sir James Bruce of Kinnaird, something would have been accomplished for his family. With his friends' advice he drew up a memorial to the King recording the offers made him before he set out on his travels. For support he relied on the name of Bruce. Among King George's Lords of the Bedchamber was Thomas Brudenell-Bruce, Earl of Ailesbury and Lord Bruce of Tottenham. The English nobleman's relationship to the laird of Kinnaird, indeed his links with the land of the Bruces, was remote indeed. He may have been surprised to find that, in the name of kinship, a Scotsman would count on him as his natural spokesman at court.

He was disappointingly slow to place James Bruce's petition to the King. Before there could be any answer to it George III collapsed into his first prolonged fit of insanity, and though the memorial was finally passed to the Prime Minister, the young William Pitt, it had no result. James Bruce's hopes were disappointed again.

He pressed on with the making of his book. He had journals that covered part of his years in Ethiopia, the long strips of paper on which he had noted distances, dates and some happenings on his journey through the Sudan, Balugani's records, innumerable letters to remind him of the details of his journey; but at last he was in a hurry to see the work done and he preferred to rely mainly on his memory, which was vivid but sometimes patchy. He chose to dictate rather than to write. He would sit for hours, for days on end, pouring out descriptions of men and places, opinions, lively incidents, long reported conversations, while an assistant took down his words.

One vivid, though not altogether convincing, account of his methods of work was first printed more than a hundred and thirty years after it was written. It is a statement by the Rev. Benjamin Latrobe, of the Moravian Church, Fetter Lane, London. This pastor claimed to have been engaged by Daines Barrington to help Bruce during a visit to London in May 1788. Dictation began day after day, he says, before eight o'clock in the morning and lasted till nine at night, with scarcely a break for meals. Bruce told his story fully and fast, 'leaving it to my own judgement, in a great measure, in what words I should express his ideas'. This exhausting labour continued for more than a year – at intervals, evidently, for the traveller certainly did not spend all those months in London. When it was finished, on June 28th, 1780, the Rev. Mr Latrobe at last pressed for payment, and Bruce, who seemed surprised at the suggestion, offered an insulting five guineas.[1]

It is difficult to know what to make of the story. James Bruce seems to have known the pastor for some time before they worked together. He had twice given him a subscription to the Brethren's

[1] *Notes and Queries*, October 25th, 1924.

Society for the Furtherance of the Gospel – the Moravians were then the most active of Protestant missionary bodies. He had consulted with Daines Barrington before asking Laporte to help him. Barrington was doubtful about this, but finally approved.[1] Bruce was not a mean man. Any secretary who successfully imitated his lively though often not very correct English style must have had remarkable literary skill. But whatever the truth may be in this case, Latrobe's account does suggest how the *Travels to Discover the Source of the Nile* expanded in a stream of talk, memories and ideas. Everything went into it – autobiography, history, topography, scientific data, portraits of people and peoples, theories and opinions.

It turned out to be much longer than its author had planned or expected. All the details of publishing were carefully considered. Bruce was anxious that specially cast type, special paper, even ink if possible, should be made in Scotland. This produced yet another law case.[2] In 1790 the five handsome quarto volumes appeared, with a dedication to King George.

It may surprise Americans and perhaps some students of British imperial expansion to learn that, in 1790, he could praise George III as the first great ruler who had encouraged the exploration of the world without aiming at military victory and colonization. 'Pride, ambition and an immoderate thirst of conquest' had been the motives of the earliest voyages of discovery, he declared; later 'avarice led the way in all expeditions; cruelty and oppression followed; to discover and to destroy seemed to mean the same thing; and, what was still more extraordinary, the innocent sufferer was styled the Barbarian; whilst the bloody, lawless invader flattered himself with the name of Christian.

'With your Majesty's reign . . . began the emancipation of discovery from the imputation of cruelty and crimes . . . In place of hearts confused with fantastic notions of honour and emulation, which constantly led to bloodshed' Georgian explorers like himself 'were filled with the most beneficent principles, with that noble

[1] Receipt (1776) and letter of April 10th, 1789, at Broomhall.
[2] Memorial, Broomhall MSS.

persuasion, the foundation of all charity, not that all men are equal, but that they are all brethren; and that, being superior to the savage in every endowment, it was for that very reason their duty to set the example of mildness, compassion and long-suffering to a fellow creature, because he was weaker, and, by no fault of his own, less instructed, and because he was therefore perfectly in their power.'

No modern critic of imperialism could have written more forcibly. But Bruce had his own claim to make.

'Although one of the least considerable of your Majesty's subjects, yet not the least desirous of proving my duty by promoting your Majesty's plan of discovery, as much as the weak endeavours of a single person, unprotected, forlorn and alone, or at times associated to beggars and bandits could promote it, I undertook this desperate journey and did not turn an ell out of my proposed way till I had completed it.'

This was a proud and justified boast.

With readers the book was immensely successful. Most of the edition was sold within thirty-two hours. It was translated into French and German. Cheap printed summaries were published. But at once all the doubts, all the unbelief and ridicule of fifteen years before, flared up again. There were, indeed, friendly critics, and magazines gave long accounts of the travels. But the attitude of most scholars and literary men was sceptical. Dr Johnson was dead, but his view of Bruce was not forgotten and now that the whole story of the travels was set down in print there were innumerable things to be pointed at which seemed too strange to be true.

Without waiting to finish Bruce's first volume, Horace Walpole wrote (June 30th, 1790) that he was 'sick of his vanity and (I believe) of his want of veracity'. It was the accepted point of view among people who had taken no more trouble to justify it than he had done, even among some who enjoyed the *Travels* as a record of romantic adventures and tall stories. Bruce became a butt for professional humorists. A supplement to the story of Baron Munchausen 'humbly dedicated to Mr Bruce the Abyssinian traveller' was brought out in which the favourite comic character and type of all extravagant liars was taken to Africa, where he encountered sandstorms and eaters of raw meat as well as more fantastic marvels, among them a magical carriage in which he was able to cut canals at Suez and Panama. The rhymer John Wolcot (Peter Pindar), who had made a prosperous livelihood out of satire, largely aimed at King George, produced *A Complimentary Epistle to James Bruce, Esq.* He himself, he complains, had been as far as Madeira, and yet he had seen no such wonders as Bruce described.

> To thee how kindly hath thy genius giv'n
> The massy keys of yonder star-clad heav'n
> With leave, whene'er thou wishest to unlock it,
> To put a few eclipses in thy pocket!
> No loaded camels, to provoke my stare,
> Sublimely whirl'd, like straws, into the air;
> Nor, happy in a stomach framed of steel,
> On roaring lions have I made a meal . . .
> Alas, I never met with royal scenes!
> No vomits gave to Abyssinian queens . . .
> Nor, blushing, stript me to the very skin
> To give a royal blackamoor a grin . . .
> Nor have I been where men (what loss, alas!)
> Kill half a cow and turn the rest to grass.

It was all a good joke with no particular malice behind it – simply the assumption that the name of Bruce was something to be laughed at, that nothing the traveller wrote need (or, indeed should) be taken seriously by anyone. When Kay, the Scottish caricaturist, made a drawing of the gigantic laird of Kinnaird he showed him speaking to little Peter Williamson, compiler of the first Edinburgh street directory, whose account of his own sufferings among American Indians was generally thought to be incredible. In the caption Williamson was made to declare, 'There is more truth in one page of my Edinburgh Directory than in all your five volumes 4 .' [*See* Plate 15.]

It was the end of ambition for James Bruce, or almost the end. Some learned writers did, indeed, praise and quote his book as the authoritative account of Ethiopia, the Sudan and the Red Sea. His friends stood by him and pressed him for a new edition. He set about a revision, correcting points where his memory had misled him. But attacks on his good faith continued. In 1792 the eccentric Edward Wortley Montagu, who had lived long in Egypt and the Levant and so carried some weight in spite of the erratic behaviour which made his own relatives consider him mad, asserted in print that Bruce had never gone to Ethiopia, but had spent the years when nothing was heard from him in Armenia or thereabouts.

Bruce said to his daughter, 'The world makes a strange mistake when it supposes that I would condescend to write a romance for its amusement.' He did not expect to live long enough to find himself righted, but she, he believed, would probably 'see the truth of all I have written completely and decisively confirmed.'[1]

He still lived actively enough at Kinnaird and Ardwhillery, though he was growing stouter and heavier, so that the country folk felt pity for the horse he rode, whose back was bent with his weight. Often he would be seen walking round his estate with a turban on his head and a tall staff in his hand. His neighbours thought him a strange being. He had built a little observatory for his telescopes.

'God preserve us!' one of them said. 'The laird's gone daft: he sits up a' nicht keekin' at the starns!'[2]

The French Revolution shocked this ardent royalist who had a fellow-feeling for kings, and he wept when he heard of Louis XIV's execution.

'There's Kinnaird,' said the old housekeeper at Airth, where his half-uncle, William Graham, was still living, 'greetin' as if there was nae saunt on earth but himsel' and the King o' France.'[3]

Friends and travellers came to see him and the museum room

1 Kay's *Original Portraits*.
2 Nimmo's *History of Stirlingshire*, 3rd edition; Kay's *Original Portraits*.
3 Ramsay's *Reminiscence of Scottish Life and Character*.

where his drawings, manuscripts and relics of his journey were displayed. They were usually welcomed and hospitably entertained. For some of them he would show his marksmanship by shooting one of the little herd of fallow deer that he kept in his park at Kinnaird. But a casual visitor could be infuriating. There was one who refused to believe that beef could be eaten raw and demanded that Bruce should prove his own story. Bruce sent for a steak, salt and pepper and prepared a 'cartridge' of meat in the Ethiopian manner.

'Now you must eat this,' he said.

The tourist was horrified: it was Bruce, he insisted, who should take this test.

'You came here a stranger and insult me in my own house', said the furious giant. 'I must prove my statement in my own way. You see my staircase there. If you do not empty that plate I shall fling you from the top step to the bottom.'

The tourist did prove that raw meat could be eaten.

The idea of a fall from a stairway must have come naturally to James Bruce's mind. He had once jokingly suggested a similar punishment for his rival 'Lord Rosemary'. But the thought did not forewarn him of his own fate. On April 26th, 1794, there were guests at Kinnaird. He was helping an elderly lady to her carriage that evening when he slipped and pitched down six or seven steps to the floor. His own weight knocked him senseless and the next morning he was dead.

They buried his great body under the monument he had raised for his wife beside the church which his ancestor, the great Presbyterian leader Robert Bruce, had founded at Larbert. It is something very typical of that time, poised between classicism and industrialism – a remarkably graceful obelisk of cast iron with delicate reliefs rather in the Adam style.

The inscription tells that

> His life was spent in performing
> useful and splendid actions;
> He explored many distant regions,

He discovered the fountains of the Nile,
  He traversed the deserts of Nubia.
He was an affectionate husband,
  An indulgent parent,
An ardent lover of his country.
By the unanimous voice of mankind,
  His name is enrolled with those
              who were conspicuous
For genius, for valour and for virtue.

22

Post-mortem

'The voice of mankind' on James Bruce was certainly not unanimous when he died. It was only by very slow degrees that the essential truth of his own story was confirmed. His book fired the imagination of poets – 'the flashing eyes, the floating hair' of Coleridge's Xanadu are surely those of Takla Haymanot in his encounter with what Horace Walpole had called 'the bramble' and the Abyssinian 'damsel with a dulcimer' in the same poem is evidently a Brucean phantom. Southey, too, took ideas and images from Bruce. Much later Victorian novelists, particularly Rider Haggard, borrowed heavily from the *Travels*. But it was long before the cloud of scepticism which hung over his name began to lift.

'The learned Hartmann', a German orientalist, warned his readers that Bruce was apt to contradict himself and should not be relied on where his statements were unconfirmed by other people. This almost total distrust was taken seriously by some of Bruce's Scottish fellow countrymen – the scholar-poet John Leyden, for instance – who may have been apt to remember that Scots law demands corroboration for all evidence. For the moment there could be no corroboration of much that Bruce said and wrote, because there was no West European witness of his travels after Balugani's death and Balugani's written testimony was still unknown in 1794. And it was indeed true that the traveller could invent – as in the case of the toast to Maria at the source of the Abai – and that he sometimes gave a date or an hour wrongly when a reference to his own notes made at the time would have set him right.

Corroboration could, indeed, come from Africa, and was to do so, but twenty years after his death scarcely any news of Ethiopia had reached the Western world since he left the country. The very name of the reigning emperor was unknown – this is scarcely surprising, perhaps, since emperors of that time came and went very quickly and scarcely ruled beyond Gondar. The first explorer inspired by Bruce's book, William George Browne, set out in 1792, hoping to reach Ethiopia by way of Sennar, but war diverted him to Darfur, far in the west. He did meet Ethiopians who had known or heard of Yagoube and confirmed his doings at Gondar and his governorship of Ras el Fil, though some denied that he had reached the source of the Blue Nile. A few years later a second traveller, E. D. Clarke, met an Ethiopian priest in Cairo who gave similar confirmation. General Sir David Baird, who commanded a force sent from India in 1801 to oppose the French invaders of Egypt, declared that the safety of his troops on their Red Sea voyage had been due to the accuracy of Bruce's chart and sailing directions. In spite of this the first British civilian traveller who covered the route into Ethiopia by Massawa seems to have set out with a determination to prove that the Scotsman had been hopelessly inaccurate and unreliable.

This was George Annesley, Viscount Valentia, who, luckier than Bruce, was able to make most of the journey which took him as far as India in 1802–6 in the East India Company's ships. His *Voyages and Travels* is a pompous and ill-natured book. He quarrelled repeatedly with the captains who were unlucky enough to have to convey his party, notably when they persisted in saying that Bruce's sailing directions were the best guide. He insisted that Bruce had made every possible mistake not only in calculating distances and counting the number of old water cisterns on an island but also in handling such people as the Naib of Massawa – until he learned by experience that naibs could show lack of respect even to a viscount. Bruce had grossly misplaced the island of Macowar, he declared: it was not till thirty years later that another traveller pointed out that Lord Valentia's Macowar was a different island from Bruce's.

Valentia had with him a much more intelligent observer, Henry Salt, by whom most of the more serious work of exploration on the journey was actually done. He, too, it is obvious, was expected to find mistakes in Bruce's record. He decided that the road into Ethiopia across Mount Taranta was not really so steep as the Scot had made out and picked what holes he could in other statements; but the farther he went the more often he was forced to admit that Bruce was, on the whole, a reliable guide. Four years later he was sent back to Ethiopia by the British Government. This time he found an Ethiopian scholar (Doftar Esther, he calls him) who remembered Bruce in Gondar, but denied that he had commanded troops or been governor of a province and declared that the story of the grotesque Galla chief Gouangoul was an invention. Salt did not succeed in reaching Gondar himself. On the strength of this man's reminiscences of what had happened more than thirty-five years earlier he told Sir Walter Scott that Bruce had 'considerably exaggerated his personal consequence and exploits', though most of his story was true.

It was 1815 before Salt gave his comparatively favourable verdict. Ten years before something much more important for Bruce's reputation had already taken place.

His family were anxious to destroy the legend of 'the Theban liar'. His son James also thought of the copyright of the *Travels* and the documents stored at Kinnaird as a valuable piece of property. The second edition for which Bruce had made corrections had never been published. The first was long out of print and there was still a strong demand for unauthorized summaries. Archibald Constable, the enterprising – finally too enterprising – Edinburgh publisher reached an agreement with the new laird of Kinnaird. He found an editor for the book who is an important figure in the history of Bruce's fame, though the two men can never have met.

Alexander Murray was a shepherd's son, born in a remote Galloway glen in 1775. In his boyhood he had only thirteen months of formal schooling, but he possessed an extraordinary talent for languages and letters. From the few books he could lay hands on he

managed to pick up a good deal of Latin, some Greek and Hebrew
and at least a smattering of French and German. Friends took him to
Edinburgh, where the Principal of the University was startled by
his knowledge and ensured him the means of study. The memoirist
Henry Cockburn remembered him in one of the classes as 'a little
shivering creature, gentle, studious, timid, and reserved'. But
behind this shrinking manner were an iron determination, considerable wit, and a mind which he was training to exact scholar-
ship. He became a remarkable philologist, a journalist for a while, a
parish minister in his native province, finally Professor of Oriental
Languages at Edinburgh – though for less than a year before over-
work killed him. A tall monument among the Galloway hills still
records his countrymen's admiration for this 'lad o' pairts'.

In 1802 Murray was one of the very few in Britain to have mas-
tered the Ethiopian languages, partly, no doubt, from the specimens that Bruce himself had given. He knew those tongues, like
so many others, exactly and grammatically. In his views of history
he was equally stern and exact.

He went to Kinnaird determined to examine the documents in
the fullest detail. It was a sad experience for himself and his hosts.
Young James Bruce and his wife could not understand why this
curious little man should wish to pry into letters and other writings
which, they thought, could have no interest for the world at large.
They had no idea of an historian's need to know all sides of a man
or a question. They held back papers from him that were finally
extracted from them only after appeals to the contract with Constable which the laird feared to break. From his side there were
complaints that little Mr Murray, immovably set on his task, was
'treating my house like an inn'.[1]

Ten weary months certainly did not blunt Murray's critical
faculties. He found inconsistencies and mistakes in Bruce's book
itself – some are not hard to find – and contrasts (which are not
necessarily contradictions) between the journals written in Ethiopia and descriptions of the same events dictated more than fifteen

[1] T. Constable, *Archibald Constable and his Literary Correspondents.*

years later. James Bruce had certainly been an imaginative man, and Alexander Murray distrusted imagination.

'At the close of life, after twenty years' repose and much domestic affliction', he finally wrote in his preface to the 1813 edition, 'the Author of these Travels seems to have viewed his former life as in a dream. Each interesting event found a glowing place in his description, though indolence often preventing him from fixing, by his journals, the true time and place.'

'As I was appointed by his family and my friends to examine his papers,' he told Henry Salt, 'it could not be expected that I should write a commentary of the most disagreeable kind on the work – however, I did not judge it to be for the interests of truth and science to conceal absolutely the defects of a celebrated book. As I had perused the Journals[1] with attention I saw a number of things stated with too little regard for fact.'

Murray's work on the *Travels*, was, indeed, magnificently thorough and comprehensive. It should have been decisive for Bruce's reputation. By printing Balugani's Italian letters and records he destroyed the last excuse for thinking that Bruce had never been to the source of the Abai. Other well-selected documents authenticated most of Bruce's movements. His sparing notes clarified the vast, half-digested epic of travel. The short life of Bruce which he used as a preface made it possible to follow the explorer's plans and doings much more easily than in his own writing, often as full of confusions as of colour. Every book that has mentioned James Bruce since has drawn on Murray: in some ways no one will ever know his subject so well as he did.

But the faintly menacing air of his letter to Salt, with its hint that he could have torn the whole *Travels* to pieces if he had wanted to, suggests that he had no great sympathy with his subject. This is surely true. Bruce was a romantic and Murray distrusted romance so strongly that he even displaced the stories of the Emperor Bakaffa's discovery of his wife, Mentwab, and of her most faithful supporter, the Galla Waranya, though, even if these are half

[1] Now at Broomhall.

legendary – and, apart from their picturesqueness, there is no compelling reason to doubt them – they were an important part of the political background of Ethiopian life in Bruce's time.

In some ways Murray knew more than Bruce about Arab affairs, rarely about African ones. It seemed clear to him, for instance, that the traveller's command of Ethiopian languages, even of Greek and Arabic, had sometimes been weaker than he supposed. But, after all, Bruce had been in Africa, he had talked to hundreds of people there. Murray had not: he was a little apt to suppose that his theoretical knowledge must carry more weight than Bruce's practical experience. He was too much inclined to think that anything not in the journals or in other notes actually written in Ethiopia or the Sudan might be a mere embroidery. These documents, brief and disconnected, are, in fact, memoranda of things seen and heard and have very little to say of Bruce's own actions or thoughts.

The sense of disapproval, the hint that it would be possible to criticize Bruce much more severely than he had done, lingered in his careful comment and can be felt there still. It is, in fact, a misleading hint. One after another the chief doubts about the explorer's claims have been cleared away. British travellers in Egypt found the tomb from which the famous 'Theban lyre' had been copied – Bruce's own name, it is painful to add, was scratched on the painted rock.[1] Murray and Salt had had doubts about the traveller's part in battles of Sarbakusa. 'A prince who left Bruce at home if he could have brought him out neglected the most able-bodied associate you ever saw', was Walter Scott's comment on this piece of scepticism. In fact, when the traveller's granddaughter and her husband were looking for material for a new publication, a letter[2] from the minister of Kirkpatrick-Juxta, Dumfriesshire, told of an

[1] The sarcophagus, Bruce's 'finest vase in the world', was removed by Henry Salt, who, as British Consul-General at Cairo, became an active dealer in Egyptian antiquities.

[2] The Rev. William Singer to C. L. Cumming-Bruce, M.P., 1835, Broomhall MSS.

Ethiopian who had been questioned in India by a distinguished neighbour of his, Sir John Malcolm. The man had never heard the name of Bruce, but when he was shown an engraved portrait he at once recognized Yagoube, under whom he had served in those battles and who had been Governor of Ras el Fil – another point still disputed in Britain.

Throughout the nineteenth century, indeed till our own day, travellers and historians have found themselves forced to rely on James Bruce's guidance. Some things in his record are uncertain, and always will be. How far do conversations reported long after they were uttered, and without the benefit of shorthand or tape-recorders represent exactly what was said in Arabic or Amharic? How far (if at all) did Bruce exaggerate storms, searing winds, the vivisection of cattle for a banquet, the sheer malice of some of those he met, the admiration of others for himself? The Theban liar is, indeed, a myth, but even today writers are apt to refer to him with an air of patronizing dubiety to which they would not be tempted in dealing with other explorers of his quality.

His own self-delusions help to make that possible. As important is his attempt to combine two sorts of truth in the story of his travels. There is the objective, the scientific truth of masses of observed facts and measurements. There is the human, the literary truth of a vast pageant of strange lands, strange societies, surprising men and women – of his portrait of himself, which is true even in its exaggeration. To men of exact learning, like his editor Murray, the pageant can be an embarrassment. Others today can give us scientific facts about Africa better than Bruce could do, though he gave many. His unique record of remote nations in crisis when our modern age was scarcely dawning, and of his dealings with them, is something which no one can replace and which makes him one of the great figures in Europe's discovery of Africa.

INDEX

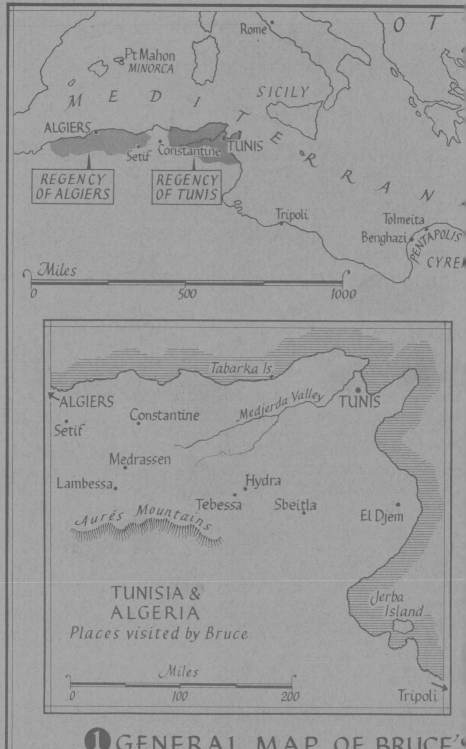

1 GENERAL MAP OF BRUCE'S

W.Bromage